HAPPINESS IS.

Happiness is.

Unexpected Answers to
Practical Questions in Curious Times

Shawn Christopher Shea, M.D.

Health Communications, Inc.
Deerfield Beach, Florida

www.hcibooks.com

Library of Congress Cataloging-in-Publication Data

Shea, Shawn C.
    Happiness is : unexpected answers to practical questions in curious times / Shawn
Christopher Shea.
        p. cm.
    ISBN 0-7573-0066-9 (tp)
    1. Happiness.   2. Self-actualization (Psychology)   I. Title.

    BF575.H27S46 2004
    170—dc22

                                                                                2004047392

Publisher: Health Communications, Inc.
            3201 S.W. 15th Street
            Deerfield Beach, FL 33442–8190

Cover design by Larissa Hise Henoch
Inside book design by Lawna Patterson Oldfield

Dedicated to Susan, Brenden, and Ryan
my three favorite kaleidoscopes

and

To the clinicians and casemanagers
of our community mental health centers
who embody the meaning of compassion

Contents

Acknowledgments

I would like to begin by thanking Peter Vegso, the president of Health Communications, Inc. (HCI), for offering me the chance to write for his wonderful publishing house.

Two individuals at HCI deserve particular thanks in the inception and development of *Happiness Is*.: Tom Sand (senior vice president) and Bret Witter (chief editor). Tom, your warmth, wisdom, and insight are embedded in every page of this book. I cannot thank you enough for your belief in both myself and our "little" project, which you helped to conceive. Bret, you are simply the best. You have an almost uncanny knack for intuiting how a book's structure should flow, knowing exactly what needs to be cut and precisely what needs to be added. You are one of those rare editors who sometime seemed to know better than even I did what I wanted to say, and you knew exactly how best I should say it. Many thanks. I would also like to express my sincere gratitude to everyone at HCI including marketing, production and design, and sales for your great support.

I would like to thank my good friend Laurie Walkling Brown for her unwavering enthusiasm and feedback, as well as George and Sally Cahill for theirs. A special thanks to Paul Farmer, Brian Hershberger, Ed Hamaty, and Drew Smith for their love and laughter over the years as well as their belief in the project. A very special thanks to Bonnie Rossello, whose support of my clinical mission for the last decade has been instrumental in giving me the time and motivation to create *Happiness Is*. Of course my great appreciation goes and will always go to Ria Romano, without whom this book would never have been born.

I couldn't imagine ending my acknowledgments without thanking Ellen and all the great staff at Brewbakers café, where a goodly number of these pages were created.

Finally, my deepest thanks goes to Susan, my wife, for her wise, pithy, and unerring editing of the manuscript, which has been instrumental in both the initial direction and final polish of the book. Her efforts and sacrifices—as the writing demanded so much of my time—are also greatly appreciated as is the much valued support of my boys, Brenden and Ryan. Thanks to all.

Introduction

*"As a matter of fact, happiness is something dynamic, a reality
that must continuously be struggled for, but which, once we attain
it, cannot be diminished by the external circumstances of life . . .
which is why it's a reality that each of us can achieve."*

THE MONKS OF NEW SKETE

Happiness. Some would argue that it is the most elusive of human
quests and that, like a unicorn, it may not even exist. The wizened
Monks of New Skete do not seem to think so. Nor do I.

As a psychiatrist, I have asked hundreds of patients what happiness is.
I have received hundreds of different answers. But despite the fact that each
person may ultimately view happiness differently, I am convinced that
there is a common thread—a most unexpected one—to be found in all
those who have established an enduring sense of happiness. Through my
clinical work, my readings, and my personal experiences, the nature of this
thread has become clearer and more tangible. It is a thread that is of the
utmost utility. It is the thread that leads to happiness.

In the following pages we will meticulously track down this thread. We
will sculpt a definition of happiness that provides us with a compass for
better understanding how to pursue it. Our quest will lead us to search for

the very nature of man, where we will uncover a new and exciting model—the human matrix. This contemporary model of human nature will show us what it is that limits our ability to find happiness and what it is that allows us to transcend those very same limits.

In our quest, we will pull upon a vast array of resources, trying with every step to see the world anew from as many perspectives as can shed light on our pathway. We will hear from saints and sinners, quantum physicists and poets, avatars of analytic thought and those who trust more the realm of magic and hope. We will also tap the wisdom of my patients and the wisdom I have gained through my own quirky encounters with the strange wonderment we call life. As we call upon all of these resources, we will find ourselves exploring the nooks and crannies, the nuances and shadows, the details and the unknowns of everyday existence, for it is in such nuances that wisdom often waits.

I should also mention what the book is not. Our book is not a scholarly or academic treatise filled with case studies and statistics. I believe in such writings, and, indeed, have spent much of my career writing them. But the goal of this book is not proof. It is provocation. It is incantation. It is an invitation to think creatively, to view our very existence with a new lens. And with this fresh lens—the human matrix—to search for the type of applied spirituality where we find bits and pieces of our self and our purpose in our daily encounters.

The answers to finding an enduring sense of happiness, the type of happiness to which the Monks of New Skete allude in our epigraph, must be spontaneous, imaginative, and flexible. Indeed, the answers to finding happiness are often unexpected. They are not so much things to do as they are ways of thinking, manners of conceptualizing, and approaches to understanding. They are not just concrete suggestions for action, but methods of understanding how and when to take these actions. They are not just habits to be grown but perceptions that allow one to break those habits that hinder growth. Happiness is not a static thing to achieve but a vibrantly resilient way of being that allows us to achieve.

As we wrap up this introduction, you will note that I keep using words such as "our book" and "we shall uncover," as if you, the reader, were, in reality, one of the authors of the book. The reason for this choice of words is a simple one—you are.

Not in the sense that you are writing the words, but in the sense that only the reader can determine the final meaning of the words. Each reader puts his or her own stamp on a book's meaning as surely as any editor puts his or her stamp on its words. Many gifted writers have been keenly aware of this fact—that their final period does not end the creative process. It begins it.

The goal of the writer is to spark creativity and excitement in the reader, to create movement. In truth we really are cocreators of this work. As the author I am fully aware that I am not the one who has ultimate control of the creation. You are. In that sense I hope that you have great fun with it and that you create marvelous works of living art in the pursuit of your quest for happiness.

The gifted novelist John Fowles wonderfully captures the peculiar nature of this cocreation between writer and reader. From the very first time I read the following excerpt, it had a strange fascination for me. It seemed to hint at the magic that occurs between an author and a reader, for I truly believe it is a magic of sorts:

> *I don't want some passive thing: to be sold, to be read. Writing is active, and the kind of writing I have always admired, and shall always want to achieve, makes reading active too—the book reads the reader, as radar reads the unknown. And the unknown ones, the readers, feel this.*

As you read this book, I hope that you palpably feel this tension between the writer and the reader, between you and me, between you reading the book and the book reading you. *Happiness Is.* will read you in the sense that it will trigger memories, moments and laughter that are unique to you and no other reader. This coming face-to-face with one's own story is critical for understanding the unique pathways that each of us must find in our pursuit of happiness.

In the following pages the explorations of some of my patients, as they sought the meaning of their stories, are told. In all instances their names have been changed, and, at times, distinguishing characteristics or facts have been altered to further protect their identity without disrupting the essential reality of our work together.

As we conclude, I am reminded of a Zen parable. In it, the attributes of a man of true wisdom, a monk of the highest order are described. The list of attributes is a surprisingly short one. Great masters seem to share the following three traits: (1) they are very funny and particularly good at laughing at themselves, (2) they are driven by an intense sense of compassion, and (3) despite years of practice, they approach every aspect of Zen with a "Beginner's Mind," always open to new ideas and fresh solutions.

I believe this is a good standard by which to judge our cocreation. If we both do our jobs, we can only hope that when we are done, that the writing and the reading of *Happiness Is.* will have made us laugh loudly, stirred our sense of compassion, and opened our minds to the endless wonderment of our never ending ability, as Homo sapiens, to be both the creator of our problems and the designer of our solutions.

Part I

Defining the Goal
of the Quest:
The Meaning of Happiness

"The purpose of our lives is to be happy."

THE 14TH DALAI LAMA

*"Happiness is like a sunbeam, which
the least shadow intercepts."*

CHINESE PROVERB

Prelude: The World at Our Fingertips

*"Will Mulder find happiness? No. That's not for him.
He's a questing hero."*

A FAN'S COMMENT FROM A WEB SITE ON *THE X-FILES*

The Nature of the Beast

We are questing beasts. Our lives are frequently a delightful, and sometimes not so delightful, series of quests. Indeed, our lives are not so much a neat series of well delineated quests as they are, more often, a tangled mass of conflicting quests that simultaneously demand our attentions.

Our quests are sometimes ordinary and downright primitive in nature. We search for food, shelter, safety, and sex. Our quests are sometimes elevated and important in nature. We tirelessly work to become school teachers, doctors, entrepreneurs, and homemakers. Our quests are sometimes viewed as trivial in nature — but this does not change how hard we pursue them. We relentlessly search for the golf swing of Tiger Woods, a set of abs like the ones on those annoyingly handsome men smiling astride their Bowflexes, or a wrinkle-free forehead thanks to the wonders of Botox. Our quests are sometimes interpersonal. We look for a good set of friends, colleagues we like and partners to cherish. Finally, our quests are sometimes grand and spiritual in nature. We pray to be compassionate, find the right religion or touch the face of god.

Put all these pressing pursuits together, and it is no wonder that we are frequently tired and just a bit out of sorts. We're pooped. Moreover, by simultaneously pursuing too many of these goals it is easy for any given human being to sabotage his or her ability to successfully pursue one of the most basic yet critical of all the quests—the quest for happiness.

Whether we are working eighty hours a week to get the money to secure our child the best college education that money can buy or relentlessly hunting down a Beanie Baby whose soaring value will undoubtedly secure that very same education, we are preoccupied with a massive set of quests. Not all of these pursuits support each other nor are they necessarily good for ourselves or other creatures on this planet. And, compared to the other creatures on the planet, we seem to spend an inordinate amount of time discussing, prioritizing and, ultimately, picking our quests.

Having practiced clinical psychiatry for over twenty years, I have come to believe that this "questing business" has a good deal to do with our eventual happiness or unhappiness. Indeed, when people enter my office, although they seldom use the word quest, their pains are almost always rooted in this "questing business." They are unhappy about what quests they are on, what quests others have foisted upon them, the fact that they are failing with their quests, the fact that others feel they are failing with their quests, the fact that they are afraid that others will feel they are failing with their quests, the fact that they can't pick the right quests, the fact that they have become boxed into pursuing the wrong quests, or the fact that they have picked too many quests. And the most common bottom line is often a simple one: The quest for happiness has eluded them.

Mulder's Dilemma, Spirit's Secret and Happiness Machines

In the historical sense, it is our questing nature that has driven us to achieve some of the most marvelous feats of civilization such as building the Cathedral of Notre Dame, discovering the atom, landing on the Moon, preventing polio, elucidating the concept of democracy, and, of course, creating *The Simpsons*. But, as we have already hinted, there is a dark side to all this questing business. It is this dark side that brings people into my office. If we want to understand the nature of finding happiness, it is worth our while to explore this dark side in a little more detail.

The dark side of our quests emerges when they become our fixations or our obsessions, when we spend so much time in pursuit of one of them (or several of them) that the most important ones are left starving for our attention. Even noble quests—religion, gold medals, careers, love—can become dangerous if they become a fanatic focus that leads us away from what really matters—God, self-respect, productive work, family, friends and compassion.

It is at such times that we risk becoming like Mulder of *The X-Files*, who as our perceptive fan cogently stated in the opening epigraph of our chapter, will never be happy, because he is just too ferociously preoccupied with this alien thing. In some respects we are all Mulders. Our culture floods us not with aliens but with pressures to tackle an enormous number of quests, some of which may be alien to our own natures and skills. We frantically—one might say fanatically—try to cram them all into one lifetime. The advertising industry aids this nasty process by transforming simple desires into pressing needs. Before one knows it, life is no longer a quest for happiness; it is a mass of unhappy quests.

So where does all this leave us? It leaves us with the knowledge that questing is pivotal to human nature, which can be both good and bad. Good—if our quests are wisely chosen, manageable and obtainable. Bad if our quests are poorly chosen, unmanageable, and unobtainable. It also leaves us with the reassuring knowledge that, if falling prey to our own quests leads to unhappiness, it also follows that the ability to more wisely choose our quests may lead to happiness. Truth be told, because we have the ability to choose our personal quests and how much time we allot to each of them, we have the ability to determine—to a surprisingly large degree—the extent of our own happiness.

I am reminded of one of my favorite lyrics from the Age of Psychedelia as it played itself out in Los Angeles in the early 1970s. The lyric is from a song entitled "Prelude: Nothin' To Hide" by Spirit, an underground rock band that had developed a bit of a cult following in the new and vibrant clubs of LA that seemed to spring to life as heroin brought death to the cafes of the Haight-Ashbury up north. Back in 1969, if you were in the know about music, you knew about Spirit. In any case, I liked them, and the lyric of interest to us goes like this:

> *"You have the world at your fingertips.*
> *No one can make it better than you."*

This lyric seems to capture the essence of our chapter in its simple yet elegant truth. We have every reason to feel a sense of hope, for in a very real sense, I believe that we can shape our own happiness—we have the world at our fingertips—for we, alone, are the ones who have the power to make it better. We have this power because we have the ability to choose both our quests and the game boards upon which we pursue them. But there is a catch here, for the choosing and the handling of these quests is a complex business filled with pitfalls and traps.

Perhaps the greatest of these traps is to lose sight of the fact—which the Dalai Lama made clear in our opening epigraph—that "the purpose of our lives is to be happy." It is deceptively easy to lose this focus while watching an ATM machine eat one's bankcard or when getting a summons to meet with the teacher of one's child about an "unfortunate incident" at school. But without this focus, happiness is indeed fleeting.

Our book is about learning how to maintain this focus so that we are in the best possible positions to achieve happiness. It is useful to look at the strategy that we will use to pursue our quest, for the strategy itself sheds light on the actual feasibility of transforming the world at our fingertips into a better place.

The first prerequisite is that we must decide upon a clear, concise, and practical goal. Nothing to chance here. No assumptions allowed. We must come to a sophisticated understanding of what it is we are seeking. We must define happiness. To begin without a clear definition is to risk being sidetracked by the innumerable number of feelings, moods, and beliefs that frequently masquerade as happiness but are, at best, only bits of the real thing and, at worst, fragments of an illusion.

When questing, the second step is to thoroughly understand what tools are available to pursue the goal of the quest. More germane to our point, once we have defined happiness, we must seek out a sophisticated understanding of the nature of the questing beast, for we are our own tool. What are we made of? What attributes do we bring to the quest? What are the limitations and strengths of the machine we call a Homo sapien to find happiness? Just how happy can the questing beast be?

In this regard, none could deny that we Homo sapiens are vastly more marvelous than the machines we ourselves create. Unlike our microchips and spaceships, we are not only made of atoms, polymers, and packets of protein and plasma. We are equally made from bits of soul and belief, fragments of thought and dream, orchestrations of government and culture. We are splendidly complex machines filled with nuance, shadow and ambiguity. Nevertheless, we are machines. We are "happiness machines." It behooves us to take a look at our blueprint, for such self-knowledge will prove to be an invaluable tool in the pursuit of our quest.

The third step in a successful quest consists of gaining a sound working knowledge of "the rules of the game." Once we understand what the happiness machine is made of, we must put it through its paces. What makes it tick? What rules govern how a human being can go about the business of finding happiness? How exactly is the game played? What are we allowed to do and what are the potential consequences of doing it? What is it sometimes best not to do?

Once we have achieved a knowledge of how to play the game, we are ready to take our fourth and final step, a most critical step in the completion of a successful quest. We must "put it all together." What are the strategies for most effectively using our tools to achieve happiness? Do some tools work best in combination, and, if so, what combinations lead to happiness? Even more important, how do we learn to flexibly create even better strategies that may solve the unexpected problems of tomorrow? In the real world of jobs, bosses, partners and deadlines, what strategies can best help us to find happiness amidst life's daily doses of chaos?

As a psychiatrist I have had the opportunity to use this four-part strategy with hundreds of patients over several decades. I have seen it yield remarkable results in the quest for happiness. Consequently it is to these four steps—mirrored by the four sections of our book—that we shall turn in the following pages, a process we should start at once.

To begin our hunt for a definition of the word happiness, it may be of value to look at the relationship of happiness to another word that we encounter on a daily basis—success. These two words form such a common point of reference in our everyday language that most people bandy them about as if everyone else is, undoubtedly, in agreement with what they mean. But as we shall soon see, the true meaning of these words is as elusive as the Cheshire cat. As soon as we get close enough to grab their meaning by the tail, there is no tail to grab.

As we examine the relationship between happiness and success, we will find an unexpected wisdom laying hidden, waiting for our footfall, if we dare to walk the curious path that connects them. I wish I could tell you that I had expertly shared this wisdom with one of my patients and that it had forever changed his life, but the truth is that the wisdom was spoken by one of my patients, and it was he who forever changed my life.

The Tense Young Man
Who Didn't Know That
He Already Knew

2

"The trouble with being in the rat race is that
even if you win, you're still a rat."

LILY TOMLIN, COMEDIENNE

The Rat Made Flesh

Buddhas, saints, prophets and self-help gurus are madly popping up about us like mushrooms after a summer rain. Like mushrooms, some are pretty, some are interesting, most are benign and a few are poisonous. They are winking at us from nearly every page on Amazon.com and pitching their wares at us on almost every flickering TV channel. No doubt much wisdom can be gained from these sources if the foolish chaff and commercialism is screened out by our intelligent understanding of how books and media work.

From spiritual gurus peering out with a winning smile from seemingly every bookshelf in Barnes & Noble to pop psychologists manning the mikes with hot-shot advice on the talk show circuits, spiritual and psychological wisdom is readily available. Such contemporary sound-bite wisdom is as ubiquitous today as indulgences used to be in the Renaissance Catholic Church, and with the same stipulation—money. We buy wisdom today like churchgoers used to buy indulgences, with cold hard cash.

Curiously, even though I have learned a tremendous amount from my readings in philosophy, religion and spirituality, for which I am truly grateful, the most powerful bits of wisdom have come from the most unlikely of sources—everyday people who have managed to survive life's difficulties with some type of unassuming gracefulness. My best buddhas have often been those who did not know they were a buddha. And their wisdom came free. It was a wisdom that, born of pure hard-earned experience, held the promise of pure hard-to-beat practicality. So it was with Timothy.

Timothy entered my office on a Friday afternoon, with the cool winds of autumn launching their many colored kites into the blue skies of Pittsburgh. As a chief resident in psychiatry, I was housed in a small but cozy office just off the emergency room, where occasionally the quiet of the office would be interrupted by the muffled wailings of an approaching ambulance or police car bearing an involuntarily committed patient.

Timothy had nothing to do with my emergency room. He was a self-referred private patient, who by risking therapy with a resident in training was able to benefit from markedly lower costs per session. For patients, it was a bit of a crap shoot. If you happened upon a talented young therapist, you won. If you happened upon a not so talented young therapist, you lost. For most patients, it was a naive leap of faith. But for some patients, who were forearmed with a bit of inside information, it was less risky. In Timothy's case, I had been suggested by someone who knew my work well—his brother—so the risk seemed less.

Timothy was a junior in college, struggling with a few inner demons, not of the psychotic nature but of the everyday nature, those anxieties that we all encounter and sometimes simply don't know how to battle effectively. He was a tad short but well built with an animal grace that proclaimed "athlete" with every movement. Indeed, he was an All-American. He was also an honors student and respected among his peers.

Timothy had just the right amount of ugliness to his face to be handsome in a rugged sort of way. His handshake was firm, his eye contact genuine. He was upfront, appropriately anxious for meeting his first shrink and clearly motivated to succeed in therapy. He had a new quest to conquer—knowledge of the self—and deserved real credit for having the courage to enter psychotherapy. He approached one of my comfy chairs then looked about the room with a furtive glance like a soldier checking out the lay of the land. He looked at me, raised his eyebrow, nonverbally asking whether this was the correct place to sit. I nodded my head. And he plopped into the chair. Therapy had begun.

After our introductions I asked him what had brought him to my office. His answer was given with a quick and certain sureness, for Timothy was not a young man of hesitations or second guesses. He had mulled over this opening volley over and over on the nights before our current moment of introduction: "I seem to be succeeding at every thing I want to, but I'm not very happy." He paused, and then with his first smile, almost sheepish in nature, he continued, "Sort of weird, isn't it?"

There was something so earnest and serious in his demeanor, yet refreshingly naive, that I immediately liked Timothy. Here was a young warrior in life, sincere and hardworking, who was just plain battle fatigued. And to Timothy life was indeed a battle. People needed to be tough. If you weren't tough, the answer was simple, you got tougher. No matter what the cost, you pick your quests and then you better damn well succeed in them. That was the key to happiness. The only problem was—it wasn't working. He had done his part for twenty years now, succeeding with every task, but life was not doing its part, providing a feeling of happiness.

As I took his history it became apparent that Timothy had more than his fair share of the typical stresses routinely associated with the simple fact that one has parents and siblings. If we are honest about our evaluation of them, families are great gifts but are sometimes equally great curses. It is not that families are by nature dysfunctional. It is merely that families by nature are composed of people. And people are often problematic, so no family is free of jealousy, hidden agendas and politics. We just hope that, in our families, these negative attributes are far outweighed by feelings of acceptance, open affection and genuine loyalty. Sometimes they are, sometimes they aren't. I'm not telling you anything new here.

Timothy had taken upon himself the not so useful belief that love from his father was essentially based on success in his endeavors. For Timothy, the words "I'm proud of you, Son" were equated with the words "I love you, Son." This confusion, a very common confusion between fathers and children—especially sons—leads to an ever-spiraling heat on a child to succeed in grander and grander fashions. If you letter in a sport, that is great, but now its time to be an All-American. If you have a 3.6 grade point average, that is wonderful, but why don't you have a 3.9? It's a nasty game, where the winner is always destined to be the loser, for the winner can never be good enough.

As our interview proceeded, Timothy loosened up. His posture moved from a soldier "at attention" to a soldier "at ease," but it was still military all the way. A few more smiles slipped from his lips, and we even managed a chuckle or two. Near the end of the interview, I questioned myself whether I should formally test his memory and concentration, for he was concerned that deficits in these areas were hurting him in his tests at school.

In an initial interview with an elderly client I routinely test such cognitive functioning, for dementias can be easily missed and may masquerade as depressive or anxious states. It is less common to do such testing initially with young clients such as Timothy, especially if, as was the case with Timothy, they are carrying a 3.8 grade point average at one of the most difficult universities in the country. On the other hand, Timothy seemed concerned about these deficits. More important, I was having an intuition. My gut was telling me to do the formal cognitive testing, even though my mind did not see the immediate need. In psychotherapy, one learns to listen to the gut, for the gut often sees a patient's soul better than the mind.

The cognitive testing proceeded quite nicely. As I suspected, although some of his depressive symptoms were straining his concentration abilities, no striking cognitive deficits were present. But I was struck by a growing change in Timothy's demeanor. He had moved from being "at ease" to a state somehow even more rigid than being "at attention." His back had stiffened. His gaze intensified. And he nervously bit his lips. Something was up.

I reached a point in the testing, called digit spans, where we give the patient a set of numbers and then ask the patient to repeat them back. We move from one number to usually around seven numbers in a row. It is merely a method of testing the patient's ability to concentrate and to employ his or her short term memory. Our conversation went something like this:

Dr. Shea: Doing great. Try this one, Timothy: 2–4–3–9–8–.

Timothy: 2, 4, 3, 9, 8 (his voice countered in a rapid-fire staccato, a bit like a Gatling gun bearing down on poor General Pickett at Gettysburg).

Dr. Shea: Okay. 4–6–3–5–7–1–.

Timothy: 4, 6, 3, 5, 7, 1 (said with such intensity, that I looked up from my clipboard to find myself face to face with the barrel of the Gatling gun. The gun barrel was still smoking. Timothy was looking right through me, hunting for my soft spot. It was the type of look a pro quarterback might see in the eyes of a linebacker, say Ray Lewis. It wasn't a friendly look. I remember thinking to myself, "Okay, we seem to be taking this a little bit more seriously than may be necessary."

Dr. Shea: 3–2–7–1–5–8–4–.

At which point Timothy said something that I had never had a patient say until then and have never had a patient say since. He said, "Dr. Shea, you are not going to beat me at this, no matter how hard you try."

Here was an unexpected breakthrough. My testing had not found the cognitive deficits it was designed to uncover. It had uncovered something profoundly more important—a deficit of the soul. Our testing had, in Timothy's mind, somehow been malignantly transformed from a technique to help us both uncover whether or not his depression was causing significant concentration problems to a celebrity death match in which one man and only one man would be left standing. Deep inside Timothy's soul, the sands of self-respect were so unstable that even the slightest challenge was a threat to self-respect and, hence, to being loved.

Dr. Shea: Timothy, I'm not trying to beat you.

Timothy: Yes, you are.

Dr. Shea: No, I'm not. (pause) I'm trying to help you find out if your concentration may be hurting you in your studies, something you wanted me to do for you. I'm not mad at you at all, and I'm not hoping you will make mistakes (Timothy relaxed a bit in his chair). Honest.

Timothy: Well, it felt like you were against me, like you wanted to beat me (Timothy smiled sheepishly again). Sorry.

Dr. Shea: No need to be sorry. It is what you were feeling. (pause) How often do you feel like this?

Timothy: (Timothy took a deep breath and shook his head in self-wonderment.) Every day.

Dr. Shea: Every day?

Timothy: Every day.

Dr. Shea: Really?

Timothy: Every day, Dr. Shea.

Dr. Shea: Give me an example.

Timothy: Well, let's say I'm at a party or something, and I'm talking with a girl. If some guy comes up, even a friend, and starts talking with us, I'll feel like he's trying to make me look stupid or something, like I thought you were doing. So I feel like I got to beat him, you know. You know I'm not that good looking, so I got to try harder. You know. Any time I meet a guy, I feel I got to prove myself to him. You ought to see me when I'm taking a test, man. I'm like going to war or something, I don't know what.

Dr. Shea: That sort of sounds unpleasant.

Timothy: Yeah, (pause) it is.

Dr. Shea: You know what?

Timothy: What?

Dr. Shea: I don't think it's necessary.

Timothy: You don't?

Dr. Shea: I don't (I smiled, and Timothy smiled back and sat back in his chair, letting out a sigh. At which point he said one word). Wow.

And here is where our story begins to tie in with the relationship between success and happiness. For with Timothy we have our perfect example of a good human being, who was highly successful in the eyes of society, who was desperately unhappy, for success had made a rat of him as Lily Tomlin notes so wittily at the beginning of the chapter.

Our society is geared to put us all in the rat race, where worth is determined by how many quests we succeed in achieving. It has even begun to malignantly invade our preschools where, instead of enjoying play and socializing, our children are, quite literally, pushed to learn, and if you don't do this task, you are a failure at age four! How sick can we get? The answer is: pretty sick. There is a multimillion dollar business in "Learning Toys," one of the uniquely weird oxymorons of all time. The goal of such toys is to learn while you play. I don't know about you, but that doesn't sound like playing to me. That sounds like learning, you know, schoolwork. Maybe I'm missing something here.

By the way, God help you these days if a fellow parent turns to you and asks, "What are your kids doing this summer?" and you don't answer with something like, "Preparing for the 2020 Summer Olympics. I have my kid enrolled in soccer camp, swimming lessons, bike repair (in case he becomes a tri-athlete), and intensive reading of important twentieth-century authors that might be important in college board preparation. You never know. I think he's going to have a great summer. It'll be a lot of fun."

I made the mistake of answering this question honestly once by commenting, "You know, I'm just going to let the boys relax this summer. You know, do nothing. Just play. They worked hard at school. I think they deserve a break." Silence. Then I heard, "Oh, that sounds great," said with the tone of enthusiasm that one would expect had I informed them I was sending the boys to have a sex-change operation over the summer months. That night I kept waiting for a knock on the door from Children and Youth Services saying that my neighbors had filed a charge of child neglect. I'm not kidding, it's getting ugly out there. And the people who lose are our kids, for they are no longer allowed to be kids. They are becoming rats.

You see, the culture is fixated upon this idea of questing for success in multiple endeavors. We all get put in the rat race and, naturally, we try to win. But as Tomlin suggests, winning is really losing in such races, for one is being trained to be a rat. In essence, my patient Timothy was Lily Tomlin's theoretical rat made into the flesh. And it hurts. It hurts bad. In fact, some adolescents and young adults hurt so badly that they attempt and sometimes complete suicide, driven by the gut feeling that they are, and always will be, losers in this quest for the gold.

In this regard popular culture seems to love to make rats of us. For instance, outlandish statements—sometimes taken completely out of context—have a knack for landing on inspirational posters such as this beauty:

Winning isn't everything, it's the only thing.

Vince Lombardi, former head coach, Green Bay Packers

There's a nice quote. That must have been hanging on the walls of the Enron executive suite.

Pulled out of context—spoken to a roomful of professional athletes who hopefully understand that the statement is a motivational exaggeration—such a phrase can easily become less a dramatic ploy than an accepted truth. Plopped onto the wall of a junior high locker room, Coach Lombardi is suddenly transformed from a brilliant motivator into a brilliant rat maker.

And here is another beauty attributed to Bertolt Brecht:

Why be a man when you can be a success?

Delightful! No guilt production here. And what about this problematic motivator from the gifted former baseball manager Sparky Anderson, who I doubt was aware of its darker implications:

Success is the person who year after year
reaches the highest limits in his field.

At first glance it doesn't look so bad—almost sounds logical; but take another look. Such a statement tells all young athletes who are playing to the best of their abilities, that if their play does not land them at "the highest limits," they are not a success.

These are the kinds of statements that create "Timothys." Beneath their adulation of winners, they house the metacommunication that one is never good enough, unless you win. And sometimes, even if you win you are not good enough, because you didn't win the way you should have.

Thankfully, there are people—highly successful people—who disagree, as witnessed by the following quote from Arthur Ashe, one of the greatest tennis players of all time:

> *Success is a journey not a destination.*
> *The doing is usually more important than the outcome.*
> *Not everyone can be Number 1.*

And here is one from Jennifer James, author of *Twenty Steps to Wisdom*:

> *Success is not a destination that you ever reach.*
> *Success is the quality of your journey.*

And, finally, leave it to Bob Dylan to capture the essence of our argument with his inimitable no-nonsense wisdom:

> *A man is a success if he gets up in the morning*
> *and gets to bed at night, and in between*
> *he does what he wants to do.*

This does not mean that one doesn't want to succeed with certain quests in life. We do. It just means that it is important to pick such quests, limit the number of such quests, and realize that we are not failures if we are not the best in all of our quests, rather it is much more important to realize that we tried to do our best in such quests even if we finished last. In the end, the most important quest is to enjoy our quests.

A Rat Transformed, Misleading Road Signs
and the First Piece in the Puzzle

For a moment let us return to that first session with Timothy. From the above discussion we can see how an overemphasis upon success can clearly backfire. But we need to dig deeper. You will recall that our goal in this chapter was to examine the relationship between success and happiness. It is Timothy who, despite all of his maladaptive anxiety and his extreme intensity, may hold a revelation concerning the relationship of success to happiness. It is a revelation that, as they say in Zen literature, is splendid in its simplicity.

After months of therapy, Timothy entered my office with a smile on his face (for the first time ever) and quipped, "Dr. Shea, I got the answer." He promptly plopped himself into the chair. I was pleasantly taken back by his casualness, his lack of tenseness, or a need to impress me. He looked happy.

Timothy proceeded, "Now I don't know exactly how important this really is, but there is a part of me that thinks this is what we we've been look-ing for. I just feel that I have a better idea of what is important in life." And then he said the following. It was simple. It was accurate. And it ultimately changed my life:

"You know what, Dr. Shea?"

"No, what, Timothy?"

"Success isn't happiness. Finding happiness is success."

He sat back. "You are a successful man if you are happy, not if you have accomplished all sorts of things. I've had it backwards all these years. That's why I've achieved all these successes, and I've not been happy. I need to sit back and find out what will make me happy, what I like to do, and how I want to do it. Then I need to set those things as my goal. Being happy will be my goal and making other people happy too. I think I can be productive this way. I just think it's better. You know, I think I sort of knew this all along, but I didn't really know I knew it, what it really meant, I mean. What do you think?"

I answered, "I think you are on to something. I really do."

Timothy smiled. He was a rat transformed.

Here is where the plot thickens, for as I said those words, I felt a twinge of jealously towards Timothy, for he really had discovered something, something that he had not read or heard from me, but something that had arisen from his own soul. I knew the words, but I had not felt the words—not like Timothy felt them, for his feeling was the feeling of stumbling upon a truth, not just understanding it intellectually but knowing it in your gut. And it made me think.

It was one of those rare junctions in therapy in which the therapist knows that it is the patient who is saying something that the therapist needs to hear. These are wonderful moments, moments in which two souls meet. They say the greatest joy for a teacher is the moment when the teacher realizes that the student has become better than the teacher. So it is in psychotherapy.

Timothy has taken us one step closer to understanding why it is so easy to lose sight of the ultimate goal, why it is so easy for questing beasts to get lost on their way to happiness. Apparently, not infrequently, the road signs are wrong. In particular the sign labeled "success" often points to the wrong town. If one doesn't keep Timothy's wisdom in mind, that "Success isn't happiness. Finding happiness is success," it is very easy to become preoccupied with quests that follow roads to fame or fortune, but not to happiness. Timothy has given us the first piece in the puzzle of the meaning of happiness. We have come a giant step closer to defining happiness by defining what it is not.

By the way, Timothy is not alone in this assertion. He is accompanied by quite an array of big guns in the world of philosophy:

> *Happiness is the meaning and the purpose of life,*
> *the whole aim and end of human existence.*
>
> Aristotle

Happiness is the only sanction of life: where happiness fails,
existence becomes a mad lamentable experiment.

George Santayana

How to gain, how to keep, and how to recover happiness is
in fact for most men at all times the secret motive for all they do.

William James

By heaven we understand a state of happiness infinite
in degree, and endless in duration.

Benjamin Franklin

And, finally, Timothy will be pleased to know that he and Albert Schweitzer, the Nobel-Prize winning physician and humanitarian, were on the same track:

Success is not the key to happiness.
Happiness is the key to success.

Now how does all this help us to find happiness? I believe it is probably best for me to simply show how it helped me. About four years after Timothy ended his therapy, I was still involved in my job at a well-known and highly respected academic center. Success, by the standards of Vince Lombardi, was coming my way. I had been told by the chairman of the department that I was one of a handful of young turks that they were grooming to be national leaders in psychiatry. I had a book published at a very young age. I began presenting on a national level. Like Timothy, success after success was coming my way.

On the other hand, loaded down with administrative duties and research pressures, my work hours had become extreme, my time with my family less and less. And when I was home, I wasn't home—my mind was still at work. I felt as if I was losing sight of my own clinical mission. Over the preceding two years I had slowly come to realize, to my surprise, that I wasn't so happy anymore.

It was then that I started thinking of Timothy. I had this fantasy that I walked into my office and Timothy was in my chair. I sat down, and with a tremendous sense of happiness, I turned to him and said, "You know what, I just figured something out."

Timothy turned to me and said, "What's that?"

I answered, "Success is not happiness. Finding happiness is success."

Timothy just smiled and said, "You got it."

Three months later I changed jobs, moved to New Hampshire to focus on providing clinical care for the indigent in a community mental health center and never looked back once. In my academic career, the time constraints, politics and research pressures had outstripped my ability to use my time in a satisfying fashion. What I discovered upon moving to New Hampshire was that I was much better suited, by nature and temperament, to handle the unique and equally demanding stresses of community mental health work. I was happier.

As Timothy pointed out, one only succeeds in life's quests—developing careers, finding rewarding relationships or gaining financial security—to the degree that one has the time to enjoy pursuing these quests while doing them. Paradoxically, these seemingly all-important goals are meaningless unless they help one to stay focused on the ultimate goal—finding happiness. Aristotle knew it. Santayana knew it. William James knew it. Benjamin Franklin knew it. Albert Schweitzer knew it. Timothy knew it. And, now, we know it.

We are now ready to hunt down the next piece to the puzzle of happiness. To find it, we must leave our cozy psychiatrist's office in Pittsburgh and travel to a place that is not only distant in miles but also in years. It is a place where one of the most powerful leaders in history casts her rather corpulent shadow into the nooks and crannies of cities as diverse as London and Bombay. It is in these shadows that the next piece of our puzzle—a most elusive piece—awaits us. It is to England and its great monarch, Queen Victoria, whose unmistakable silhouette cast this great shadow, that we now turn.

3   Heaven Inside Hell

"The mind is its own place, and in itself, can make
a Heaven of Hell, a Hell of Heaven."

JOHN MILTON

Flames in Paradise

We shall continue our search for the meaning of happiness at Piccadilly Circus, an intersection of bustling London streets. The year is 1886. All of London, and, indeed, much of the world, is aglow with the intrigues and marvels of Queen Victoria and her sprawling British Empire.

Victoria had come to the throne at the remarkably young age of eighteen. Now, almost fifty years later, it was not only the Empire that was sprawling, so was the Queen. At the age of sixty-seven, the body of the Queen had morphed into its now famous silhouette that would remain her hallmark throughout the rest of the century. As the Queen's girth had exploded, so had the population of London itself. In the first eighty years of the nineteenth century, greater London had grown from an impressive one million inhabitants to a staggering 4.5 million people.

As we stand here at Piccadilly Circus, near rush hour on a Friday in 1886, it looks like all 4.5 million of them are racing our way. The intersection is a blur of speeding hansoms, cursing cabbies, spinning cart wheels and yelling bobbies. If we could take a peek at the people who are being hauled about in these hansoms and cabs, we would find a rare collection of both the great and the infamous, culled from all four corners of the world. The catch phrase of the day is, "The sun never sets on the British Empire." In point of fact, it didn't. Victorian gunboats and lances had made their inroads from Peking to Johannesburg, from Darjeeling to Toronto. British imperialism was at its peak.

For those lucky people who were rich and famous, or who wanted to become rich and famous, the streets, theaters and brothels of Victorian London were a veritable paradise. Indeed, the gods associated with wealth and fame flocked to its pearly gates as rapidly as today's elite flock to Hollywood Boulevard. Charles Dickens created Ebenezer Scrooge here. Karl Marx dreamed up *The Communist Manifesto* here. Florence Nightingale drafted the first recruits into the Red Cross here. And Oscar Wilde went straight to jail here for professing the "love that one dare not name." Unfortunately for Oscar, he named it.

Even at night, London was a heaven for the more nocturnal of angels. The streets were aglow with the eerie light cast by thousands of flickering gas lamps. This was the shadowy London made famous by fogs so green with the smog of the mills that they were called pea soup. This was the London where one could hear the footsteps of Holmes and Watson fading into the distance as they chased the evil Professor Moriarty. This is the London that the philosopher George Santayana captured quite well when he quipped, "London is the paradise of individuality, eccentricity, heresy, anomalies, hobbies and humours."

But it was a paradise with a dark side—a dark side that flickered not so much with gas light as with flame light, for if you were not rich or gifted, pretty or intelligent, witty or well-connected, London was not so much a heaven as it was a hell. Indeed, it was the romantic poet Percy Bysshe

Shelley who dared to flat out say it, when he wryly commented, "Hell is a city much like London—A populous and smoky city."

To this hell we now turn for a closer look. Within its horrors we shall find a man busily at work transforming hellish flame into heavenly music. He will provide us with not one but several pieces to the puzzle of the meaning of happiness. To appreciate the enormity of his task—the brilliance of his workmanship—we must first learn more about the intensity of the flames surrounding him.

To do so we must leave the fashionable district of the West End of London and wander into the East End, where the slums await us. In places like Whitechapel and the parish of St. Georges, we find the London of Charles Dickens in the flesh, filled with the jetsam of humanity tossed ashore by the glitter of the fashionable. Just how bad is this place?

First, it is a tad on the crowded side. In 1844, in St. George's, Hanover Square, there were about 1,465 families living in exactly 2,174 rooms. Rooms—not apartments, not houses—rooms. In one room local inspectors found fifty people living in a space that measured twenty-two by sixteen feet. In London general, nearly fifty thousand families were living in single rooms. Second, it is on the smelly side. As one can imagine—with crowding of this magnitude—privacy was a bit of a problem. Plumbing was more of a problem. Daily hygiene was, shall we just say, a severe problem. Third, it is on the unhealthful side. There are more spirochetes and typhoid bugs swirling around here than paparazzi trying to get a shot of Madonna on a nude beach. Children in particular were at high risk. In 1855 over one-half of all deaths were to children under the age of eight. In short, the neighborhoods were rife with crime, filth, disease and hunger.

Our statistics become even more disturbing when they become specifics, when we put some faces on these numbers. In this regard, Charles Dickens made us well aware of the atrocities of workhouses, coal mines and industrial mills, but there is one example of Victorian misery, which Dickens mentions in *Oliver Twist*, that is worth revisiting—the plight of chimney sweeps. It is here that we shall find our faces.

When a modern reader first thinks of chimney sweeps, it is easy to picture the smiling mug of Dick Van Dyke. Dick has just popped out of a chimney pipe, as if shot by some circus cannon. He is quickly joined by the wondrous voices of a myriad of high-stepping young laddies dancing atop the rooftops of London, all of this magic occurring under the approving eyes of a Miss Mary Poppins. Don't get me wrong, I loved this Academy Award-winning fantasy from Hollywood as much as the next guy, and *Mary Poppins* remains one of my favorite musicals. But *Mary Poppins* is not the best place to go for a look at the life of a real chimney sweep.

It wasn't for naught that Percy Bysshe Shelley said that London and Hell were both filled with people and smoke. The 4.5 million inhabitants of London needed to cook their food and heat what little bathwater they were using. To do so, their stoves sent millions of chimneys into the heavens. They were small-bore chimneys that would twist and turn as they wound skyward. They were, of course, pitch black inside and someone had to clean them. The "someone" turned out to be five- and six-year-old boys.

The small children would toughen their skins with sea brine to help them withstand the inevitable cuts and bruises they would sustain as they climbed into the labyrinth of chimneys. Lung poisoning was common, as was injury from falling masonry and the actual stunting of growth that sometimes resulted from the unhealthful working conditions.

High in the twisting turns of mansions, sometimes forty or fifty feet in the air, the unthinkable would occasionally occur. The chimney sweep would become disoriented and lost, and, perhaps, even stuck. It is difficult to imagine what such terror must have been like to experience. Not a few chimney sweeps did not return to the ground.

Naturally, five- and six-year-old boys were not eager to ascend such death traps, so their ever obliging employers, called master chimney sweeps—nothing more or less than slave masters—would pierce the boys in the butt with large pins or perhaps apply a little enthusiasm via the application of live coals to the aforementioned butts. It was not until late in 1875, long after France and North America banned the use of children as chimney sweeps, that England passed a bill (sponsored, ironically, by a man named Lord Shaftesbury), that banned children from this atrocious practice.

In short, all was not well in Victorian London—at least not in the East End. It is clear that the intensity of the flames surrounding our protagonist was remarkable. Yet, out of all of this misery, he was able to become remarkably happy. How he got to be that way is the guts of our story.

Angels in Hell

The historical figure, who will introduce us to our protagonist, was himself pretty nifty. He also happened to be hanging out in the nifty side of London. His name is Sir Frederick Treves. He was the "top scalpel" at the most prestigious hospital in all of the city—London Hospital. Sir Frederick was as equally gifted at cutting a fine figure on the dance floor as at cutting off a bit of necrotic leg in the operating room. Gifted at conversation, writing and partying, Sir Frederick, if alive today, would undoubtedly have achieved that most remarkable of triple crowns of celebrityhood—making it on the covers of *Time*, *Newsweek*, and *People*.

But here was the really refreshing news about Sir Frederick. He was a nice guy. Not full of himself, not a superstar, not a big shot—he wouldn't have wanted to have been on all of those covers. In fact, Sir Frederick was a remarkably compassionate man, as reflected by the fact that he spent nearly every Sunday, not on the cricket fields, but on the back wards of London Hospital caring for the indigent.

John Merrick—our protagonist—was one of these indigent. Frederick Treves took him under his wing, bringing him to the London Hospital, where Merrick would live in two small rooms for the remainder of his life. It is John Merrick who offers us some unusually rich insights into the definition of happiness. I believe him to be one of the most courageous and dignified people I have ever had the pleasure to learn about.

Merrick was born in 1863. He would live a brief twenty-seven years in the part of Victorian London that comprised the Hell of our chimney sweeps. But if being born into the squalor and poverty of Victorian London was not enough, John Merrick had the great misfortune of being born into a body ravaged by a rare disease known as the Proteus syndrome.

This genetic disorder was identified in 1979 by Michael Cohen Jr. Subsequently, in 1983 a German pediatrician, Rudolf Wiedemann, gave the disorder its almost science fiction-sounding name. Wiedemann gave this name in honor of the Greek god Proteus, an Olympian who had the notable distinction of being a polymorph—a creature that can appear in many shapes and guises, sort of a Greek prototype for John Carpenter's creature in *The Thing*.

In the Proteus syndrome, the main problem appears to be a renegade set of engineers. But the engineers in question are not your typical set of computer geeks with black-rimmed glasses and a ten-year subscription to *Popular Mechanics*. No, these engineers are inanimate. They are also on the small size for engineers, being only a couple of molecules thick. And they don't work at Sony. They work inside the cytoplasm of the innumerable cells of the human body. They work as messenger boys for our genes.

Our miniscule messenger boys have the daunting task of telling our cells when to start making new cells, how many of them to make and what they should look like after one goes to the bother of making them. In Proteus syndrome, the engineers get it all wrong. Like mad scientists sucking on a few tabs of LSD, they send an incessant blur of faulty messages to the cells' factories. With bad blueprints onboard, the factories have no recourse but to go berserk. The result is not pretty to look at. The cells go into a manic overdrive, producing disfiguring growths and tumors that poke through the skin all over the body.

John Merrick had Proteus syndrome in a bad way. As a two-year-old he began sprouting unsightly tumors from his face. As the years progressed, Merrick's head became an enormous growth that was covered with convolutions and folded skin that for all the world looked like a creation by the horror writer H.P. Lovecraft, without Lovecraft's trademark tentacles. By the end of his life Merrick's head had ballooned to be the size of the circumference of a normal man's waist.

But there is perhaps no one better qualified to describe John Merrick's deformities than the man who helped him to cope with them—Dr. Treves. In a tiny tract of only about thirty pages, Treves wrote a magnificent monograph that is hard to beat in its intensity, poignancy and sense of compassion. I cry most every time I read it. In this monograph Treves described Merrick as follows:

> *The most striking feature about him was his enormous and misshapened head. From the brow there projected a huge bony mass like a loaf, while from the back of the head hung a bag of spongy, fungous-looking skin, the surface of which was comparable to brown cauliflower. On the top of the skull were a few lank hairs. . . . From the upper jaw there projected another mass of bone. It protruded from the mouth like a pink stump, turning the upper lip inside out and making the mouth a mere slobbering aperture. . . . The nose was merely a lump of flesh. . . . The back was horrible, because from it hung, as far down as the middle of the thigh, huge, sack-like masses of flesh covered by the same loathsome cauliflower skin. . . . The right arm was of enormous size and shapeless. . . . The hand was large and clumsy—a fin or paddle rather than a hand.*
>
> *. . . To add further burden to his trouble the wretched man, when a boy, developed hip disease, which had left him permanently lame, so that he could only walk with a stick. He was thus denied all means of escape from his tormentors. As he told me later, he could never run away. One other feature must be mentioned to emphasize his isolation from his kind. Although he was already repellent enough, there arose from the fungous skin-growth with which he was almost covered a very sickening stench which was hard to tolerate.*

Like one of our misfortunate chimney sweeps, suddenly lost and trapped inside the hardness of a chimney, John Merrick was forever lost and trapped inside the softness of his own flesh. It should be added that

Merrick, because of the enormous size of his deformities and the subsequent weight they placed on his body and joints, was in nearly constant physical pain. If ever there was a candidate to represent the living embodiment of the Job of the Old Testament, John Merrick would be at the top of my list.

Of course his treatment by others was, unfortunately, predictable. Merrick was ridiculed, beaten, harassed and piteously displayed as "The Elephant Man," a repugnant misnomer that hopefully will forever fade into oblivion, for it in no way captures the elegance of John Merrick's soul.

To understand the extent of Merrick's interpersonal pain, we should turn again to the actual writings of Treves as he describes first seeing Merrick alone in an abandoned shop, where Merrick was being abusively used as a perverted side show:

> The showman pulled back the curtain and revealed a bent figure crouching on a stool and covered by a brown blanket. In front of it, on a tripod, was a large brick heated by a Bunsen burner. Over this the creature was huddled to warm itself. It never moved when the curtain was drawn back. Locked up in an empty shop and lit by the faint blue light of the gas jet, this hunched-up figure was the embodiment of loneliness. It might have been a captive in a cavern or a wizard watching for unholy manifestations in the ghostly flame.
>
> The showman—speaking as if to a dog—called out harshly, "Stand-up!" The thing arose slowly and let the blanket that covered its head and back fall to the ground. There stood revealed the most disgusting specimen of humanity that I have ever seen. . . . He was naked to the waist, his feet were bare, he wore a pair of threadbare trousers that had once belonged to some fat gentleman's dress suit.

Sir Frederick would prove to be a most wonderful friend. He sheltered John Merrick at the London Hospital for all of his remaining years, visiting him almost daily. In addition, Treves understood the intense interpersonal pain that Merrick had undergone and carefully, sensitively, sought ways of relieving it. For instance Treves realized that his friend had never had a woman meet him without a look of utter disgust on her face. Indeed, it was not uncommon for women to shriek at his sight if not appropriately fore-warned of his appearance. Here is how Treves handled this situation:

> *Feeling this, I asked a friend of mine, a young and pretty widow, if she thought she could enter Merrick's room with a smile, wish him good morning and shake him by the hand. She said she could and she did. The effect upon poor Merrick was not quite what I had expected. As he let go her hand he bent his head on his knees and sobbed until I thought he would never cease.*

Because of his career and position, Treves was able to muster an enormous amount of support for Merrick, who would receive visitors as famous as Ellen Terry, one of the most gifted of actresses on the London stage, to Queen Victoria herself, who visited Merrick many times and sent him a Christmas card each year that always contained a handwritten message.

Despite the fact that Merrick had great difficulty speaking because the malformations of his lips made his pronunciation almost indecipherable, he was quite intelligent. And he used his intelligence to make the most of the kindnesses that Sir Frederick and his friends offered him.

For instance, Merrick was a reading maven. He made his two modest rooms into a miniature library. His books took him to faraway worlds. In these worlds Merrick was neither ugly nor an object of derision. He was a Victorian dandy. He was a Persian prince. It did not matter.

Together, these two angels—Treves and Merrick—using compassion, intelligence and imagination, had managed to begin the transformation of Hell into Heaven. But it was up to Merrick to do the hardest work. It was he who would ultimately display the most dazzling pieces of the puzzle of happiness.

Every Hour of the Day

What exactly does Merrick have to teach us? Undoubtedly he lived in much better circumstances due to the extraordinary compassion of a bevy of Londoners, but let us not kid ourselves. He still coped with constant pain, he couldn't look into a mirror because of his own hideousness, he never left his two rooms without a hood on his head, and he existed with the continual awareness that to the vast majority of his fellow human beings he was a living monster.

A simple vignette helps to illuminate how difficult Merrick's daily existence was. His head was so enormous and heavy that he dare not lay back in his bed to sleep, for his spine could not support his head. Consequently, Merrick slept each night in a most peculiar and uncomfortable fashion. He sat against the bed board with his knees bent upwards. He then carefully, using his hands as support, would set his head forward onto his knees, a position that would be his only respite throughout the night.

Our point is simple: If ever there was a man who should have been unhappy, it was John Merrick. And it is the following words from Treves' monograph on Merrick that have always fascinated me the most, that haunt me in a pleasant sort of way, like a house ghost that adds whimsy to an upstairs guest room. They haunt me because they seem unbelievable. They haunt me because they don't seem to fit our facts. But I have no doubt that they are true. Treves wrote, "Merrick, I may say, was now one of the most contented creatures I have chanced to meet. More than once he said to me: 'I am happy every hour of the day.'"

John Merrick's first contribution to our search for a definition of happiness cannot be overstated, for Merrick proves without a shadow of a doubt that happiness is not determined by external circumstances. Happiness is determined by internal attitudes.

Merrick is the living proof that, as John Milton suggested in the opening epigraph of our chapter, the human mind really can create a Heaven inside a Hell. But Merrick also shows us something more. He demonstrates the curious fact that "happiness" cannot be equated with feeling good, being joyful or being without pain, for John Merrick was seldom without physical pain. Yet John Merrick was happy.

Merrick, more powerfully than perhaps any man I have studied, taught not by his words but by his actions, his very being. One is reminded of the enigmatic words from the *Tao Te Ching*, a wonderful book of Taoist wisdom, that was written by a Chinese sage named Lao Tzu about five hundred years before Christ was born:

> *Therefore the Master*
> *acts without doing anything*
> *and teaches without saying anything.*

By these standards John Merrick must surely stand as a dazzling example of a Taoist Master, who just happened to be hanging out in the London of Queen Victoria. Merrick did not tell us how to be happy; he showed us what it is to be happy.

Of course words also can play a role, as guideposts of a sort, in our spiritual quests. It is reassuring to see that some very respected thinkers from differing traditions and religious backgrounds agree with our discovery, via Merrick, that happiness is not based upon external circumstances but upon internal reflections.

I am immediately reminded of some of the passages written by the philosopher Alan Watts in one of his more obscure but brilliant books, *The Meaning of Happiness*. For those not familiar with Watts, he was a San Franciscan luminary who for several decades, including during the 1950s and 1960s, demonstrated an almost uncanny knack for translating Eastern thinking, especially Zen Buddhism and Taoism, into terms that made sense to Westerners. What was most remarkable about Watts was his ability to appeal to everyone from Manhattan stockbrokers, hustling the markets of Wall Street, to the long-haired adolescents sprouting flowers from their heads in the back alleyways of Haight-Ashbury—no mean feat. When it came to Eastern philosophy, no matter who you asked or where you asked it, Watts was "da man."

Watts was, indeed, a great wordsmith, one of the most eloquent writers I have come across, and he knew exactly how to cut through the crap of most philosophical jargon—both Eastern and Western. In his preface to *The Meaning of Happiness*, Watts adds something new to our understanding, for he points out that happiness need not be fleeting, especially

> . . . that complete kind of happiness which does not depend on external events, which belongs to the very nature of the individual and remains unaffected by suffering. It persists through both joy and sorrow, being a spiritual undertone which results from the positive and wholehearted acceptance of life in all its aspects.

This passage seems to have captured exactly the type of spiritual undertone that we stumbled upon in the heart of John Merrick. A few pages later, Watts provides a pearl of wisdom that will, undoubtedly, help us in our search for the meaning of "happiness." It is a simple statement of fact. It is a statement that Merrick did not write, but lived: "All men suffer, now as well as in ancient times, but not all are unhappy, for unhappiness is a reaction to suffering, not suffering itself."

Notice how remarkably similar the bottom-line message is from a Christian perspective, as eloquently stated by the Reverend Billy Graham:

> The happiness which brings enduring worth to life is not the superficial happiness that is dependent on circumstances. It is the happiness and contentment that fills the soul even in the midst of the most distressing circumstances and the most bitter environment. It is the kind of happiness that grins when things go wrong and smiles through tears. The happiness for which our souls ache is one undisturbed by success or failure, one which will root deeply inside us and give inward relaxation, peace, and contentment, no matter what the surface problems may be. That kind of happiness stands in need of no outward stimulus.

Let us review for a moment what Merrick has shown us. I believe that through his actions, we have uncovered three key pieces to the meaning of happiness:

1. Happiness is not determined purely by external circumstances.
2. Happiness, both its presence and its absence, as well as its depth, is greatly determined by internal attitudes.
3. Happiness might even occur during periods of suffering.

If these three puzzle pieces alone were all that John Merrick provided us, it would have been well worth the time we have spent on his life, but Merrick also had a more intangible gift to give us. It is a metacommunication provided by the example of his life, itself.

This message is not so much a piece of the puzzle as it is the picture on the box of the puzzle—the promised reward of all our hard work. It is a message that, in the last analysis, has been vastly more meaningful to me than any philosophical idea or inspirational passage that I have encountered. It is a message that motivates us to continue with our work, our lives, our missions. The example of John Merrick's life gives us that most precious of gifts. It gives us hope.

Merrick's hope is not hackneyed. Merrick's hope does not require a specific religious belief. Merrick's hope is not imagined. Merrick's hope is concrete, real and irrefutable. John Merrick showed us that no matter how painful life's experiences may be, there is always the hope that one can still find happiness. One man did it. It is irrefutable. It is real. And, during tough times in my own life, I have thought of it often.

There is no "should" to the message of John Merrick. It is not that we should be happy while dealing with tough times. It's okay if we are not. It is simply greatly reassuring to know that it is possible to be happy during tough times. John Merrick did it. And the fact that he did it inspires a clear and wonderfully real sense of hope. This is not Ivory Tower hope. This is blue collar hope. The question now is—how did he do it?

The Brain of a Man, the Fancies of a Youth
and the Imagination of a Child

Part of the answer to our question is to be found once again in the writings of Sir Frederick, for they provide our most immediate picture of who John Merrick really was. In this regard, one can imagine that secondary to Merrick's extreme isolation throughout his life, there were certain types of social engagements that most people take for granted, that had always been out of his reach. Merrick experienced life like a small boy who sees a Nintendo gaming console in a shop window but knows he will never have enough money to buy it.

One such tantalizing occasion for Merrick was his dream of going to the theater. Once again Sir Frederick masterminded a method of bringing this dream to his friend. In the dead of night, hidden away behind the drawn blinds of a racing carriage, Merrick was secreted up a back stairways to a special box seat provided by the wonderful actress and human being Mrs. Kendal, who arranged the entire evening at the request of Sir Frederick. The theater was the famous Drury Lane Theatre, and the play was a pantomime. Merrick peered down at the stage, hidden behind a carefully selected group of patrons who occupied the front seats of the box to function as blinds to hide Merrick from other theater patrons. Sir Frederick describes the evening as follows:

> One has often witnessed the unconstrained delight of a child at its first pantomime, but Merrick's rapture was much more intense as well as much more solemn. Here was a being with the brain of a man, the fancies of a youth and the imagination of a child. His attitude was not so much that of delight as of wonder and amazement. He was awed. He was enthralled. The spectacle left him speechless, so that if he were spoken to he took no heed. He often seemed to be panting for breath. I could not help comparing him with a man of his own age in the stalls. This satiated individual was bored to distraction, would look wearily at the

stage from time to time and then yawn as if he had not slept for nights; while at the same time Merrick was thrilled by a vision that was almost beyond his comprehension.

Part of Merrick's happiness was the direct result of his ability to see the world through the eyes of a child, to be alive to the moment at hand, to be open to the sensation of wonderment. So powerful is the concentration of the human being during periods of awe and wonderment that I doubt that Merrick was even aware of the pain in his joints and limbs as he sat in that booth.

In a similar fashion it was the rolling hills and valleys of rural England that provided Merrick with perhaps his greatest days of happiness and that provide us with yet another example of the awesome power of wonderment. Merrick had always dreamed of seeing the farms, villages, fields, birds and foxes of rural England. Sir Frederick, through the graciousness of a wealthy patron named Lady Knightley, was able to offer Merrick a holiday home in a cottage on her estate. Sir Frederick captures the moment with the immediacy of a photograph:

> *There is no doubt that Merrick passed in this retreat the happiest time he had yet experienced. He was alone in a land of wonders. The breath of the country passed over him like a healing wind. Into the silence of the wood the fearsome voice of the showman could never penetrate. No cruel eyes could peep at him through the friendly undergrowth. His letters to me were the letters of a delighted and enthusiastic child. He gave an account of his trivial adventures, of the amazing things he had seen, and of the beautiful sounds he had heard. He had met with strange birds, had startled a hare from her form, had made friends with a fierce dog, and had watched the trout darting in a stream. He sent me some of the wild flowers he had picked. They were of the commonest and most familiar kind, but they were evidently regarded by him as rare and precious specimens.*

In these passages we see that, once again, it is a sense of wonderment that kindles much of the luminosity of Merrick's style of happiness. And herein lies one of the secrets for finding happiness that Merrick passes on to us. For Merrick shows us that wonderment is the gateway to gratitude. Perhaps "wonderment" and "gratitude" are even words for the same thing. And it is this gentle sensation of gratitude, a sensation that I truly believe we can cultivate within ourselves, that may offer us one more hint of the pathway to the more enduring sense of happiness described by both Alan Watts and Billy Graham. Perhaps it is to this importance of gratitude that the curiously wise English mystic, Meister Eckhart, was alluding when he wrote way back in the 1300s words that still ring true today:

If the only prayer
you say in your entire life
is "Thank-You,"
that would suffice.

The Sweeping of the Swallows and the Bending of the Grasses

I have obviously spent more than my fair share of time thinking about John Merrick. During those times many associations have come to my mind. I would like to share one of the more puzzling of them.

It is while I picture Merrick wandering about Lady Knightley's fields and woodlands that I have found the following image popping into my head. I don't know exactly where it comes from, but I have often found that the curious burpings of my subconscious are often better guideposts to my soul than the more refined musings of my conscious awareness. So let's take a look at it. Perhaps, in its own strange way, it will provide us with one more piece to our puzzle concerning the meaning of happiness.

The curious image is of a very distant field in a very distant time from the Victorian Era of Lady Knightley's estate. The year is A.D. 1221. The field sits outside a small town in Italy. It is filled with gracefully bending grasses. On this field, in the winds—filled with the searing heat of a Mediterranean day—there stands a wide-eyed individual, uncommonly simply dressed. He is apparently viewed by the local citizenry as a wise man of sorts, and, at the moment, much like John Merrick, seems to be utterly entranced with the world about him. He is watching a pair of swallows darting in the air, and with the "brain of a man, the fancies of a youth and the imagination of a child," he stands awestruck by the beauty of their wing beats and the gracefulness of their dives.

The man is Saint Francis of Assisi. He believed, with the same gentle naivete of John Merrick, that he could talk with these swallows. There are many people, not the least of which is the Pope, who also believe that he could do so. It is the image of Saint Francis of Assisi that keeps popping into my mind as I picture John Merrick enjoying the country estate of Lady Knightley.

Perhaps I am reminded of Saint Francis because I find him to be so similar in temperament to John Merrick. There is one feature in particular that these two saints, separated by four centuries, seem to have shared: They both had a profound sense of wonderment and gratitude.

It was Saint Francis who wrote the *Canticle of the Creatures* in which, with the sincerity of John Merrick, he praised Brother Sun, Brother Moon, Brother Wind, Brother Air, Sister Water and Sister Earth, as if God had given each of these wonderments to him as a personal gift. Saint Francis, like Merrick enjoying his pantomime, was filled with an intense gratitude for every creature that he had ever come across, good or evil, tame or wild—for all were miraculous in the very act of their existing.

There is another reason that Saint Francis was so enthralled by the universe about him. He was a mystic. Most mystics believe that, whoever is responsible for cooking up the idea of the universe, whether god, goddess or a more nebulous "godhead," the maker can not only be seen in what he or she has made, the maker is what he or she has made. In short, God is marvelously present in all of creation, including swallows and blades of grass. From the mystical perspective, it should also be added that since we humans are part of creation, ipso facto, God is also present in us.

In itself this is not so unusual a perspective. It is the type of thinking that most of our religious leaders have touched upon at some point in their teachings, whether Christian, Buddhist or Jew. It is probably what Christ was hinting at, regarding the feeding of the poor, when he commented, "I tell you the truth, whatever you did for one of the least of these brothers of mine, you did for me." One can easily see how, for mystics such as Saint Francis, this ability to perceive god in all things fosters not only a sense of wonderment but a feeling of vibrant compassion.

This perspective also helps us to understand an important part of the puzzle we have not yet addressed: How does one make wonderment endure? When John Merrick sat speechless in the theater, we saw the power of a new experience—never before encountered—to create moments of wonderment. Saint Francis, on the other hand, had seen a lot of swallows in his day. Yet, on this day, in this particular field, each swallow was experienced as if it were something new. As we have just seen, part of his ongoing wonderment with "old swallows" probably came from his mystical perspective. When Saint Francis watched swallows sweeping from the clouds, he did not hear the flutterings of wings. He heard the whisperings of God.

But if we push further into an examination of how Saint Francis managed to create a world of enduring wonderment, yet another new piece to our puzzle emerges. It is a piece of the puzzle that is at the very heart of our ensuing chapters. But as a preview, let me say that the ability to craft an enduring sense of wonderment seems to be partially dependent, not only on a mystical sense of compassion, but also on something much more mundane—the ability to enter into the present moment without the baggage of the past.

It is here that, yet again, the lives of John Merrick and Saint Francis seem to dovetail, for one of the greatest roadblocks to entering the present moment—filled with the promise of wonderment—is the presence of hate.

One of the greatest gateways is forgiveness—a favorite topic of Saint Francis. Sir Frederick was so struck by the quality of forgiveness in John Merrick that he describes it in great detail:

> *It would be reasonable to surmise that he would become a spiteful and malignant misanthrope, swollen with venom and filled with hatred of his fellow-men, or, on the other hand, that he would degenerate into a despairing melancholic on the verge of idiocy. Merrick, however, was no such being. . . . He showed himself to be a gentle, affectionate and lovable creature . . . free from any trace of cynicism or resentment, without a grievance and without an unkind word for anyone. I have never heard him complain. I have never heard him deplore his ruined life or resent the treatment he had received at the hands of callous keepers.*

I have no doubt that the wonderment that we have been describing as an integral part of the meaning of happiness is tied into Merrick's ability to let the past be, to forgive the many who had harmed him.

As we close our musings on John Merrick and Saint Francis, it is apparent that the burpings of my unconscious were there for a good reason. Both men had a great deal in common. Both, in their own way, have contributed important pieces to our understanding of the nature of happiness. As further evidence of their affinity, one need only look at the following prayer, one of my favorites since childhood. If John Merrick had been a man predisposed to write down his thoughts, he most certainly would have penned this prayer. In actuality, it was Saint Francis who wrote it. But I have come to believe that it was John Merrick who lived it:

> *Lord, make me an instrument of thy peace,*
> *Where there is hatred, let me sow love,*
> *Where there is injury, pardon,*
> *Where there is doubt, faith,*
> *Where there is despair, hope,*

Where there is darkness, light,
Where there is sadness, joy:
Divine Mother, grant that I may not so much seek
To be consoled as to console,
To be understood as to understand,
To be loved as to love,
For it is in giving that we receive,
It is in pardoning that we are pardoned,
It is in dying that we are born to eternal life.

Married to the Surprise

A Nun in the Closet

As we begin this chapter we find ourselves back in the Middle Ages of Saint Francis. It is within these curious times—not so different from our own—that we will uncover a very important piece of the definition of happiness. The particular piece that we are looking for is an "attitude"—an attitude towards life.

It is an attitude that will allow us to more frequently experience the delicious brew of wonderment, forgiveness and compassion that we described in our last chapter. It is also an attitude that enhances the likelihood that our happiness will not be just a fleeting shadow. It will become an enduring state that is present even during times of suffering. And it is an attitude whose essence was summed up in a single sentence penned by a remarkable woman. She was the first woman to ever write a book in English—Julian of Norwich.

Let us begin our search for the wisdom of Julian of Norwich by getting a better feel for the times in which she lived and why she ended up in a closet. They were not good times. Pestilence, war and famine were the name of the game. Everybody had to play. Getting out of bed in the morning was a giant gamble. And the odds of wining big at Vegas today are a good deal better than the odds of surviving to age fifty in England back then.

So bad was the Scottish famine of 1310 that one of the contemporary chroniclers noted that the Scots were forced to feed, "on the flesh of horses and other unclean cattle." If that were not bad enough, in a few short years across the Channel, dinner entrees were about to get a good deal worse. During the Great Famine of 1315 to 1322, the Irish were apparently "so destroyed by hunger that they extracted bodies of the dead from cemeteries and dug out the flesh from their skulls and ate it."

Although it is doubted by some contemporary historians, it was the scuttlebutt of the day that occasionally people were also feeding on each other. Nasty. It has been estimated that 5 to 15 percent of the population died without food in their mouths. But these numbers are a pittance compared to what was to come.

Shortly after these famines, a long since forgotten, but historically speaking, incredibly important rat entered the picture. The year was 1347. The rat in question scampered across a ship's plankway in the port city of Avignon, in France. In the wake of its little furry paws, the Black Death swept across Western Europe, exterminating human beings with the same ferocity as a can of Raid stomping out a stream of unhappy ants. With the cruel efficiency of our current plagues—where AIDS has killed twenty-eight million and TB takes another two million every year—the Black Death devastated everything in its path: friends, neighbors and enemies.

Twenty million people died in Europe during the first outbreak of the plague between 1347 and 1350. In England upwards of five million may have died during the same years, a number representing 30 to 50 percent of the population.

From our recent parlay with anthrax, we are, unfortunately, keenly aware of what a genuine fear of pestilence feels like. We can now better imagine the abject terror that a villager of Western Europe must have experienced when half of his or her village disappeared in a matter of months. It doesn't make heading out to the old workplace, where who knows how many infected neighbors are waiting, seem like such a smart idea. Production, farming and the occasional cocktail party took a nose dive, unless your name was Prince Prospero.

More to the point of our story, no part of Europe was more ravaged by plague than England, the home of Julian of Norwich. Between 1300 and 1400 the Black Death hit the bonny good shores of England five times. Three times the plague infested the town of Norwich itself. We don't know to what extent Julian lost loved ones, for we know very little of her life before the age of thirty. But the plague first hit when she was six years old, and, if she had married around the age of sixteen, as was common, she may well have lost a husband or two as well as a few children to the snapping jaws of the pestilence.

By the way, I do have a reason for reviewing all of this grim stuff. In just a little bit, Julian of Norwich is going to be sharing a trade secret of sorts. She is going to describe the attitude that is so critical for creating an enduring sense of happiness. More specifically, she is going to share with us some very useful information on how to handle bad times or, as Julian describes them, "periods of woe."

I just want to make the point that, when Julian of Norwich is talking about "bad times," she is not talking about a glitch on her newest piece of software from Bill, nor is she ruing the fact that her cable company is removing Nick at Nite from her standard package. No, when Julian of Norwich is talking about "woe" this nun means "WOE" in capital letters.

Complicated times require unique adaptations. Bizarre times, as I believe the fourteenth century can be safely called, may require extreme solutions, and the fourteenth century had its share of them. At one point, little tribes of up to a thousand people, known as flagellants, could be found trekking from city to city, whipping themselves into a bloody frenzy—the idea being that since the plague was obviously God's punishment for some horrendous disobedience by humankind, if we beat God to the "punishment thing" we might get commuted sentences. God was unimpressed. At best the flagellants were rough on shirts. At worst they would morph into frenzied mobs that would murder large masses of Jews and others who they felt were surely poisoning their wells.

Julian of Norwich also participated in a rather extreme, yet decidedly more humane and peaceful, bit of medieval problem solving. Julian was an anchorite. Anchorites were people—about 214 of them in England during the fourteenth century—who decided to devote themselves to a life of contemplation and mystical experience by being walled into a room attached to a local church. Space was a tad tight, for the prescribed size of the cell was generally twelve square feet—about the size of a large walk-in closet in the Beverly Hills of today.

Concerning the closet market—as with picking one in which to vanish forever—it would appear that, as we see in the real estate markets of today, "location" was everything. One poor guy in Compton, Surrey, clearly in need of a different real estate agent, got stuck living the rest of his life in a cell measuring six feet, eight inches, by four feet, four inches. Oh yeah, I forgot—the church threw in a sleeping loft. Ouch.

Anchorites were generally allowed three windows. One narrow slit provided a view of the church altar so you could participate in mass, receive Holy Communion, and confess whatever pathetic sins you might be able to muster living in a twelve by twelve foot cubby. A second slit provided the opening for your food. The third slit was actually not a slit but a more reasonably sized window to the outside world. Even with this window it was deemed "good karma" to keep it covered with a shade. As one can see, the life of an anchorite was a life of considerable darkness.

At some level closet life wasn't so bad: The local bishop assured you three squares a day, some anchorites got two rooms, it was not uncommon that you might be allowed a stroll or two in the garden, the plague bacillus was less likely to visit your bloodstream and people from all over the countryside thought you were "pretty neat." But there was a catch. As an anchorite you had to stay in your closet for the rest of your life at the risk of being excommunicated from the church—a punishment guaranteeing an afterlife in Hell.

These anchorites, as they entered their closets, and the clergy that supported them were so serious about the finality of their current life on this planet that it was common practice to give them "the last rites" and to wish them bon voyage with a "mass for the dead." With all of this talk of hell fire and masses for the dead, as one can well imagine, most anchorites kept their word. Once in their closets, they stayed in them.

With regards to accommodations, our anchoress, Julian of Norwich, did a good deal better than some. She had two rooms, probably her own altar, and a maid that brought food and water, cooked up meals and attended to the fire. Through her one outside window she could talk to people, people who were seeking her counsel and the wisdom that was to result from her meditations and prayers. She also probably had a cat and was allowed a garden walk now and then. But we should keep in mind that Julian, like all anchorites before or after her, lost that most precious of gifts—her freedom. Hers was a simple, tough and regimented life that lacked any hope for change whatsoever.

She lost all chance to touch another human being, cuddle, have a family, go to the market, buy anything, travel anywhere. Hour after hour, week after week, year after year, she could go nowhere. She could not walk more than thirty yards in one direction. Period. Ever. Her life was lived within the radius of a fifteen-yard circle. I don't care how you cut it. This doesn't sound like fun.

Like John Merrick before her, only more so, her life was confined to two rooms. Yet there is an important difference, an almost excruciatingly perplexing difference. It is a difference that is of immense importance to our understanding of the meaning of happiness, for John Merrick was condemned to his way of life by his destiny. Julian of Norwich chose hers. Not only did she choose it, by all accounts, she was extremely happy with it. Once again, the question is how.

Part of the answer lies in who Julian of Norwich was, or more explicitly what she was. You see, Julian of Norwich, like Saint Francis from our last chapter, was also a mystic. Since college I have been reading the writings of mystics, and since college I have been impressed with what they have to say. What they teach goes to the bull's-eye of what we seek—the meaning of happiness.

Mystics and Heavy Metal Bands

In our last chapter we briefly touched upon what it means to be a mystic—a person who believes in the tangible presence of god in all things both human and non-human. Before exploring Julian's mystical writings, I believe it is wise to more clearly define the word, for it is often bandied about.

What is a bit unusual about mystics is the intensity with which they pursue the presence of god. Mystics are into this god-quest big time, for mystics believe that God can be both felt and touched by the human soul. During these mystical moments, which they maintain are beyond words, there is apparently a wonderfully enthralling sense of peace, timelessness and wholeness, as one experiences the infinity of the godhead itself.

From these transcendent moments, it is believed that the mystic returns with more than his or her fair share of wonderment, compassion and wisdom—the wisdom to find happiness. It is exactly this type of wisdom that anchorites were supposed to discover and share with the rest of us. It is exactly this type of wisdom that had people lined up for counsel at the window of Julian of Norwich, like she was the Dr. Phil of today. And like the Dr. Phil of today, Julian of Norwich did not disappoint.

One thing I should add about most mystics is that unlike Saint Francis, who wrote with such simple and direct words that he could create the immediate magnetism of the prayer that closed our last chapter, most medieval mystics were a bit more obscure in their writings. Well, more than a bit.

Let's be frank; mystical writings sometimes sound like gibberish. They are the type of writings that can seem pretty well irrelevant in our day and age, until, out of nowhere, a certain phrase catches our eye. Suddenly, as we understand what the mystic was really trying to tell us, our hectic and complex world of cell phones and stock options suddenly seems at once both more simple and less hectic. Don't get me wrong. Julian of Norwich, although clearer in language than most mystics, is still quite capable of gibberish. Inside that gibberish, though, she has some real good insights. Let's take a look.

Once inside, the first thing we notice is Julian herself—the woman behind the writings. We had mentioned earlier that she was happy with her meager existence. In actuality, she was more than happy. She was very happy. And Julian of Norwich made other people happy. By all accounts, the people who lined up at her window went away satisfied customers. Somehow she had provided them with solace.

Let's keep in mind that this was no small feat considering who was popping up at the window. These were the survivors of bubonic plague, horrifying periods of starvation, and the killings, rapes, and other atrocities that were part and parcel of a medieval time ravaged by war.

Moreover, many of these people were also burdened by the nagging question of Why? Why would God allow this? Why had God abandoned them? Why would God allow pain into the world? Why would God allow such a thing as unhappiness in the universe? And surely an all-powerful God would not have a need to allow all of this pain simply because some guy named Adam got into trouble with some girl named Eve over some lousy apple.

Such questions are very reasonable and many a theologian and philosopher have lost some sleep over them. For people as deeply religious as the people of the Middle Ages, the wrong answers to these questions were quite literally devastating. If one truly believed that somehow or other God had abandoned them or betrayed them, life was without meaning. Life without meaning is life without hope. Such was the demoralized outlook of many who sought the counsel of Julian. This is not an easy crew to put a "happy face" on. To see how Julian did it, let us turn directly to her writings.

At the beginning of this chapter I stated that there was a single sentence of Julian's that held an important clue for us. It is:

> During our lifetime here, we have in us a marvelous mixture of both well-being and woe. . . . And now we are raised to the one, and now we are permitted to fall to the other.

At first glance it sure doesn't look like much of a mind blower, does it? Julian simply seems to be saying what is already painfully obvious—there are good times and there are bad times in life. So obvious is this fact that even Led Zeppelin got it right in "Good Times/Bad Times," the name of a hit song from their first album. So what's the deal here? If a big-gun mystic like Julian of Norwich can't give me any more insight into life than Jimmy Page and Robert Plant, we are wasting some serious time here.

The deal is what Julian of Norwich made of these "good times" and "bad times." The deal lies hidden in a single word—"marvelous"—that is sitting unobtrusively within eight nondescript words in the first sentence. If you don't look twice, you might not even notice "a marvelous mixture of both well-being and woe."

What exactly is that supposed to mean? I don't see anything "marvelous" about woe. Do you? I don't want any woe in my life, especially not the type of woe Julian is tossing out. But, apparently, Julian of Norwich did. She did, because she knew that she had no choice. None of us does. Julian's "well-being" versus "woe," Led Zeppelin's "good times" versus "bad times." We all have them. And here is where Julian is sharing a trade secret: We all need them. Both of them.

Life is not marvelous because it is filled with well-being. According to

Julian of Norwich, it is marvelous because it is "a mixture of well-being and woe." It is the mixture that gives life its zing.

It's not that one wants to have bad times. It is that one accepts that bad times are the reflectors that make our good times feel so damn good in the first place. Bad times, like bad guys in a movie, serve a purpose. There can be no heroes unless there are villains. It's as simple as that. Bad times give birth and meaning and intensity to good times.

Mystic after mystic—Christian, Buddhist, Hindu, Islamic, Jewish and Taoist—all say the same thing. Life is made up of polarities. There is no such thing as only good.

One cannot even imagine a world that is all good. It is unimaginable because good can only be conceived as a contrast to something that is bad. If there is good, then there must be something that is "not good." What is a heaven without a hell? Good times and bad times create each other. As Led Zeppelin so handily pointed out, there are no good times, there are good times/bad times. Life is made up of opposites that define each other, and life is the marvelous flowing from one extreme to the other. This then is the "marvelous mixture" that Julian of Norwich was so acutely aware.

I want to emphasize that we are not being cute with words here. It is the simple truth. Each end of a polarity would literally not exist without the other. Lightness is unimaginable without darkness. Joy is vacant without sorrow. Winning is meaningless without defeat. A human being, literally, cannot conceive of what it is to be dry, unless there is prior knowledge of what it is to be wet. Dryness does not exist unless wetness brings it into existence. Strange but true.

Although not a particularly smart way to do it, some people have achieved this realization, not through religious experience, but with the help of a few drops of LSD. Back in the now-distant 1960s a few legitimate scientists were experimenting with LSD to see what it could tell us about human nature and the functioning of the brain's neurochemistry with the hope that perhaps this curious liquid might actually be usable as a way of routinely helping people in psychotherapy. The answer proved to be a resounding "no." But some genuine insights did fall out of the research, as with this excerpt by the well-known nutritionist Adelle Davis, writing under the pseudonym of Jane Dunlap, concerning her first time dropping acid:

> Another conviction quickly arose: it was that each positive emotion and its negative antithesis indeed constitute one quality rather than two . . . in the same way the dark colors in a painting give beauty and contrast to the pastels, the negative emotions are equally necessary to give depth and meaning to the positive ones; that one could not truly appreciate love without first knowing hate, or beauty without having seen ugliness, or any positive emotion without awareness of its antithesis.

"Dunlap" does a nice job of highlighting the fact that the degree of enjoyment is dependent upon the depth and meaning it is given by the depth of its opposite. Picture for a moment the true pleasure we have all experienced when drinking down a glass of sparkling cold water on a hot summer day after exercising. It is wonderfully delicious.

But contrast our enjoyment with that of a man who quite literally has been lost in a desert, close to death from dehydration, when he drinks down that glass of water. His thrill, his pleasure, his utter ecstasy is beyond comparison to ours. In short, I am not capable of experiencing that type of pleasure over a glass of water, simply because I have never had the depth of pain associated with not having water. Not only are the positive points on life's many polarities defined by their opposites, the depth of the bad times often determines the heights of the good times.

I am reminded of the people I have met through the years who have recovered from their alcoholism. They are some of the happiest people I have ever met. I am convinced they are that happy because they truly know—from the depths and horrors of their alcoholism—just how bad life can be. From this depth of pain they achieve new heights of pleasure in even the simplest of things—a human smile, waking up refreshed, a chance to have a job. They have an intense gratitude—much like John Merrick—for the loveliness of life because they have real knowledge of just how hideous it can be.

Bottom line: To build a universe where people can have pleasure, you have to build a universe where they can also have pain. And the greater the potential experience of pain, the greater the potential experience of happiness. There is no other way. Chuang Tzu, a delightfully insightful Taoist sage, put it bluntly:

> *Those who would have right without its correlative, wrong: or good government without its correlative, misrule,—they do not apprehend the great principles of the universe nor the conditions to which all creation is subject. One might as well talk of the existence of heaven without that of earth, or of the negative principle without the positive, which is clearly absurd.*

And this realization brings us back to Julian of Norwich and the unbelievably damaged people who came to her window for solace. Julian of Norwich could not take away the loss of their families to the Black Death. She could not take away the pain of their poverty or hunger. She could not right the horrible wrongs done to them by marauding soldiers. But she could take away one thing. She could take away their anger at God. And as she did so, she gave them back that most precious of gifts—hope.

How did she do it? We don't know for certain, but I have a hunch that Julian of Norwich, after first having shared some of the material we have just explored, with the impeccable timing of a gifted psychotherapist, leaned forward and whispered something like this:

> *You see, God didn't abandon us. He loves us dearly. He allowed pain, because it was the only possible way that we could ever experience pleasure. He doesn't want us to feel pain, but he knows that we can only feel happiness if we also know unhappiness. To give us pleasure, he had to allow pain. You see, He had no choice.*
>
> *And God does everything He possibly can to allow us to experience minimal pain—just enough pain—that we can experience all of the*

beauty of a lake, the ecstasy of a lark's song, the excitement of a kiss. But there are times when the world deals out much more pain than is necessary or that God would want. And now, we are in such times. They pass. And God will help them to pass as quickly as possible.

With such simple words Julian of Norwich released all of the anger that had kept these desperate people from their god. In one session, armed only with common sense and logic, Julian of Norwich gave them back faith and hope. Julian of Norwich was a master therapist. Move over Dr. Phil. This nun is the real deal.

But what if one does not believe in a god or goddess? How can this psychological truth be of any practical value in the search for happiness outside of talk of God? Surely, I'm not suggesting that when one has bad things happen, that the pain will go away simply because I understand that, in the greater scheme of things, this tragedy will make me more appreciative of what I have? As my twelve-year-old son Ryan would say, "That sounds lame Dad." No, the truth is both more gentle and more compelling.

Whether one believes in a god or not, there are two side effects to "bad times" that often, in a very real way, make them much worse and much more difficult to bear: anger at life that the bad times happened and anger at life that more bad times may be on the way. The latter anger is often accompanied with a great deal of anxiety, which in itself is quite painful. Bad times breed anger and anxiety as surely as good times breed laughter and calmness.

But the anger against life is as senseless as the anger against God. There have to be bad times or there simply would not be good times. This psychological rule is the reality of the human mind whether one is a theist, atheist or agnostic. As our Taoist sage, Chuang Tzu, would say, "It's just the way it is. Period."

The acknowledgment that good times and bad times are a wonderful and necessary mixture in life can, once this wisdom really sinks into one's soul, help one to eliminate much of the anger that is easy to direct at life itself, an anger that is neither necessary nor helpful. By understanding the painful yet useful role of bad times, then one is more accepting of their appearance and, paradoxically, more capable of enduring and transforming them.

It is in the acceptance of pain that one finds the resilience to lessen it. It is in the acceptance of bad times that one is better able to find good times. Julian of Norwich has given us an incredibly important piece of the puzzle of human happiness. Julian of Norwich has made us, with eight little words, both less bitter and less fretful. But our nun in the closet is not done. She's on a roll.

The "Hazelnut Thing" and the Wizard of Oz

When she was just turning thirty, Julian of Norwich had a series of powerful mystical visions, which she called "showings." Her recording of these mystical experiences resulted in the first book in English ever written by a woman, a text subsequently known as, *A Book of Showings to the Anchoress of Norwich*. In our search for the meaning of happiness we are particularly interested in one of the more eccentric of these visions.

One day, while just minding her business, Julian suddenly found herself in the presence of God—this is the type of perk that one gets if one does the mystic thing. In any case, she peered down into the palm of her hand. To her surprise there was something laying in it. The something, we never know exactly what, was perfectly round and the size of a hazelnut. She felt a great trepidation about its future and began to wonder exactly what it might be.

And here is the part that gave her the same thrill Dorothy and her companions felt when they first saw the magnificent Wizard of Oz in the Emerald City. God, who you will recall is still hanging out in her room, looks directly at Julian. He simply says, "It is all that is made." And He vanishes. Poof.

At this point Julian of Norwich recounts that she had an intensely felt sense of hope and safety, for she suddenly realized that God intended to keep the little hazelnut thing safe. Forever. Symbolically, it would always be there, in the palm of her hand, safe and sound, for God loved it.

Then the hazelnut thing vanished too. Poof poof. The life of Julian of Norwich was never the same again, for Julian of Norwich learned, inside that vision, a lesson she could not easily forget. She discovered an attitude toward life that would transform her life. Julian of Norwich learned to trust.

Good times, bad times, it really doesn't matter. They come, they go. But no matter what happens, the little hazelnut thing—all that is made, including Julian, you and I—will always be safe for God loves us. God protects. God always was and always will be, and so shall we.

It really was a defining moment for Julian of Norwich, exactly the kind of thing mystics are looking for if they want to launch a career. It was much better than a visit to Oz, because this time, when Dorothy pulled back the curtains, there really was a wizard standing there. When Julian pulled back the curtains, she saw God. She saw his love. She saw his infinite strength and His infinite compassion. She knew that no matter what misfortunes life threw at her, in the end, she would be safe, because she was with the "Big Guy."

I should add a very curious thing about Julian, for she spoke of God in a symbolic sense as both masculine and feminine, a way cool convenience if one is of a feminist persuasion. She sensed that whatever God was, He or She was well beyond our full comprehension, so she would refer to him as Father or Mother, depending upon which trait she was discussing, more traditional masculine traits such as strength or more traditional feminine traits such as compassion. It made no difference to Julian, male or female, a Father or a Mother, the godhead was all wonderful. No set of words could do it justice, so let's not quibble over labels.

But back to our hazelnut thing and Julian's vision. I have always wondered what that little hazelnut thing really looked like. Perhaps she saw a miniature crystal ball or perhaps the lovely mosaic of green, blue and white cloud that we call home. We will never know. But one thing that we do know. This little hazelnut thing gave her—and us—a most significant piece to our puzzle concerning the nature of happiness.

In my psychiatric practice, in my personal life and in my studies of historical figures such as John Merrick, St. Francis of Assisi and Julian of Norwich, I have found that people who have successfully developed a more enduring sense of happiness share a single defining characteristic. It is the wisdom that Julian gained from that hazelnut thing in her palm. They have a profound sense of trust.

Julian found it in God. Taoists find it in the Tao. Others find it in the wonderment of Nature itself. And some people find it in the magic of compassion and mission. And some, like Mulder from *The X-Files,* find a curious sense of trust in the idea that the answer is out there somewhere, and the very fact that it is unknowable fills them with an awe, and this awe with a reassuring trust that the world is most definitely a place of wonderment, not fear. I cannot tell you which source of trust is right for you. I can only tell you that all happy people seem to have it, no matter what its source.

It is this attitude of trust that seems to allow them to approach life with a lively anticipation that they can handle whatever life may bring—good times or bad times. They exude a gentle yet robust confidence. There is no need to fret about the future, for they are confident that they have the skills and beliefs to handle it with whatever tenaciousness and gracefulness it may require.

This sense of gentle trust may very well be the force that enables one to meet life one moment at a time. Armed with this trust one can move forward always confident—not that life will bring only good things—but that life is a wonderful mixture of the good and the bad. This acceptance that life is supposed to have good and bad—so that we can experience happiness—coupled with the trust that one will handle gracefully whatever bad times come our way, is remarkably releasing. It releases us from arguing with the past. It releases us from screwing up the present with fears of the future. So ingrained was this outlook for Julian of Norwich that she was perhaps best known for the following sentence that captures it perfectly, "All is well, and every kind of thing will be well."

It also brings us to the end of our chapter and, paradoxically, back to its beginning, for the astute reader will have noticed that the first two lines of our opening epigraph sounded familiar. They were the lines from the rock group Spirit that became the focus of our very first chapter. But in this chapter, we've added two more lines from later on in the song. Let's see them altogether again, for they have something—in fact a great deal of something—to do with Julian of Norwich:

> *You have the world at your fingertips,*
> *No one can make it better than you . . .*
> *No, we've got nothing to hide,*
> *We are married to the surprise.*

You see, Julian of Norwich had the world at her fingertips, even though she lived inside a closet. She was a profoundly happy person who made her own miniscule world inside that tiny cell better, all by herself. Perhaps even more important, she made others happy. She had nothing to hide, her strengths and her weaknesses were there for all to see, for she had a profound trust that all would ultimately be well.

She had a delicious love of life in all its tapestry from good times to bad times. She understood the value of both. She understood the necessity of both. And it was her profound sense of trust that stripped the future of all its frets.

It was this trust that allowed her to step spritely throughout the world even though she could not take a single step into that world. It was this trust that allowed her to touch people profoundly even though she could never touch them physically. It was this trust that allowed Julian of Norwich to eagerly anticipate each unfolding moment. You see, because of her trust, Julian of Norwich was married to the surprise. She was wonderfully free to be surprised by life in all its beauty and fury, in all its ugliness and its rapture. And never, not for a single moment, did she ever regret what life brought to her.

5 Not Necessarily a Magician

". . . for the meaning of happiness consists in three elements—freedom, gratitude, and the sense of wonder. These three elements can be present in the most ordinary of lives; the free man is not necessarily a magician, a seer or a 'mystic'. . . ."

ALAN WATTS FROM *THE MEANING OF HAPPINESS*, CIRCA 1940

The Buddha in the Limo

I like my buddhas to be chubby, which is why Benny caught me off guard. Even though I am not a Buddhist, I can still express my admiration for the myriad of calorically challenged buddhas that seem to dot the temples of Japan, with the ubiquity that McDonald's golden arches dot the highways of America. In my opinion, the images of Western saints are often all too sleek and slim, if not altogether anorexic appearing. I have an innate distrust of any saint whose very body habitus suggests that I am sinning on an all too regular basis.

Now, a chubby buddha is a different thing altogether. Considering the middle age propensities of my belly, here is a saint whose body shape suggests that I am heading in the right direction. I like that in a saint. I also like the fact that Eastern buddhas are often shown smiling and laughing. Such representations reinforce the all too often forgotten truth that, like beauty, wisdom and laughter can come in any size body, despite Hollywood's current preoccupation with malnourished waifs, the so-called "heroin addict chic."

I remain absolutely convinced that wisdom hides in the sounds of laughter, and that one should turn off the television set on any minister or New Age guru who doesn't make one laugh. I am certain of one thing: Christ, Saint Francis and Julian of Norwich were lovers of laughter. What I don't understand is why the gospel writers and church scribes, who adored them so, did not choose to record their wit and laughter as well as their wisdom and serenity. Surely, Christ loved to make children giggle and surely, part of Julian's popularity lay in her power to make people laugh during times of plague.

But Benny was thin. Wiry thin. Although this was probably okay because, like any buddha worth his or her salt, Benny had no idea he was a buddha. I have gotten ahead of myself, so allow me to backtrack.

Our chapters thus far have taken us on a circuitous search for the meaning of happiness. Indeed, with the wonderment and courage of John Merrick, the gratitude of St. Francis, and the profound trust of Julian of Norwich, we have already collected many of the pieces of our puzzle. We now have in our paws a goodly number of the concepts needed to arrive at a useful definition of happiness, a definition that will allow us to pursue more effectively our ultimate goal in this book, an enduring sense of happiness. But there remain a few missing pieces, and even a single missing piece in a jigsaw puzzle dooms one to an unhappy ending.

Thus far, we have gleaned most of our insights from the lives and beliefs of extraordinary people, such as John Merrick, or saints and mystics such as Saint Francis of Assisi and Julian of Norwich. The question is—will all this stuff work for the everyday Joe? Will it work for the typical parent trying to hold down two jobs while holding together a marriage? Will it work for the divorced mother, who just got home from work and is desperately trying to get three different kids to three different soccer games? Put bluntly, will it work for you and me?

For instance, would our ideas—such as welcoming both the good times and the bad times or nurturing a sense of trust—deliver happiness to an everyday person? For instance, take Timothy, our patient from the first chapter who realized the difference between happiness and success. Will these ideas offer Timothy a practical way for pursuing happiness? And, if an everyday person such as Timothy, living in our currently frenzied world of dotcoms and sitcoms, can experience happiness, what does it look like? What does it feel like?

We need to find an everyday, reasonably happy schmoe to see what this "happiness thing" looks like in real life, 24-7. In the presence of such an everyday human being I believe that we will find one or two of the missing pieces to our puzzle. They are important pieces that can't be tapped by looking at historical figures like John Merrick and Julian of Norwich.

Hence an interstate highway in Iowa. Hence a limo with a broken air conditioner. Hence a seemingly endless string of cornfields on a humid August day topping ninety-five degrees. Hence me. Hence Benny, the limo guy. The year is no longer 1356. We've clicked our ruby red slippers. We're back home again, Toto. The year is 2000.

As a speaker and consultant, I'm on the road over a hundred days a year. I love my work and believe in my mission, but it can be exhausting. I've garnered so many Marriott points that my next option is to own a Marriott hotel for free—city of my choice, Hawaii excluded. I've also logged more than my fair share of miles in taxis and limos, and that is why I was caught off guard by Benny's opening comment as he was about to reach for my door in the back of the limo. "How would you like to sit up front with me? We got a good three hour ride and with a broken air conditioner, it might go faster with somebody to talk to."

I had already logged two flights that day, had argued briefly with a snitty man at the ticket counter and had been fretting all day about a consulting job I was concerned I wasn't going to land. Needless to say, at first glance, I did not find the idea of having to make chitchat with a total stranger for three hours too appealing. So, like an idiot, I said, "Yes."

After nestling into a gray limo that had clearly seen better days, I had the chance to eyeball my abductor and his surrounds. Benny sat comfortably in his daily workplace. There were some tapes scattered about from pop icons like Kenny G and Madonna. The dashboard had the customary share of knickknacks, loose change and gum wrappers. But I was struck that, despite its age, this old limo was otherwise meticulously clean.

I casually asked, "How old is this thing?"

A smile shot across Benny's face, "It's got over 200,000 miles. And it purrs like a kitten. This ole babe and I have been around." I nodded my approval.

It was obvious that Benny loved "this ole babe" and had put in many an afternoon vacuuming, cleaning and polishing her innards and outtards. Unlike many limos, this was not one limo in a fleet of thirty owned by some bored businessman looking for a tax write-off, this was *the* limo in a fleet of one. The limo belonged to Benny, and Benny belonged to the limo. Benny was no fool, he danced with who brought him to the dance.

Of course, we talked about all sorts of junk, the obligatory weather stuff, questions about the countryside, discussions about when we should stop to eat—Benny's response was a quick, "When we're hungry." And soon I noticed I was feeling sort of perky.

This guy, with the easygoing smile and the matter of fact chit-chat was making me feel kind of comfy, as if Benny had not invited me into a limo but into his home. That's it. I felt like I was careening up Interstate 35 in Iowa, not in a limo, but in some guy's den on wheels.

Benny had Kenny G softly doing whatever Kenny G does in the background, the wind was zipping through my hair, I could feel the powerful but strangely reassuring heat of the mid-day sun on my arm, and we were sailing. If I had been feeling anymore free, I would have been looking across not at Benny, but at Peter Fonda on a motorcycle with Steppenwolf pounding out the chorus of "Born to Be Wild" in the background.

Benny and I eventually stopped—when we were hungry—at a truck stop. I stuffed myself on some dead cheeseburgers with lots of ketchup, a big order of fries and some Mountain Dew. Before hitting the road again I grabbed a few beef jerkies and a Twinkie. I called over to Benny, "Can I get you anything?" Benny shook his head, smiling in disbelief, "No thanks, I don't eat that crap." And he laughed. And then I laughed. And he was still chuckling as we were crawling back into "ole Babe" as I now called her.

It was then that I realized, with a sudden startle, that I had forgotten something. I had left something somewhere, and I had no idea where. Somewhere before we hit the truck stop, somewhere about thirty minutes outside of the airport. I had forgotten something that I almost always had on me, that I had grown so used to carrying, that I felt uneasy without it. I had forgotten my worries.

Somehow there was just not room in "ole Babe" for Benny, me and my worries. And, with that sudden realization, I smiled, slammed the door as fast as I could, and said, "You should try some of this junk. It's great stuff!" And Benny just shook his head in wonder.

As cornfield after cornfield sped past us, we continued our carefree chatter. At one point after a big diesel rig blew past us, I asked Benny, "You know, you seem pretty happy. What keeps you going?"

Benny checked his side mirror, adjusted the volume on Kenny G and said, "I don't know. I've certainly had my ups and downs, but I do keep going." He paused, then turned to me with a smile, "sort of like the Energizer Bunny."

I replied, "Sounds good to me." I paused for a moment and then asked, "What do you mean you've had your ups and downs?" God love me—the shrink inside just couldn't keep his mouth shut.

"Oh my gosh, oh my gosh. I know what down is. I was a terrible alcoholic. But I've been sober for seventeen years. AA saved my life."

A huge smile came over Benny. I smiled back and commented, "That's really great! One day at a time, I suppose." I was quoting a very common and very wise saying from Alcoholics Anonymous.

Benny quipped back, "Oh no, not one day at a time: one minute at a time. Just one minute at a time. I find if I just pay attention to what I'm doing right now, this very instant, things turn out pretty good." There was a pause. "I really enjoy life. There's a lot to enjoy."

As you can see, in this limo in Iowa, we have come upon our everyday human being who seems reasonably happy. Don't get me wrong, Benny had times of sorrow and pain. He certainly had his share of stresses. He was still rebuilding from some of the devastation caused by his alcoholism. He had five children and some significant debts from paying for their college educations. And even though Benny was putting in sixty hours of work a week, and often much more, being a limo driver is not the road to big bucks.

I was impressed with Benny. I was impressed with how he seemed to find a gentle happiness during considerably rough times. I was about to become more impressed.

I asked Benny about his wife, Patty, and once again you couldn't have seen a bigger smile, "She's wonderful. I couldn't ask for a better friend." Benny went on and on about Patty in a pleasant sort of way, especially about how much fun they had together, and then he commented, "She's had it tough though."

And here is where I got a surprise. When Benny says, "She's had it tough," think Julian of Norwich and what it would have meant if Julian had just said, "Patty has had her share of woe." Patty didn't have the bubonic plague, but she had had just about every other disease in the book. For years Patty had been dealing with diabetes, rheumatoid arthritis, lupus erythematosus, and a strange autoimmune disease known as Sjogren's syndrome, which leaves your eyes incredibly dry and tearless, so much so that there is almost constant irritation and discomfort.

Apparently, Patty's immune system had declared war, not on just one organ system in her body, but on her entire body. Most people only suffer from one of these afflictions, some unfortunately get two, but it is relatively rare to get such a long list—an unfortunate situation sometimes called pan-autoimmune dysfunction. Without getting technical, let's just say that Patty was one sick lady. Every day she would feel intense pain in her joints, and she was not even able to blink an eye without discomfort. In addition she experienced an almost deadening sense of weariness, while coping with the always present awareness that almost any one of these diseases could kill her.

I was taken aback. As a physician, I had some inkling of just how devastating to daily life this slew of woe actually was. Yet here was Benny, a person who not only did not appear to be unhappy, he had the knack of making me feel happy.

I asked, "How do you do it?"

"Do what?"

"Cope with all this stuff. How do you keep going when every day you and Patty our dealing with such difficult diseases?"

Benny paused for a moment. It was very clear that he felt I had asked a legitimate question, but it was equally clear that it was one to which he had not given much thought. He shrugged his shoulders and said something that I have never forgotten. They were words of great meaning to me, for I had a son with a serious illness as well, so I knew all to well what it was like to deal with an illness in a loved one. Benny said, "When Patty is well, we rejoice. When Patty is sick, I try to help her." He paused and added, "What else would you do?"

I merely nodded and said, "Yeah, yeah. I guess that is all you can do." But I knew all too well from my own personal experience that it was not true. There were all sorts of dysfunctional things you could do. You just had to be creative. For instance, when my son was well, I often found myself fretting about his getting sick again, leaving absolutely no room for rejoicing. And when he was sick, I found myself wishing he was well and getting angry that he wasn't. Such wishing and shaking of my fists left me really beat, so beat that I was sometimes not as effective as I could have been at helping my son. It was then that I realized that Benny was not just a limo driver. Benny was a buddha.

He demonstrated, in the flesh, the gentle acceptance of both the good and the bad of life espoused in the writings of Julian of Norwich. As Julian of Norwich had predicted, it was Benny's acceptance of life that allowed him to live it moment by moment. When one does that—lives in the here and now—all sorts of the marvelous things we have been seeking begin to happen, including wonderment and compassion. That is why my worries couldn't fit inside the limo with Benny. This state of alertness and concentration to the minute by minute momentum of life creates a feeling inside a person, a feeling that is contagious—a feeling that one just might be tempted to call "happiness."

This contagious quality of true happiness cannot be felt in a book, but I sure could feel it inside that limo. I could see its impact on Benny in his laughter and in his smile. I could feel its impact on me as I found myself laughing and smiling.

Here then was one of the pieces of the puzzle for which we have been looking, a piece that only a living, breathing, talking human being could teach. You see, Julian of Norwich and Saint Francis of Assisi could not directly touch me with their happiness. Benny could. I could speculate on the idea of happiness from Julian of Norwich and Saint Francis through their words. I could know the meaning of happiness from Benny through the twinkle of his eyes.

Benny's simple absorption in the moment—as he said, minute by minute—not only changed him, it changed the people around him. Because Benny, the limo driver, was living in the present moment, Shawn, the limo passenger, found himself there as well. And being in the here and now—living in the present moment—Shawn the limo passenger was free of his worries.

This realization is one of the most important pieces in our puzzle. If you live in the present moment, you are psychologically free. You are free to decide what to do with the present moment, to decide to fully experience its good or to creatively transform its bad.

As Watts said in our opening epigraph, one will recognize happiness by its three calling cards—a sense of freedom, gratitude and wonder. From John Merrick, Saint Francis, and Julian of Norwich, we knew that happiness was often a bedfellow with the last two. But it was up to Benny to really bring home that the act of living in the present moment was one of the keys to fully appreciating what Watts saw in the relationship between happiness and "a sense of freedom."

Happiness occurs by living in the Now, the Present Moment. What we saw in Benny was somebody actually doing it. And when one does this simple act, one is free of both the regrets of the past and the frets of the future, for there is no room for them. What did Benny say? "When Patty is well we rejoice, when Patty is sick, I try to help her." Simple as that.

Benny also proves that the everyday human being, the truck driver, the nurse, the lawyer, the businessman, the homemaker, the school teacher, can learn to live in the present moment, despite concurrently experiencing great stresses. These stresses try to yank us back into the past or jettison us forward into the future. But we do not have to be at the mercy of life's stresses. Like John Merrick, Benny provides hope. If Benny can do it, then you and I can do it. To understand how, it is useful to see the various ways in which people who have mastered the knack of living in the present moment have described this curious state of being.

New England Sages, Spiders from Mars and Whirling Dervishes

Benny is certainly not the first sage to point out the benefits of living in the present moment. It is such an important point that sages and people in the know have been saying it for centuries. Each sage uses a slightly different lens, and each lens releases a slightly different secret worth our attention, for living in the present moment is not quite as simple to achieve as it might at first glance appear. In fact it is often quite difficult to do. To peel away some of its secrets, we will begin by examining what some of the icons from our popular culture have had to say about it.

Our first icon, if he were alive today, would be approximately 200 years old. He might sound a bit dated, but, in my opinion, few have captured the importance of living in the present moment with a more piquant freshness. Our icon is none other than Ralph Waldo Emerson, a hiking buddy of Henry David Thoreau of Walden Pond fame. They were part of a clique known as the New England Transcendentalists, who have the remarkable distinction for American philosophers of still being talked about today.

These New Englanders are our American all-stars, philosophically speaking. While trudging about the glorious autumn forests and stone-walled vales of New England, they managed to stir up not only some of the dead leaves but some new ideas, or at the very least gave new vibrancy to some old ideas. Here is how Emerson captures the importance of living in the here and now in one of the most famous of all American essays, "Self-Reliance":

> These roses under my window make no reference to former roses or to better ones; they are for what they are; they exist with God today. There is no time for them. There is simply the rose; it is perfect in every moment of its existence. Before a leaf-bud has burst, its whole life acts; in the full-blown flower there is no more; in the leafless root there is no less. Its nature is satisfied and it satisfies nature in all moments alike. But man postpones or remembers; he does not live in the present, but with reverted eye laments the past, or heedless of the riches that surround him, stands on tiptoe to foresee the future. He cannot be happy and strong until he too lives with nature in the present, above time.

Not only does Emerson elegantly describe the importance of living in the present moment, he provides compelling metaphors that alert us to the dangers of becoming preoccupied with either the past or the future. It is wise to avoid standing on tiptoes more than is absolutely necessary.

Our next popular icon is a little less dated. In contrast to Ralph Waldo Emerson, who probably dressed in somber shades of black and white, our next icon is sporting a hot-blue spandex suit with neon sparkles in his hair.

The time is the early 1970s, and the icon in question is doing a damn good impersonation of a rock star supposedly visiting from another planet. Our alien pop hero goes by the handle of Ziggy Stardust. He is backed up by his band, the Spiders from Mars.

David Bowie—aka Ziggy Stardust—had the misfortune of finding himself looking at life from the inside of a bottle, where more drugs were floating around than even the bong-bearing Caterpillar from *Alice in Wonderland* could have imagined. In the opening years of the 1970s, Bowie was part of the raucous and not so healthy cultural maelstrom known as "Glam Rock." In fact, David Bowie essentially invented it. Fortunately, like Benny, Bowie successfully popped out the other side of his addictive bottle. Once out of the bottle, like many ex-addicts, he displayed, and still does, that same refreshing gratitude for life that Benny exuded. Here is how David Bowie succinctly puts it all together:

> *It's about this moment, . . . You can't live with ridiculous expectations of the future. And you can't continually look back and say, 'What if?' It has to be a question of how you live today. I don't get terribly excited about the future. I'm quite happy to paddle my canoe around in the nooks and crannies of now.*

There is a matter of fact quality to Bowie's quote, as one imagines him paddling lackadaisically about the nooks and crannies of the present moment, that I find very appealing. Bowie makes the point rather bluntly that if one is looking to cull happiness from daily life, living outside the present moment is simply not very practical.

His imagery also suggests a characteristic of those who have learned the art of living in the present moment that we have not yet encountered. They are not in a rush. To uncover the secrets to be found in the nooks and crannies of life, one must take the time to see. Over the years I have come to realize that one seldom comes upon life's most delicious secrets by traveling in straight lines at great speeds. They are more reliably found by moving in curving lines at slow speeds, with spirals and hitches. The Buddha was not a speed skater. If one moves too quickly, the present moment—and all of the wonderments within it—can be lost in the blur.

Bowie, by the way, was not the first guy dancing around in unusual duds who found it impractical to live outside the present moment. About five hundred years earlier, in the deserts of the Middle East, a group of Islamic mystics called Sufis beat him to the punch. A quick perusal of Sufi wisdom will show us that, no matter what the religious tradition— Christian, Taoist, or Islamic—or who the pop icon—New England Transcendentalist or MTV fixture—the dangers of living life in the past and/or living it in the future are emphasized over and over again.

Sufis are a mystic branch of Islam, but if when you hear the word "mystic," visions of a serene Julian of Norwich or a contemplative Saint Francis pop into mind, one is on the wrong track with Sufis. Like all mystics, Sufis focus upon achieving a direct union with the godhead. Unlike Julian or Saint Francis, they achieve this state through a tantalizing mixture of meditation, intricate breathing patterns, pounding drums and swirling dance movements.

You might be more familiar with Sufis from their popular name, whirling dervishes, a most appropriate appellation for Sufis, who often create their mystical states by whirling in circles, with their right hands gracefully upturned towards the heavens and their left hands open to the soul of the earth below. Their movements are graceful, their flowing white robes wonderfully designed to billow in the winds of their gyrations. If you are a Sufis you get to meet God face to face and stay in shape at the same time. For a mystic, it doesn't get any better than this.

Sufis not only dance a delightful dance, they write wonderfully good bits of wisdom that shed some direct light on our own search for the secrets of living in the present moment. In this regard, of all of the Sufic mystics, perhaps the best known writings are those of the fourteenth century poet Rumi. It is to his writings we now turn.

Rumi was the Alan Watts of his day. Not only could he convey vision-ary wisdom, he could convey it with grace and beauty. One would be hard pressed to find a more eloquent single sentence description of the value of the present moment than in the following piece of wordsmithing:

> *Past and future are shutters covering the window*
> *through which streams God's sunlight.*

As was the case with Alan Watts or David Bowie, in the next breath Rumi could move from the poetic to the starkly obvious, whacking one on the head with the swift strike of a Zen Master's bamboo stick:

> *How long are you going to worry about what*
> *has already happened and can't be changed and what*
> *has yet to come and can't be controlled.*

Rumi has hit upon a new slant here—concerning Julian's concept of trust—that is well worth closer attention. Both in my personal life and with my patients, I have found that it is sometimes difficult to put the abstract idea of "nurturing trust" into practice.

It sounds like a great idea, but its manner of implementation is not always immediately obvious. Paradoxically, one of the major stumbling blocks to learning to nurture trust is the fact that, to do so, we must first be able to rec-ognize when we are not doing it. Moving through life without trust is like all bad habits. In order to transform it, we must first acknowledge that we have it. But how does one recognize those moments when we move without trust?

Here is where Rumi adds a particularly practical piece to our puzzle. He does so by giving us a surefire hazard light that alerts us when "past and future are shutters covering the window through which streams God's sun-light." We know that the shutters are closed—we are not moving with Julian's sense of trust—when we are ferociously trying to control the people and the stuff around us.

There is a right time and a right place to try to control aspects of the universe—the bad times of Led Zeppelin—but it is dangerously easy to make a habit of this practice during the good times as well. I am amazed at how often I find myself, and my patients, worrying about how to control this and that during periods of everyday activity when nothing particularly bad is happening. Control freaks abound in this life. And, if we are honest, we all have a bit of control freak residing inside us, sometimes more than a bit.

With his emphasis on avoiding over-control, Rumi has given us a much more concrete way to spot those times when it is best to "just let go" and realize that "all is well" as Julian would say.

I am reminded of the wise saying from Richard Carlson, Ph.D., "So many people spend so much of their life energy 'sweating the small stuff' that they completely lose touch with the magic and beauty of life." With practice it becomes progressively easy, thanks to Rumi, to spot moments where we are needlessly sweating the small stuff trying to control "what has yet to come and can't be controlled." Once I spot such a moment, I have found the following simple thought to be both gently reassuring and surprisingly effective at returning me to the present moment:

There is absolutely nothing really bad happening right now. Relax.
There is nothing you need to control. Nothing. Nothing at all.

Sometimes significant others can help with this process of spotting moments when one has lost a sense of trust. For instance during those good times when I find myself pacing about the house as if I were smack-dab in the middle of bad times, my wife, Susan, will frequently help put a stop to it all. She will invariably happen upon me muttering to myself (indication of agitation) and twirling my hair (nervous habit). She will gently stop both the mutterings and the twirlings, put her hands on my shoulders, look me in the eye and say, "You neurotic moron. Get a grip."

Works for me! With the loving yet firm hand of a smallish Zen monk yielding a surprisingly big piece of bamboo, her frank wisdom registers in my soul. It is as if Susan—who at such moments invariably has one of those smiles that says, "I know who you are and I love you just the way you are but . . ."—had just pulled a cork from my body.

All of my unnecessary anxiety pours into a gentle pool of nothingness. I inevitably let out an appreciative sigh. It is the same sigh I emit after returning from a long and arduous lecture tour, as my feet find footing upon the familiar planks of my front porch. I am home again. I am back in the warm embrace of the present moment.

At such moments, I don't know who to thank more: Julian, Rumi or Susan. But I do know we have stumbled upon another valuable piece of our puzzle. Whether we catch these moments of lost trust ourselves, or with a little help from our friends, Rumi has given us a practical method for nurturing Benny's ability to live life minute by minute in the present moment. Rumi has helped us to spot those moments in time when it is wisest to gain control by yielding it.

Yet another Middle Eastern voice—the voice of Judaism—echoes the Sufi belief of the critical importance of the here and now. The words come from a contemporary Kabbalist—the Kabbalah being a Jewish mystical tradition that seems to be finding a new chic in our contemporary world. Our Kabbalist is Rabbi David A. Cooper, who wrote the engagingly wise book, *God is a Verb, Kabbalah and the Practice of Mystical Judaism*. The religions may be different, but, once again, the truths sound surprisingly similar:

> *We are never "here" because we are always trying to be "there," wherever that is. But understand this important teaching: When we accept each moment as a new opportunity for fulfilling our purpose, we are always present, always succeeding, always changing the world for the better. And we are always "here."*

It consistently amazes me that one could quite literally list all of these quotations from the world's great religious traditions, and, if you did not list their sources, you would have no idea which quote came from which religion. So why, one might ask, am I taking such a long look at all of these traditions, when they seem to be making the same point? Because I want you to believe. I want you to believe that these ideas are not just intellectually interesting fodder, but the real McCoy. Somewhere inside them, part of the mystery of finding an enduring sense of happiness resides.

Living in the present moment works. Julian of Norwich hinted at it. Rumi danced it. Ralph Waldo Emerson wrote of it. John Merrick lived it. And David Bowie still believes it. Their words all point towards one curious fact about the relationship between living in the present moment and finding happiness.

Living in the present moment brings happiness, not so much because of what it adds to life, as to what it takes away. It takes away worry. It takes away fretting. It takes away anxiety. It is through the door of the present moment that we enter the limo of Benny. Once inside, we find wonderment, gratitude, compassion, forgiveness and acceptance. Outside, we leave behind our frets, our worries and our fears.

Why Gods Hide and Rain Cannot Be Caught

Here is where we turn to a paradox well worth our attention. It is quite clear that living in the present moment is desirable, practical and, most important, obtainable in everyday existence. On one level, it is also difficult to do, for our fretting dismantles it. On a different level, it is the only thing that we can do. There exists only the present moment for human beings.

You see, it is not so much whether we live in the present moment or not; it is whether we allow ourselves to enjoy living in the present moment or not. As human organisms we can only experience the present moment. Even fretting about the past or the future occurs only in the present moment. Worry and anxiety are moment by moment co-creations of the swirling chemicals in our brains and the whirling machinations of our souls. They are happening right now. The past and the future are out of reach of human touch and perception. Even our memories are manifestations of the present moment.

Alan Watts captures the wonderment of this paradoxical fact of human existence in the following quote from his provocative book, *The Wisdom of Insecurity:*

> *But what about memories? Surely by remembering I can also know what is past? Very well, remember something. Remember the incident of seeing a friend walking down the street. What are you aware of? You are not actually watching the veritable event of your friend walking down the street. You can't go up and shake hands with him, or get an answer to a question you forgot to ask at the past time you are remembering. In other words, you are not looking at the actual past at all. You are looking at a present trace of the past.*
>
> *It is like seeing the tracks of a bird on the sand. I see the present tracks. I do not, at the same time, see the bird making those tracks an hour before. The bird has flown, and I am not aware of him. From the tracks I infer that there have been past events. But you are not aware of any past events. You know the past only in the present and as part of the present.*
>
> *We are seeing, then, that our experience is altogether momentary. From one point of view, each moment is so elusive and so brief that we cannot even think about it before it has gone. From another point of view, this moment is always here, since we know no other moment than the present moment. It is always dying, always becoming past more rapidly than imagination can conceive. Yet at the same time it is always being born, always new, emerging just as rapidly from that complete unknown which we call the future. Thinking about it almost makes you breathless.*

Why is this so? A Zen monk might quickly respond, "Because it is so." As a Westerner, I am both simply too analytical and too curious to accept such a bald statement of faith. I want to know why, scientifically speaking, I only experience the present moment.

Fortunately, the answer is a surprisingly simple one. We are confined to experiencing only the present moment, for the same reason that we are limited to what waves of the electromagnetic spectrum we can see. Our sense organs and brains do not allow us to experience anything but the present moment.

The world in its totality exists out there—somewhere. How much of that world I get to see is entirely dependent upon the perceptual apparatus with which I am born. This limitation is set not only by the limited abilities of my sense organs to gather data but also by the processing power of my brain to interpret the data which these sense organs bring to it.

All organisms, including humans, only see a part of the world. A dog cannot see the color red, but red exists. An ant cannot see a house one hundred yards away from it, but the house exists. We cannot see infrared, but infrared exists.

In a similar sense our brains are geared to only experience the present moment. Period. When it comes to reality, all humans live in cages. We don't see the bars of our cages, because the bars are behind our eyes. The bars are in our brains. Our brains limit what we can see, hear and even experience. In this instance, our brains severely limit our experience of time to the present moment. For a human that's all there is—the present moment. Experientially, for humans, the past and the future literally do not exist. They are merely concepts.

There is an extremely intriguing corollary to this fact that is worth a bit of a sidetrack. Once you understand the simple fact that the biology of our brains clearly has something to do with setting limits on what we can experience, one comes smack-dab to the following provocative realization. Perhaps our neuronal architecture and neurochemistry limits not only what we can perceive, but also what we can conceive.

Clearly, ultraviolet and infrared light exist, but I can't see them. Clearly, ultrasonic and radar waves exist, but I can't hear them. Clearly neutrons and neutrinos exist, but I can't feel them. But what of God? Are there thoughts, conceptions or even beings that could exist that we cannot know because we do not have the neural hardware to conceive of them?

What does our science say about whether or not one can ultimately disprove the existence of a god or a goddess? The answer is straightforward: Logically speaking, we cannot ever disprove the existence of god, for, if there is a god or a goddess, it is quite possible that he or she exists in a form that our brains do not allow us to see or even conceptualize. An all-powerful god could easily create a world in which only tiny bits of itself could be perceived or conceived by the human brain—or none of it at all. Depending upon the limitations of our neurological hardwiring, God could be as invisible as an electron. We just don't know. As Billy Crystal would say, "Mahvelous. Simply mahvelous."

By the way this does not prove that a god or goddess exists. It simply confirms the fact that neither logic nor science can ever disprove god, for we humans are limited to the perceptions and thoughts that our brains allow us to produce. If indeed a god or goddess exists, we may not be able to perceive or even conceive the actual form of the god, except to the extent that the godhead might choose to reveal itself.

Looked at in another light, if some thoughts are created primarily by neurochemistry, then there may be thoughts that we simply cannot have—there may be thoughts in the universe that, for humans, are unthinkable. Just as an ant does not have the neuronal hardware to see a house a hundred yards away, a human may be able to see the house but not the god that hides within it. As the enigmatic French filmmaker Jean Cocteau so aptly commented, "Mystery has it own mysteries, and there are gods above gods. We have ours, they have theirs."

Returning to our main topic of this chapter, the essence of happiness lies somewhere in the constantly unfolding mystery of the present moment. Learning how to more continuously experience this moment is clearly at the heart of developing an enduring sense of happiness that can refresh us during times of pain and disappointment. But, in a practical sense, where exactly does all of this leave us?

It leaves us with the understanding that both scientifically and spiritually, one cannot capture the past nor step into the future. Attempts to capture the past, such as photographs, yield, at best, vague phantoms of what once was. The phantoms in the photograph cannot be touched. Only the photograph itself can be touched. It is the photograph that exists, not the past. Similarly, expectations of the future create, at best, only mirages of what the future will actually be. The future cannot be lived. Only the present moment can be lived. No one can touch, kiss or hold a future image.

In this regard, trying to capture the present moment as it immediately slips into the past is as futile as trying to capture the rain from a summer storm in a silver bucket. The raindrops may pelt the metal of our bucket and fill its silver gut, but after the storm has passed what is left in our bucket may very well be water, but it is most certainly not rain. The past and the future do not exist. Only the present moment really exists. It is delightfully recreating itself with every fleeting microsecond. There is no pail made by man that can capture it.

In the last analysis, it is this fleeting quality of the present that makes it so wonderfully and deliciously precious that we dare not waste it with our frets and our fears. Ironically, it is death that shows us the fleeting preciousness of the present moment. When we try to remember the face of a loved one who has died, it is death that shows us the unreality of the past and the unreality of the future. Try as we might, our imaginations only create half pictures, night gaunts, that hint of what was but fly away as we try to touch them. As it turns out, the faces of our loved ones can only be touched in the present moment.

And like our loved ones, the present moment is a face. It is the face of God. It is the face of all that can be. It is the face of the universe endlessly unfolding. It is a face that can never be caught. Nor should it be. To try to catch it is as fruitless as catching the rain in our pail.

Like the face of our loved one, it is best, whenever the face of the present moment is near, whenever it is *now*, to touch it, stroke it, feel its warmth, wipe its tears and savor its smile, for it is the only face that really exists. When we embrace it, it is the face that provides us the freedom from our worries and regrets that Watts mentions and to which Benny points.

It is the face that stirs gratitude in our hearts. It is the face that ignites our sense of wonderment. It is the face of happiness that is always there for the taking—we need only to open our eyes and reach. One does not necessarily need to be a magician, a seer or a mystic to touch it. Benny was none of those things. You just have to be a human being. And we all qualify for that.

6

The Thief in
the Mirror

*"Everyday I fight a war against the mirror,
Can't take the person staring back at me.
I'm a hazard to myself."*

PINK, FROM "DON'T LET ME GET ME," CIRCA 2003

Texas Preachers, Hotel Moguls
and Sacred Words

How? How does one live within the present moment? Benny has ably demonstrated both that it is wise to do so and that it can be done, but his insights are only a tease unless we can replicate them. There are still important pieces missing to our definition of happiness.

As we search for these missing pieces, we find ourselves traveling to a land more wonderfully strange than the land of Oz—the state of Texas. Only this time, unlike Dorothy, we are not in search of a wizard, we are in search of a preacher. This particular preacher not only addresses our question, he does so with an elegance worthy of a Rumi or a Julian of Norwich.

To find him we will need to move from the relatively sparsely popu-
lated highways of Iowa to the tightly packed jamways of Houston, Texas. If
you scoot off one of these crawling parking lots on a Sunday morning, you
might come upon a little chapel that hosts the evangelist for whom we are
searching.

Perhaps the word "little chapel" is a misnomer. Apparently, Texans
think big whether they are rounding up cattle or congregations. This little
chapel, by my estimate, houses about five thousand churchgoers at a swat.
The sermons go out on worldwide television, reaching many millions
more.

On the stage of our church, and it is more of a stage than a pulpit, a
rather tall and lanky dynamo can be found. The speaker, the Reverend Joel
Osteen, is hard to miss. He appears unusually young to be both so famous
and so wise, but then again, he is a blast to watch.

Osteen is that rarity among speakers: Even when I disagree with a particular point he is making, I find myself utterly enthralled with how he is
making it. He pulls a member of the congregation into his pulpit with the
same skill that Frank Sinatra used to pull a member of the audience onto
his stage. Both men—Osteen and ole Blue Eyes—make you think that they
are communicating directly to you and only to you. They know your story,
and they can tell your story like no one else in the world. Neato.

In any case, Osteen gives a great talk on the dangers of living in the
past. He provides some added pith to our thoughts thus far, for Osteen has
a knack for coining phrases that stick, bits of wisdom that we will remember when we most need them, such as the following:

*You can't do anything about what is gone, but you
can do something about what is left.*

Before you let go of the old, you can't get on with the new.

Don't let the regrets of yesterday destroy
the hopes of tomorrow.

Such aphorisms are sharp, quick and pithy. They remind us of the importance of living in the present moment, if we find ourselves lost in the pains of yesterday or the fears of tomorrow. But they don't really tell us how to do it. It is the next Osteen aphorism, one of my favorites, that indirectly provides what we are looking for—some instructions on the matter:

We've got to get to the point where we trust God
even though we do not understand God.

Wow. Especially for those who picture their god as an actual being, who by definition must have a face and a personality that peeks from behind the mists of the unknown, that's a nice one. If you let it rattle around in your brain for a day or two, it has all sorts of enriching ramifications.

It is also familiar advice. Osteen is smacking us upside the head with the same word that meant so much to our nun in the closet—trust— profound trust. We are immediately reminded of Julian of Norwich holding that hazelnut thing in her palm. As she peered at it, she was certain that it would be safe forever because God loved it, and God was all powerful. She didn't know how He was all powerful. And it didn't matter. Who cares? She just knew.

I think this word "trust" may very well be a sacred word of sorts. It is a particularly important word when it comes to understanding happiness. As we have already seen, it seems to hold the secret to being able to live in the present moment. If you don't have "trust" that things will work out, it is a little hard not to be worrying about the future, for we all know that life— simply put—is tough.

Julian of Norwich did a dandy job of introducing us to the importance of trust, describing how a deep sense of trust allows one to live in the here and now. This connection, between a sense of trust and the ability to live in the present moment, is so pivotal to understanding the meaning of happiness that it warrants a more detailed exploration.

Like all good sacred words worth their salt, the more you reflect upon it, the more meanings you see in it. For instance, from the Christian perspective, the concept of trust is not about a mere blind trust in God. One is not supposed to just hang out and wait for God to provide miracles to make life easy. It is a trust not that God will provide miracles, but that God made each of us into a miracle. It is a trust that God provides each person with the skills, talents and instincts to find happiness despite all of life's adversities. *That* is the miracle.

But it is not a free ride. Whether Hindu, Christian, Jew or Islamic, to bring this miracle into fruition, one is expected to do one's share of its birthing. It is like a magic show, only God's tricks are not sleight of hand; they are real magic. God is the magician, and we are the stage hands. The show requires us to do our parts as well. God expects us to work hard and to find our skills and talents. Then the real miracles unfold. Find your God-given talents, believe in them and miracles happen.

On yet another level, this profound sense of trust may not be about God at all. Profound trust does not necessarily come from a belief in an anthropomorphic supreme being. Many people find a profound sense of trust in the mysterious and enduring quality of nature itself. Some find it in both God and nature, for they are not necessarily contradictory world views.

To Taoists, who, to me, seem to be some of the most trusting of souls, trust comes from their belief in the enduring power of the process they call the Tao. The Tao is a process beyond definition that always was, is and will be. It is the indescribable nothing from which all somethings come. It is the very stuff of the universe, and the universe takes very good care of its stuff, thank you very much.

From a Taoist perspective, the Tao and one of its manifestations—the universe—will endure forever. As a part of that universe, each person is a part of a great mystery, and being an integral part of this magnificently mysterious universe, each of us will endure forever. The Tao does not disappear; we are a part of the Tao. There is something wonderfully comforting in realizing this fact not just in the mind, but in the gut. And it all comes down to trust.

I also stumbled upon this word—trust—in a most unlikely place one evening several years ago in a Hilton Hotel in Baltimore, Maryland. I'd been on the road for days, was missing home and had achieved that unpleasant state of affairs in which one is so weary that one is not sleepy. I had finished the books I was reading, played my computer game—Heroes of Might and Magic III—with so much vigor on my laptop that the battery blew up, and I couldn't stomach the vacant blather of the television set for one more moment. But I was awake. I was desperate. I needed something to do.

Pathetic road warrior that I was, I found myself rifling through the bureau drawers beside my bed in search of who knows what. One does strange things in hotel rooms. Before I knew it, I was holding the book *There is an Art to Living* by Conrad Hilton—"the hotel guy" himself.

Finding myself in a cynical mood, I smiled thinking, *This should be worth a laugh or two.* Being my typically mature self I immediately stereotyped Hilton as a conniving, loutish, capitalist pig, even though I knew absolutely nothing about him. I felt certain that I would find some real gems of wisdom in this little baby along the lines of "Build everything you can, crush your competition, employ illegal aliens at outrageously inappropriate wages and buy half of Wall Street. If you do all this, you too will be happy. That is the art of living." Well, no kidding. If I owned half the world I'd be pretty happy too.

I began reading. Twenty minutes later, I was still reading. I was sitting up, had brewed a fresh pot of coffee, and was taking notes. Conrad Hilton had something important to say.

Hilton describes a set of ten principles that he has found useful as he has tried to crack the same puzzle that we are—what is this happiness thing anyway? The one principle that has stuck with me the most is a simple one, and I quote, "To worry about your difficulties after the sun is set and you have done all you can for the day is useless—and an act of distrust." I had always known such worrying was useless, although I did it all the time, but in a million years I had never thought of it as being an "act of distrust." It is.

Thieves on the Road to Dartmouth and Wisdom from Pink Things

Many of our sages have used the word trust, but it is Hilton who is the first to use its negative: "distrust." This use of the negative provides one more piece to the puzzle of happiness, for it hints that fretting about the past or the future may not only be an act of distrust, it may be something even more devious—an act of thievery. I found this out one morning while driving on Route 10 towards Hanover, New Hampshire. I was driving to a class that I was to teach at the Dartmouth Medical School. It was the summer of 2002.

For years I had been teaching three all-day classes on clinical interviewing skills for the psychiatric residents at Dartmouth. I live almost an hour and a half away from Dartmouth, so I had to get up around 5:30 A.M. to make this little academic exercise on time. I am not a morning person. On this particular morning, I was in reasonably good spirits, but roughly 50 billion of my 100 billion neurons were still deep asleep. I was approaching the town of Newport, the half-way point.

It was then that I remembered Jack's Coffee, a delightful coffeehouse sitting smack-dab on the main street of Newport. My savior was at hand. If nobody else could wake up my 50 billion sleepyheads, Jack could. I decided I wanted something exotic in nature, perhaps a dash of caramel or cinnamon would do the trick. I was running late, but, what the hell. Without a mug of java, I might not even make it to Dartmouth. It was an obvious question of safety. So I zipped into a parking spot.

Jack's joint is a splendid blend of green wallboards, warm wainscoting, comfy chairs and offbeat paintings. As I looked in front of me, I felt relieved to see that there was no line at the counter. Life was good.

As I approached the coffee dispensers my eyes lit up, for there was the exotic brew of my dreams—almondine amaretto. My zillion little taste buds let up a cheer, and I purchased the biggest cup I could get—a two-buck tanker. I was set. Life was more than good. And I headed for my car.

I quickly crossed the street, sat down and started up the engine. Lacking a cup holder, I had placed the warm cup between my legs. And as I backed onto Main Street, the steam from my cup was filling the car with a delicious aroma. With my senses titillated by the promise of my much anticipated treat, I could not have been more alive in the present moment.

Soon I was on the open road, heading toward my early morning rendezvous with my Dartmouth residents. As I zipped on by the local high school football field, I made the mistake of glancing at my clock. 7:00 o'clock. Later than I had thought.

I found myself thinking about whether or not the audiovisual equipment was going to be there or not. My thoughts shifted to a recent talk in Las Vegas that had been a nightmare, with two separate microphones failing during my presentation. Then I shifted to thoughts about my upcoming contract negotiations with my major client, the same client that had brought me to Las Vegas.

My mind suddenly darted back to the high school football field, and I remembered my son was just about to make a transition from a ninety-student private middle school to a 1,500 student public high school. Yeeks! I began fretting about how his transition would go.

Suddenly it hit me. I needed to pee—big time—and I had forgotten to stop back at Jack's. There was no time to stop now, I can tell you that. I had better things to do. I was skillfully beating myself into a veritable frenzy about being late. Surely the LCD projector would not be there. Surely people would be annoyed by my late arrival. I could see it all now in vivid Technicolor.

It was then that I finally remembered my cup of almondine amaretto. I reached down, pulled the delightful brew to my lips, and took a sip. My lips pursed and shuddered. My tongue darted out. What the hell was going on! The only liquid that touched my lips was the cold last remnant of Jack's best. I glanced down in the cup. Empty. Totally empty. Somebody had stolen my cup of coffee.

I frenziedly glanced to my left, as if in my sideview mirror I expected to see the fleeing culprit. I glanced back to the right peering into my rearview mirror. Perhaps I would see the thief's butt as he scampered down the fading street behind me. It was then that I caught sight of the thief in the mirror. It wasn't his butt, it was his face. The bastard was still in the car. I had inadvertently brought the worst thief I have ever known along with me on the ride to Dartmouth — me. I was the thief in the mirror.

I did not have a single memory of drinking a single drop of the coffee. By deftly pulling myself out of the present moment into frets of the past and future, I had missed the whole cup. I was out two bucks, as surely as if I had rolled down the window and given a good heave.

For the next twenty minutes I kicked myself for being so stupid, thus managing with great ingenuity to lose, during those angry ruminations about the past, yet another twenty minutes of my day. Because of my self denigrations, I now had no idea what scenery I had just passed. I had no idea I was even driving a car. I had been totally inside my head belittling myself. Another twenty minutes stolen. Damn, I'm getting good at this!

Truth be told, on a really good day, I can steal myself blind. I'll end up in the sack at night, and have insanely little idea what in heaven's name I just experienced for the last sixteen hours. I'll know what I did, but will I have enjoyed it as I did it?

And here is the sorry truth. When we do not live in the present moment we are thieves. We rob ourselves of the fun of experiencing the delicious delicacies brought to us by life and, indirectly, we rob ourselves of the delicacies themselves. These delicacies aren't always as cheap as a cup of coffee from Jack's, I might add. I once heard of a guy who bought himself a Jaguar, then fretted so much about scratching it that he never remembered or enjoyed being inside it. That's grand larceny.

At moments like this one, when I am stealing myself blind, I sometimes chuckle when I recall the lyric from the song that introduced our chapter. Pink, if you are unfamiliar with her is, well, pink, not her whole body mind you, just her hair. I think it looks good on her. I tend to be a fan of brightly colored hair on teenagers on the right kid at the right time. Not my kid. Not right now. On other people's kids—awesome.

In any case, Pink is a savvy singer with street smarts, a feisty voice and is just subversive enough to be wholesome in a strangely subversive way because she is so damn funny. Her well-crafted lyrics appeal to the "every-man" within us because they are often right on the mark regarding our human flaws. And I find that her understated humor makes these flaws just a little bit more palatable to acknowledge in myself.

And it is Pink who wonderfully captures the essence of my dilemma as I was stealing myself blind on the road to Dartmouth: "It's bad when you annoy yourself."

Ain't it the truth.

Fortunately, we don't have to do it. To understand how to avoid annoying ourselves, it pays to learn everything we possibly can about the thief in the mirror.

A Hundred Gargoyles, Two Demons, Ten Handballs and a Torture Chamber

The thief in the mirror is not alone. He or she is always accompanied by two demons who really do the dirty work. After the thief takes away the present moment, it is the two demons who keep it away. One demon forces us to ruminate about the past; his buddy compels us to fret about the future. Before we know it, we are no longer in control. We are runaways.

A rock contemporary of Ms. Pink who is also a gifted lyricist—Stephan Jenkins of Third Eye Blind—put it rather nicely in the song "Narcolepsy":

> *I'm on a train,*
> *But there is no one at the helm.*

There is a demon in my brain,
And he is starting to overwhelm.

The latter imp, the one compelling us into the future, is a particularly nasty tyke and has a lot to do with the creation of Third Eye Blind's unpleasant sense of being overwhelmed—as opposed to being fascinated—by the present moment. This demon attacks by rushing us headlong into the future, always worrying about what will happen next so that we have no idea what is happening now.

This sensation of being sucked into, what can be aptly called, the "furious future," creates the ultimate runaway train—a human being always in a hurry, cell phone in hand, e-mail at his or her back, future business meeting on the mind. Every minute of the day counted with as much greed as Scrooge counted gold. No time to laugh, barely time to cry, the world a ceaseless blur of "Hey, how you doing, catch you later," and "I'd love to talk, but . . ."

Before we know it, we not only understand the lyric by Third Eye Blind, we are the lyric. We've become runaway trains with no one at the helm. Thanks to a thief and two demons in our brains, we have become overwhelmed by the irresistible suction of the future—its fury, its menace, its nonsense.

Clearly the thief in the mirror and his two demon friends can steal both our moments of pleasure and an occasional treasured possession such as a steaming cup of coffee or a Jag. But it gets even worse. This gang of thugs can steal something even more agonizing to lose for it can never be regained.

I discovered what this something was many years ago, when I was a college student at Duke University. I discovered it in a dirty, grotty, little room we affectionately called the "Torture Chamber." The perfect place for the demon of Third Eye Blind to be hanging out.

I was a junior and was living in a curious dorm called BOG, which was an "independent house." This meant BOG housed a loosely collected group of students with quite diverse interests that, when it worked well, fostered the fun communal feeling of a fraternity without all the interpersonal anguish and pressures that sometimes, not always, can plague fraternities.

The main campus of Duke University is a tantalizing collection of Gothic towers, gargoyles and stained glass windows, all of which seem to come to life in the moonlit nights of late summer, when the sounds of the cicadas fill the humid North Carolina air with their incessant whirring. At that time, even the gym—Cameron Indoor Stadium—had a Gothic feel to it. It was to that old and battered gym, at around nine at night, that I found myself walking. I was taking part in the intramural handball tournament. I was heading towards an important match.

BOG prided itself on always doing surprisingly well in the overall intramural competition, often beating out the more well-known fraternities. We were having a great year, but the competition was getting to be fierce, and every point could prove to be important in the final standings. Everybody in the house was expected to chip in with participation in the intramurals. Naturally, the hope was that one would be chipping in with "Wins" in whatever sport you were playing.

I was a pretty good handball player, not great, but certainly well above average. I had racked up a couple of wins, and with a bit of cockiness, I felt that I was most assuredly walking towards another one.

As I climbed the stairs in the darkened gym, I was hoping that the regular-sized handball courts would all be full. If they were full, it meant that I would meet my opponent in an undersized, decrepit old court whose walls were so filthy with the black smudges of handballs, gloves and more than a few heads that it looked like the walls had been smeared with blood—the Torture Chamber.

Good players adored this undersized court, because its small size heightened the speed and ferocity of the game. If you had a weak opponent, it was great fun. I loved it.

Handball, if you have never played it, has a primal feel. There are no rackets, referees, nets or rules of etiquette. There is just you, the opponent, six walls and, of course, that little hard black ball that stings every time you strike it with your palm. It doesn't feel so good if it hits you in the head either, I might add.

The goal is to run your opponent around and around the court chasing balls that, unless your opponent is named Michael Vick, will never feel the leather of his or her sweaty palm. If you happen to be both lucky and skilled, your opponent will soon be gasping for air. If really lucky, your opponent will also soon be sporting bruises acquired from slamming into the plaster walls of the court. Great fun! Tennis for the professional-wrestling crowd.

As I climbed the stairs I could hear the balls pounding on the walls of courts one and two with the staccato ferocity of fierce gameplay, interspersed with an occasional yell of exasperation. I smiled. There was only one court left.

Upstairs, I could hear the occasional sound of a ball striking the walls at the lackadaisical frequency of a player warming up. As I opened the door to the Torture Chamber, I smiled. There was my opponent. There stood a mildly pudgy looking guy with dark rimmed glasses and beany legs—think SpongeBob SquarePants. There was my victory.

Being a good sport he called out a friendly, "Hey, how you doing." I reciprocated with an equally genuine, "Great. Let's warm up." I truly enjoyed my opponents, for I respected them and realized that we were all just trying to win. Once we started up though, I was a competitive little dickens. My opponents morphed into "the enemy" and I had become Spartacus, a Roman gladiator. Yes, indeedy, I had too much testosterone for my own good. With age a lot of it has vanished—that's both good and bad, but let's not go there.

After warm-ups I felt delightfully optimistic, for you can usually get a pretty accurate idea of the caliber of your opponent. This guy was okay, but not up to my skills.

I was already imagining what I would be saying to Robertson, the long-haired, finely sculptured captain of all of our teams, who for all intents and purposes looked like a modern day Conan the Barbarian. Robertson was funny, easy going and tough. Although you knew he'd understand if you lost, you didn't want to, because you didn't want to disappoint him. If he kidded you about a loss, it would always be followed by a smile. But what a smile. Bottom line—you didn't want Robertson smiling at you.

He was also a great athlete, and on the handball court Conan took no prisoners. It would be great fun telling him of my victory later that might as we headed over to the Cambridge Inn, a late-night place to gobble down junk food, which we students affectionately simply called the CI.

As I expected, the first game went great. I was sharp, fast and all too clever for my gasping opponent. Score 21-5. This was going to be too easy. It was only a two out of three match, so it would be over soon, and I could already taste the pepperoni pizza that was waiting for me at the CI.

In the second game I jumped out to a four to zip lead, and then I began to think about that pepperoni pizza just a little too much. As I was popping a slice of pepperoni into my mouth, my opponent, the chunky kid, snuck by a couple of quick points. His next serve was a good one. It shot past into a back corner. He looked shocked.

My left hand was my weaker hand, and sure enough the little bastard placed his next serve in the exact same place. Shea—4; Geeky Kid—4. On the next serve, the sneaky engineer, for I felt certain he was in the engineering program, shot one to the other corner to my surprise. The only sound was the ball slapping loudly into the back corner and a terse curse. Mine, of course.

Then it happened. I imagined another voice—Robertson's voice. As usual, Robertson had a way with words, "What do you mean you lost, you Turkey shit." Smile. Zing. Point, Geeky Kid. It suddenly dawned on me, I could lose this game. At Shea 7, Geeky Kid 19, I was so far into the furious future, you'd need a spotlight to see my butt. I was a runaway train alright. I was no longer concentrating on the ball, my opponent or the game for that matter. I kept saying things to myself like, "I can't believe this. This is nuts." It was also over. Shea 7, Geeky Kid 21.

What was going on! I'm getting upset just typing this memory for I vividly remember my panic. Game three was over fast. The truth of the matter is that game three was over before it even began.

In the middle of the slaughter, I felt as if there were ten handballs, all going at once in that little Torture Chamber. Worse yet, every wall seemed to be sporting the face of Robertson, and he wasn't a happy camper. On one wall he was shocked. On the next one, I caught a glimpse of that smile that one does not want to see. On the next one, he was displaying his displeasure in a way not appropriate for description in a book of this nature. Throughout it all, his new name for me kept bouncing around in my cranium. I don't think I saw the little black ball once unless it was a blur shooting past my head as I ducked.

As we shook hands, I remember this kid, who really was a good sport, saying, "Wow, thanks for a great match. I really thought you were the better player. I bet you had a bad night or something. But it was really fun. Maybe we can get together for a beer or something sometime."

"Sure, SpongeBob. Sure." Yeah, it was a great match alright, for my thief. Apparently, I wasn't alone when I walked through the door of the Torture Chamber. My buddy and his two friends tagged along. They weren't there as cheerleaders, I can tell you that. This time the thief stole something that could never be replaced. He stole victory.

I'd choked. If you have ever wondered exactly what the phenomena of choking is, wonder no more. It is not a mystery. Choking is simply that moment when an athlete steps out of the present moment into the past or the future. Nothing more. Nothing less.

The unfortunate choking athlete either squirts into the past to bemoan an error he or she has just made, or the athlete squirts into the future to fret about that most nasty of what ifs—"What if I lose?" Choking is not a mystery. It is an act of distrust, as Conrad Hilton would say.

When we move outside of the present moment, we rob ourselves, not only of our pleasures and our possessions, but our victories. We "steal defeat from the jaws of victory" as many a sportscaster has quipped. What that pleasant engineering student taught me in the Torture Chamber at Duke was an invaluable lesson. He taught me that living in the present moment not only benefits me by what it takes away from life—unnecessary anxiety—but by what it adds to life—enhanced performance.

With this insight we are ready to uncover the last piece in the puzzle of happiness. It is a somewhat paradoxical piece for we are back to where we started our quest—the relationship between our evolving definition of happiness and the traditional meaning of success.

Back in our opening chapters we learned from Timothy, Albert Schweitzer, the Dalai Lama and a host of other great thinkers that success is not happiness, finding happiness is success. But does this mean that achieving goals and winning competitions is somehow bad?

Of course not. It is fun to win. It is satisfying to achieve goals. It would have been fun to have won that match in the Torture Chamber, and it would have been satisfying to eat my pizza at the CI without having to look at that smile of Robertson.

The art of living consists of learning how to pick our goals wisely, limit their number prudently, win them gracefully and never allow their pursuit to define who we are. If the achievement of the goals defines who we are, we have wandered off the right path. The secondary goals have become the primary goals and happiness is sure to vanish. Sometimes, quite painfully. We must now focus upon the intriguing relationship that exists between the process of keeping the finding of happiness as the focus of our lives and attending to the practical goals and achievements that constitute the everyday business of living.

In this regard, my opponent played one of the best games of his life. Unlike myself, he was living, breathing and serving in the present moment. I didn't have a chance. What is curious is that, although I am convinced he was thrilled that he won, I believe his happiness was more connected to the fact that he was enlivened by the process of winning, by the enjoyment of how well he played.

It was not so much that his victory caused his happiness. It was that his happiness—as reflected by his total involvement with the present moment—led to his victory. The victory was a consequence of his happiness, not vice versa. How this can be and why is the topic of our next chapter.

7

The Heron on
the Ski Slope

"The less effort, the faster and more powerful you will be."

BRUCE LEE, MARTIAL ARTIST

Chinese Birds, Unhappy Frogs and a
Fortuitous Chain of Events

As you can well imagine, Eastern philosophers, from old guys like the Buddha to new guys like D. T. Suzuki and Alan Watts, are pretty much into this "living in the present moment" thing. Some of the most elegant writing on the topic, especially with regard to what interests us most at this time—the curious relationship between happiness as reflected by immersion in the present moment and success in the more traditional sense of achievement—comes from Stewart Holmes and Chimyo Horioka in a tiny and obscure book. I came across it in my early twenties. It is simply called *Zen Art for Meditation*. Don't let the title mislead you. It is an art book only in the sense that it is about the art of living.

Pictures of curious landscapes, with cloud-hidden mountains and people so tiny that they seem to vanish into the rocky crags around them, are used as jumping-off points for insights into finding happiness. It is a delightful book that has a rare quality that I have seldom seen in other books on philosophy; when I read it, I not only intellectually understand the philosophy, I feel it. I tangibly change as I read the book. Bit by bit I find myself pulled into the present moment—into a sense of wonderment, gratitude, compassion and freedom.

In a chapter called "The Moment," Holmes and Horioka describe a painting of a heron in the second before he strikes at a frog. They do not pass judgment upon the heron, who is about to eat, or upon the frog, who is about to be eaten. They simply describe the moment itself. The intensity and concentration of the heron are captured with a crisp clarity by the brushstrokes of the gifted painter. With equal skill, Holmes and Horioka capture the intensity of the heron's soul in the following words:

> *Poised for a lightning thrust, this heron's whole being is concentrating on one objective: Get that frog. His long powerful neck is bent like a spring; his body is leaning forward to provide mass for the attack; his eyes are fixed unwinking on his prey; his weapon, that long, pointed bill, is aimed and ready. For him there exists no past or future—only the present. As we look at him, time seems to stop; we too, lean forward, frozen in an inner attitude of readiness, living completely in the NOW.*
>
> *How refreshing, to live concentratedly in the instant. To give over regrets, anticipations, worries, reflections, and reflections on reflections. To focus on the job at hand. How refreshing, and how loosening of prejudices and inhibitions. We are enabled to enter into a more productive transaction with what we are trying to do.*

Earlier in the same chapter they comment:

> *In the midst of a fast volley of tennis, or when we stop suddenly by a pond in spring and listen to hundreds of peepers . . . at such moments*

we are one with ourselves. All our forces are concentrated unreflectingly, unselfconsciously, on the playing, listening, watching. We are living at our best. . . . When we can move through life eating, sleeping, working, making love, without, as we do so, dwelling on the past or in the future, then we can live with all possible vigor or joy.

Herons—like our engineering friend from the Torture Chamber—don't choke. Because they live in the present moment, they get the frog.

No drug enhances performance as powerfully as living in the present moment. Steroids and stimulants don't hold a candle to the power unleashed when a human being simply trusts the moment and lives it to its fullest. Whether Broadway star, athlete, writer or heron, the best performances are achieved by living in the present moment, a moment opened to us by our sacred word—trust.

I am reminded of something Michelle Kwan, one of the greatest figure skaters of our time and a five-time world champion said during a television interview right before winning one of her numerous championships. "I am excited about the program and confident of my performance." The result, later that evening, was the human equivalent of "getting the frog." The result was victory.

Athletes and musicians have a term for these moments of complete immersion into the present that invariably lead them to peak performances. They call it being in the "Zone." Michael Jordan often played in the Zone. The Grateful Dead and Phish often jam in the Zone. Mozart composed in the Zone.

Our greatest accomplishments often occur while we are in the Zone, whether we are businessmen, surgeons, writers, concert pianists or school teachers. You will know when you are in the Zone, because time will fly when you are there.

In fact, while in the Zone, time seems to disappear, a phenomena that mystics have often described. Perhaps this relationship between peak performance and timelessness is what Ralph Waldo Emerson was alluding to earlier when he commented that we can't be happy and strong until we live with nature above time.

In the 1960s an engaging and innovative psychologist, Abraham Maslow, came up with a more scientific name for such moments of enhanced performance and timelessness. He called them "peak experiences." During peak experiences we are completely engrossed with what we are doing. Our concentration is as intense as the heron before he strikes at the frog. Our minds are totally free of worries, we are "living at our best with all possible vigor and joy." These peak experiences are sometimes lofty and enduring—composing a virtuoso violin concerto—and sometimes surprisingly fleeting and deliciously human—enjoying a good belly laugh or an explosive orgasm.

Here we have stumbled upon the resolution to the seeming paradox of viewing happiness as the goal of life while still trying to sneak in a victory or two. Indeed, we have come upon the final piece to our puzzle, the gentle tie-in between happiness and achievement. It all comes down to a fortuitous chain of events.

When we trust the world enough to uncover happiness by moving into the present moment, we frequently enhance our performance. Our enhanced performance allows us to achieve our goals with grace and ease. Our successes give us more confidence. Our increased confidence generates an even more powerful sense of trust that we can handle what life brings our way—the Good Times and the Bad Times. This enhanced trust allows us to move into the present moment more and more often, where happiness awaits. It is a marvelous positive feedback loop.

Happiness breeds happiness. And it all begins with trust.

Suddenly, the idea of developing an enduring sense of happiness—a "tough happiness" that will be there during both times of delight and times of woe—seems to be more within our grasp. Happiness need not be like a sunbeam that the least shadow intercepts.

This fortuitous chain of events resolves the apparent contradiction between viewing happiness as the ultimate measure of success while competing in those things that traditional wisdom suggests are success: the jobs we seek, the promotions we want, the financial security we desire, the gold medals we'd love to have. These secondary goals are okay to pursue as long as one does not allow them to obscure the primary quest—finding happiness—living in the present moment.

The delightful kicker is the fact that if one concentrates on uncovering happiness by living in the present moment, which Benny did as he lived life minute by minute, the secondary goals—achievements and victories—are more likely to occur. They ensue naturally from the peak performances to be found there. Our victories need not come from a brutal beating of ourselves and those around us. They naturally arise, like a flower blooming, from an acceptance of who we are and what the growing conditions are at that specific moment. Whether the results are victories or defeats, good times or bad times, we are better able to enjoy the good times and transform the bad times for we know that we did the best that was possible for the conditions at hand and will do so in the next moment as well.

I am reminded of the famous Zen archers, described by Eugen Herrigel in his tiny masterpiece, *Zen in the Art of Archery*, who as they pick up "the bow and shoot, everything becomes so clear and straightforward and so ridiculously simple." The archers focus solely upon the process of the release of the arrow. If the arrows are released with grace, they eventually pass through the bull's-eye. They do not think about the target. The primary goal is the process of releasing the arrow; the secondary goal is the bull's-eye. In life, the primary goal is uncovering the happiness waiting in the present moment; the secondary goals—achievements—will follow.

We see this when we witness great performers. So often one hears the comment, "They make it look so easy." Truth be told, despite the tremendous discipline and practice preceding the performances, the actual performances are masterpieces of ease and grace, for the performers are being who they are meant to be at that moment in time. They trust themselves to be released from the bowstring of the present moment.

Thanks to Holmes, Horioka, Maslow and a frog, we seem to have uncovered a major piece to our puzzle—the gentle relationship between happiness and achievement. To understand it more deeply so that we can use it more effectively, it is useful to explore a real-life example of the seamless integration of trust, peak performance and happiness. We need to experience the magic up close. I found it on a ski slope many years ago.

Moguls, Bruce Lee, the Secret of the Wind and Bowstrings That Cut

I became keenly aware of the power of trust to unleash the magic that we call peak performance many years ago, late at night, on top of a windswept ski slope in western Pennsylvania. As a teenager I had worked with great tenacity at becoming a talented skier. I loved the sport. It was the one sport at which I had truly become expert but . . . there was one major-league but.

I was not a big fan of riding "the bumps," a slang term for snaking through a field of "small" snow mounds called moguls. Such moguls were sometimes three or four feet tall, and at twenty miles per hour did not always look so small. And they were often treacherously covered with ice.

Such a field of moguls could create the winter wonderland equivalent of our Torture Chamber. But this outdoor chamber of horrors could prove to be a good bit more dangerous than our indoor one. In handball, if you smack yourself into an ill-placed wall, you walk away with a nasty bruise. In a mogul field, if you catch some ice and tumble viciously down a steep slope, you get carted away on a snow sled by the ski patrol. On the way down you might notice that strange looking white thing protruding from your calf—oh yeah, that's your bone. Of course, that occurs if you can see your bone. The unconscious guys don't see too much of anything on the way down.

Because of bad knees and moving down South for college and medical school, I had stopped skiing. Years later, when in my mid-thirties, I took it up again because my parents wanted the whole family to go to Lake Tahoe, California, for a family ski vacation. I decided I had better practice a bit before heading west. Soon enough I found myself standing atop Upper Wagner at Seven Springs Ski Resort outside of Pittsburgh, Pennsylvania, a resort I had frequented many a weekend in my teenage years.

Upper Wagner, by many standards is a small field of bumps, but it often had more than its fair share of ice, and with a wintry wind whipping across the bumps, it was treacherous enough. It was nighttime, one of my favorite times to ski. Powerful man-made stars cast beams of fire across the glistening snows. The air was crisp and the gusting winds slapped this crispness into my cheeks. With each breath inwards my nose filled with a fierce cold that seemed to rim my nostrils with ice like salt on the glass of an ice-cold margarita.

As soon as I skied over to the steep drop-off point that marks the top of the Upper Wagner run, I stopped. It was as if I had been transported twenty years earlier. I saw the same winds whipping tufts of snow off the mogul tops, saw the same dark shadows cast by the man-made lights, felt the same edgy fear drop over me like a shawl.

Just as I had done over twenty years earlier, I found myself anxiously peering down over the bumps trying to see where the ice might be hiding, thinking about where I might be able to pick a safe path. I pursed my lips. I was a choke about to happen. In fact, I was a choke in progress for I had already slipped out of the present moment and stood there—a demon smiling on my shoulder like a Fuseli nightmare—thinking "what if"? What if I go too fast? What if I hit some ice? What if I fall? Not only was I stuck with my old fears, I had a new one. I was an old fart. I had old knees and maybe an old heart. It suddenly dawned on me—am I having fun?

In my youth, I would have eventually shoved off and navigated a snaking path through the icy mogul field, a path that I had spent almost five minutes nervously sorting out from up top. Compared to my usual grace on the skis, I would have tightened up. My muscles would have tensed. I'd have fought each and every turn, edging my skis to slow my speed, fighting the mountain, leavened by a stifled fear. Sometimes it would go okay. Sometimes it would not. I had done this hundreds of times in my youth, and I was about to do it again, but this time on old knees.

And then, for whatever reason, I noticed something I had not noticed as a youth. I had undoubtedly seen it many times back then, but my soul—perhaps because of its fears—had never let the image register on its silver. This mogul field was surprisingly short. About seventy yards down, Upper Wagner slipped off into the type of gentle funnel-shaped slope that I had always enjoyed skiing.

I felt a surge of confidence and simply told myself, "What the hell, just ski. Your body knows what to do with these bumps. Just ski down to that snow funnel that you enjoy so much. If you hit ice, handle it. If you hit a bump too hard, absorb it. If you are going too fast, go faster. You'll be able to slow yourself down in that funnel, no sweat."

All of a sudden I felt a sense of excitement pass over me. I did something I had never done at the top of Upper Wagner before. I smiled. I was excited about the program and confident of the performance. I was the heron and the slope was my frog.

As I slipped gracefully down and through the moguls, I thought of very little. I felt the bounce of my legs as they absorbed the bumps. I sensed the carving of the skis as their edges knifed the snow. Snow-covered trees slid by in a blur of whiteness. In the distance I could hear the humming of an army of snow-making guns. It all passed in a moment's time, the crystalline stars gazing down in the pitch black sky of winter. By the time I hit the funnel I had skied one of the best runs of my life. The fears of Upper Wagner were forever behind me, and I could taste the frog in my mouth, delicious and warm.

It had all seemed so simple, so effortless. It was exactly as Bruce Lee, one of the most remarkable martial artists of our time, said at the beginning of our chapter: "The less effort, the faster and more powerful you will be." What I learned on that wintry mountain was that the less I fought the slope, the less mental effort I expended on the slope, the less fear I had of the slope, the faster I skied it and the more powerful I became.

But how did I do this? What actually happened on that slope? How could I make sure that it would happen again? What was the password that allowed me, on that night atop Upper Wagner, to slip inside a peak performance? The answers lay within the wind.

Of the sensations on that night, it was the wind that I remember the best. In all of my previous runs on Wagner, I had never noticed the wind as keenly as on this night, perhaps because fear stops one from registering life's details. On this night I felt the wind; not created by the sky, mind you, but by the speed of my body as it sliced the night's air. I felt as if the slope, my skis, my legs and the wind were all one organism. There was no time to cut and parcel the universe into itty-bitty parts. It was a delectable feeling.

Alan Watts puts it:

> *To enjoy wind you must let it blow past you and feel it against bare flesh; the same is true of time, for the moment has always gone before it can be seized, and the same is true of life which not even this wall of flesh can hold forever. To feel and understand it you must let it blow past you like the wind as it moves across the earth from void to void.*

Watts captures perfectly one of the secrets for unleashing peak experiences. To capture the wind, it is best to let it go. To unleash the power of the present moment, it is wise to trust that the present moment will take care of itself. To achieve peak performances, I have learned not to try too hard. As Bruce Lee said, "the less effort . . ."

On that night on Wagner slope the words of Herrigel and his Zen archers came back to me, but they had new meaning:

> *Bow, arrow, goal and ego, all melt into one another, so that I can no longer separate them. And even the need to separate has gone. For as soon as I take the bow and shoot, everything becomes so clear and straightforward and so ridiculously simple.*

"Now at last," the Master broke in, "the bow-string has cut right through you."

I find that it is repeatedly useful to remind myself that I must learn to release the arrow, to let go of the need to control life's challenges once I have prepared as well as I can to meet them. Only then will I, like the bowstring, cut through to the heart of the present moment.

Placing the Last Piece in the Puzzle

As Julian of Norwich and Joel Osteen pointed out, one can gain a powerful sense of trust through a belief in an all-powerful being—God. As Lao Tzu and Alan Watts have pointed out, one can also experience a sense of trust via a belief in an all powerful and enduring mystery—the universe. Both of these methods—and they are not necessarily contradictory, for many people find strength in each—are clearly wonderfully effective spiritual pathways into the mystery that we call "trust."

But our mogul field atop Wagner Mountain hints at another source of trust. This source does not replace the two spiritual sources we have already examined. It merely complements them. It is a source of trust that is available to anyone, no matter what their spiritual beliefs. It is imminently practical. It is immediately accessible. It is always available. It was the source of my trust on that mogul field that night on Upper Wagner. It is the simplest of trusts—trust in ourselves. It is the trust that we place in our own skills, talents, and gifts to get us through the mogul fields of life.

Whether one believes that these gifts come from God, the Tao, or simply the magic of the universe itself, we have been blessed with a most splendid array of skills and talents. As you learn new skills and perfect old ones, you gain a more profound sense of trust. It is this trust in our own skills that often provides the bowstring into the here and now—the bowstring that cuts directly into peak experience and peak performance.

In psychotherapy, part of the magic that I see with my patients occurs when they discover new sets of skills. With these skills in hand they begin to trust themselves to effectively manage their own problems. Knowing that one is armed with the pragmatic skills to handle difficult people, difficult tasks and difficult times allows one to let go of the need to control. At such times, as Alan Watts alluded, we can allow life to blow past us like the wind, allowing the passionate winds of life—and they are passionate—to kiss our cheeks and caress our souls.

If we try to capture this wind in a box, we are in for a great disappointment when we open the lid. Wind, wonderment, laughter, compassion and acceptance cannot be caught in a box, no matter how sophisticated the trap. But if we have confidence in our gifts, there is no need for our boxes. With trust in our talents and skills, we don't need to worry incessantly about the future, we live it now. We don't anticipate the next moment, we become it.

On that windswept ski slope years ago, I became the present moment when I said to myself, "Just ski down to that snow funnel that you enjoy so much. . . . If you hit ice, handle it. If you hit a bump too hard, absorb it. If you are going too fast, go faster." Because I trusted my skills to handle the speed—I lost my fear. And I found magic. The magic of the present moment is not created, it is discovered. It is there all the time, but it is hidden by our fears.

Having found the last piece in our quest for the meaning of happiness—the power of trusting our own talents as a gateway into the present moment—we have earned the right to take a stab at a definition. We have been meticulously interlocking all of the puzzle pieces given to us by our dazzling array of guides: John Merrick, Saint Francis, Julian of Norwich, Benny, Conrad Hilton, Alan Watts and, from nature itself, a Chinese heron and a snow-capped mogul field. Now we have the thrill of placing the last piece of the puzzle.

The following definition of happiness is not proffered as the correct one. I don't believe such a thing exists. I offer it simply as a practical one. Over the years in my clinical practice, both my patients and I have found this definition to be a useful guide as to what our quest is all about in therapy and, for that matter, in life itself. But I can give it an even more personal recommendation, for I have found the following definition to be of immediate value in my own life.

As questing beasts, seeking happiness, we stated from the beginning, that the first pivotal step to achieving our quest was to know exactly what we are pursuing. At this point, thanks to Benny and company, we just might know what happiness is.

The First Step Achieved: The Meaning of Happiness

Before proceeding we must address some limitations wrought by the English language. Our language has one set of words for attitudes and one set of words for feelings. Consequently, the English language has a hell of a time describing a human experience that is simultaneously both an attitude and a feeling.

This linguistic straitjacket poses a knotty dilemma, for I am convinced that "happiness" is just such a beast, which may explain why happiness has been such a bear for philosophers and psychologists to define. Happiness is not an attitude. Happiness is not a feeling. Happiness is both an attitude and a feeling. Happiness is an attitude/feeling. Period.

With this dual nature of happiness in mind, it is time to finish our puzzle. Our definition will echo with the insights we have gained from all of our delightful sages: Julian and her hazelnut thing, Benny and his limo, Ralph Waldo Emerson and his rose:

> Happiness is the attitude we call trust—a profound trust—accompanied by a reassuring feeling of confidence that one can effectively handle whatever life may bring, good or bad. This attitude of trust allows one to live in the present moment in which there are no frets about the past or worries about the future. This feeling of confidence is pleasant, refreshing, and steadfast.

With this definition in hand, we can see how the happiness found by concentratedly living in the present moment will naturally lead to sensations of wonderment, gratitude, freedom, forgiveness, compassion, spontaneity, and laughter, as well as episodes of creativity, peak experience and peak performance.

Moreover our definition solves many of the problems often cited when various pundits attempt to define happiness. Because Benny showed us that happiness is not only a feeling but also an attitude, happiness is not necessarily fleeting in nature, as many philosophers have lamented. Because Julian of Norwich showed us that happiness is an acceptance of both the good and the bad, it becomes apparent that one could actually be happy while experiencing difficult times. And from hotel moguls (like Conrad Hilton) to ski moguls (like those on Upper Wagner), we have learned how trust leads directly into the here and now where happiness is most likely to be found.

Happiness is. It lies hidden in each and every moment. It is not made, captured or bought. It is simply uncovered. During good times it pops up jubilantly to the surface on its own accord. But even during bad times— periods of pain, loss or defeat—happiness as defined as a sense of trust and a feeling of confidence—can be found. At such moments it waits deep inside you and me, providing us with support, hope and a sense of humor under duress.

Happiness is a tenacious blessing. One that waits only for our touch. We need only to move with trust, to slip into the present moment to find it. Julian did so. John Merrick did so. Benny did so. Saint Francis did so. And so can we.

Our definition also suggests a variety of useful correlations that might help us on our quest to find a little bit more happiness in our everyday lives. Let us take a look at some of them.

For instance, living in the present moment is not the same as saying that one never thinks of the past. You must turn to the past to learn from it or to enjoy its pleasant memories. During such reflections you give yourself over to these past images with the excited freedom and intensity of the present moment. This activity is not an example of living in the past; it is an example of creatively using the present moment to enjoy the past.

Similarly, you must think of the future. You look to the future to make sound plans or to anticipate pleasant moments to come, giving yourself over to these future thoughts with the excited freedom and intensity of the present moment. This activity is not an example of being preoccupied with the future; it is an example of creatively using the present moment to make the most of the future.

Now that we have ourselves a practical definition of happiness, we have accomplished the task of part I of this book—we have developed a more sophisticated understanding of the goal of our quest. The good news is that happiness looks obtainable, not all the time, but a goodly amount of the time. The question now is how do we find it? How do we develop an enduring attitude of trust and an enduring feeling of confidence so that we can live more consistently in the present moment?

Truth be told, it is indeed a tricky quest. Developing an enduring attitude of trust is not unlike searching for a secret passageway in a darkened room of an old Victorian house. We are holding only a candle as a source of illumination. Occasionally, as we explore the shadows, a brisk wind may snuff out the candle—divorce, financial stresses, troubles at work—and the room will grow abruptly darker. But with patience and time, we begin to see more clearly. The outlines of the family portraits and oil lamps become more distinct. We get a feel for the layout of the room—for the nuances of life. We find our matches and light our candle again. Suddenly, behind the curtain we see it, the passageway into the present moment.

Some people—Benny, Saint Francis, John Merrick, Julian of Norwich— appear to familiarize themselves with this room more adeptly than others. It is as if they knew the layout of the room before entering it. It is almost as if they possessed a blueprint that shows them where the secret passageway is hiding, a blueprint that less happy people do not seem to have. In truth, such a blueprint exists. And the people who possess this blueprint feel more confident about how to play the game of life. They trust themselves to win. So they often do, for they live more frequently in the present moment.

This blueprint is called the "human matrix." It gives us a clearer understanding, not only of the room of which we are exploring—life—but of the machine that will do the exploring—ourselves. Once we understand the ins and outs of the human machine, we can go to sleep at night content to know that not only have we done our best that day, as Conrad Hilton suggests, we are prepared to do our best tomorrow. There is nothing left to do but go to sleep with a lively sense of trust that "all is well, and every kind of thing will be well," as Julian of Norwich used to say.

In the morning we awaken to discover that there are no thieves waiting for us in the mirror or demons perching in our brains, nor runaway trains for that matter. Instead our brains, our minds and our souls are alive with the vibrancy of the present moment. We are poised, strong and graceful—ready to strike, to taste frog if we are herons, to find happiness if we are humans. The magic is in the human matrix. It is to this matrix that we now turn.

Part II

The Essence of the Questing Beast: The Human Matrix

"A man is infinitely more complicated than his thoughts."

PAUL VALERY
POET

"Everything is a matrix."

RICHARD SINKHORN
MATHEMATICIAN

READER/CUSTOMER CARE SURVEY

BB1

We care about your opinions. Please take a moment to fill out this Reader Survey card and mail it back to us.
As a special **"thank you"** we'll send you exciting news about interesting books and a valuable **Gift Certificate.**

Please PRINT using ALL CAPS

Name
First _____ MI. ___ Last Name _____

Address _____

City _____ ST ___ Zip _____

Phone # (___) ___ – ___   Fax # (___) ___ – ___

Email _____

(1) Gender:
___ Female ___ Male

(2) Age:
___ 12 or under
___ 13-19
___ 20-39
___ 40-59
___ 60+

(3) Marital Status
___ Married
___ Single
___ Divorced/Widowed

(4) Did you receive this book as a gift?
___ Yes ___ No

(5) How many Health Communications books have you bought or read?
___ 1 ___ 2-4 ___ 5+

(6) How did you find out about this book?
Please fill in ONE.
1) ___ Recommendation
2) ___ Store Display
3) ___ Bestseller List
4) ___ Online
5) ___ Advertisement
6) ___ Catalog/Mailing
7) ___ Interview/Review (TV, Radio, Print)

(7) Where do you usually buy books?
Please fill in your top TWO choices.
1) ___ Bookstore
2) ___ Religious Bookstore
3) ___ Online
4) ___ Book Club/Mail Order
5) ___ Price Club (Costco, Sam's Club, etc.)
6) ___ Retail Store (Target, Wal-Mart, etc.)

(9) What subjects do you enjoy reading about most? Rank only *FIVE*. Use 1 for your favorite, 2 for second favorite, etc.

	1	2	3	4	5
1) Parenting/Family	O	O	O	O	O
2) Relationships	O	O	O	O	O
3) Recovery/Addictions	O	O	O	O	O
4) Health/Nutrition	O	O	O	O	O
5) Christianity	O	O	O	O	O
6) Spirituality/Inspiration	O	O	O	O	O
7) Business Self-Help	O	O	O	O	O
8) Teen Issues	O	O	O	O	O
9) Sports	O	O	O	O	O

(14) What attracts you most to a book?
(Please rank 1-4 in order of preference.)

	1	2	3	4
1) Title	O	O	O	O
2) Cover Design	O	O	O	O
3) Author	O	O	O	O
4) Content	O	O	O	O

TAPE IN MIDDLE; DO NOT STAPLE

BUSINESS REPLY MAIL
FIRST-CLASS MAIL PERMIT NO 45 DEERFIELD BEACH, FL

POSTAGE WILL BE PAID BY ADDRESSEE

HEALTH COMMUNICATIONS, INC.
3201 SW 15TH STREET
DEERFIELD BEACH FL 33442-9875

FOLD HERE

Comments:

8　All Ends in Mystery

"It has been the task of science to discover that things are very different from what they seem."

Sir Arthur Eddington
20th Century British Physicist

Skating Machines and Fresh Blueprints:
A Prelude for Part II

Now that we have a good definition of the goal of our quest—happiness—it is time to get down to the business of pursuing it. Human beings may vary greatly on how successful we are at accomplishing this quest. Even an individual person may vary on a day by day basis in the ability to uncover happiness. Some days I'm pretty good at it. Other days, not so good.

From part I, it is clear that trust is a major prerequisite for uncovering happiness. Trust allows us to slip effortlessly into the eternal Now. But slipping into the present moment is not as easy to do as platitudes such as "Live in the Moment" or "NOW is the beginning of your life" may suggest. I wish it was. It isn't. Indeed, it is one thing to pick out the present moment as a destination. It is yet an entirely different thing to purchase the ticket, do the packing, and find the right train to that moment.

Part of the problem is the elusive nature of "trust" itself. What is it? Michelle Kwan, from our last chapter, may have inadvertently already given us the answer. Let us return to something she said just before she gracefully skated her way to yet another world championship: "I am excited about the program and confident of my performance."

Her statement is the very embodiment of trust. And, if we take a moment to contemplate what Michelle Kwan needed to do in order to make such a statement, I believe we will come face to face with key elements of the nature of trust itself. You see, Michelle Kwan is a skating machine.

I do not know Michelle Kwan personally, but as a skating machine questing for victory, I am pretty confident that I do know one thing about her—she knows her machine inside and out. She knows the purpose and function of her muscles and joints; she knows their possibilities and their limitations; she knows how to condition her muscles and how to sharpen the mind that controls them.

Moreover, Michelle Kwan knows what makes Michelle Kwan tick. She knows what motivates her machine; what drives it; what systems compose it. She has an exquisitely accurate internal blueprint of her machine that tells her exactly where to look if problems arise or breakdowns occur.

With this knowledge of her structure, her abilities and her limitations, Michelle Kwan gains an attitude that is very special—an unshakeable sense of trust. Armed with this attitude, Michelle Kwan becomes something that is very formidable indeed to her opponents. She becomes a supremely confident skating machine that knows only one place to skate—the endless now, where a correspondingly endless string of world championships seem to await her.

Only some of us are skating machines, but as stated at the beginning of our book, we are all happiness machines. Like Michelle Kwan on her quest for victory, the first step on our quest for happiness is to know the nature of our machine inside and out. Of what stuff are we made? How is this stuff put together? How does the nature of our stuff determine our skills, potentials and limitations for achieving happiness? The answers to these critical questions are the focus of part II.

When we are done, we will better understand the nature of the happiness machine. We will be ready to step out onto the sometimes treacherous, always fascinating, pathways of life with the same confidence that Michelle Kwan steps out onto the sometimes slippery, always magical surfaces of her ice. With a little luck, we will be equally successful.

The tool for our self-understanding—the human matrix—is a fresh blueprint for exploring the structure and nature of the happiness machine, something similar to but not identical to Michelle Kwan's skating machine. It is a tool designed specifically to help us on our quest for happiness. If we are successful, our blueprint should offer us the following insights:

1. A clear concept of the stuff of which both skating machines and happiness machines are made of that is consistent with the laws of contemporary physics and biology. We don't want any fluff in our model of the happiness machine.
2. A concise description of the human matrix that shows how all the parts of the happiness machine fit together, of what systems it is made, and what roles these systems play in our quest for happiness. We do want practicality.
3. A convincing example of the power of the human matrix to explain happiness in the real world of an everyday person facing a devastating stressor. We want evidence that our model passes the acid test—it explains happiness and guides us toward it even during times of pain and loss.

If our three chapters accomplish the above tasks, we will have the same type of self-knowledge about our happiness machine that Michelle Kwan possesses about her skating machine. We will know of what stuff the questing beast is truly made.

To accomplish this task, we must first understand the stuff of the universe—the focus of this chapter—for it is from this stuff that we are made. As Sir Eddington suggested in our opening epigram, things may be very different from what they seem.

Japanese Mini-Subs, Emerald Goggles and Roman Poets

Of what is nature, the world and the universe at large made? At first glance, the answer looks patently obvious. The world is composed of things. There are mundane things: trees, ice-cream cones and soccer balls. There are "sort of important" things: books, cats and credit cards. Then there are "real important" things: cathedrals, mountains and Wal-Marts.

Of course, in the last category—real important things—we find "people." As a thing, or as some would prefer "object," I interact with other objects. I kick soccer balls. I read books. I go to Wal-Marts.

I also realize that because I am a thing, I am by definition transient. No thing lasts forever. Like a cat, I am born and I will die. Unlike a cat, I may possess a soul that is independent of my body, and that soul may keep on truckin', but other than that issue, I am a mere wink in the drama of time.

As the saying goes, this "reality as a thing" paradigm is as old as the hills—Roman hills to be exact. It was the Roman poet Lucretius who really cemented this reality as a thing paradigm in his gargantuan poem called appropriately enough, *The Way Things Are*. It is a paradigm that has survived for centuries for a very good reason. It works. It explains how planets move, trees grow and people die; it is the blueprint that is still predominantly used today by most people watching the Super Bowl, reading *The Wall Street Journal*, or checking out eBay.

At the very heart of the theory is the idea that every thing, absolutely *every* thing, is made of littler things called atoms. These atoms are incredibly tiny marbles, much smaller than Julian's hazelnut but equally mysterious, for how they are arranged can result in bigger things as marvelously different as a human being and a hot dog. It all has to deal with how the lit-tlest things of the world—atoms—are put together to form the grandest things in the world—cathedrals and people.

By the way, Lucretius was right. It is true that the world is made up of things. They do interact with each other, whether it is a baseball with a bat or a man with a woman sitting at a bar. There is a way to hit a home run in both of these games. There are rules to these encounters that are explained quite nicely by the "world as a thing" blueprint. It is, indeed, a good blueprint. It is a useful blueprint. But is it an accurate blueprint?

Is it the only blueprint?

To find these answers, we must gain a more sophisticated understand-ing of what philosophical lens Lucretius used as he tried to answer the question, "Of what stuff is the universe made?"

We must understand, not just intellectually but in our guts, that lenses have innate problems. Not all lenses are right for all jobs. Every lens has its own unique limitations. To register this fact in our guts, we are about to go to a rather unlikely place in a rather unlikely time for a philosophical par-lay. But it will be well worth our digression. We are off to the coast of Oregon. The year is 1942.

We are bouncing about in the turbulent waves of the Pacific Ocean surf several feet below the surface of the sparkling waters overhead. We are peer-ing at the Oregon coast through the snout of a telescope that is attached to a Japanese submarine called a mini-sub. What we see will be determined by the optical lens of our telescope. It will also be determined by a second, even more important metaphorical "lens," the lens of the mind of the Japanese officer who is using the telescope, for it his mind that must give the final interpretation to what we see.

It is the nature of his lens that interests us as we begin our search for a fresh blueprint of the world. For on this mini-sub in 1942, his lens—the one inside his head—is about to make a magnificently important error, an error that from the Japanese perspective was an egregious blunder and from an American perspective was a blessed godsend.

It is a mistake that we don't want to make when we are creating our blueprint. It is a warning of sorts, a warning about the use and misuse of lenses. Let us see what this warning is all about and how it can help us in our search for an answer to the question, "What am I, of what is the happiness machine made?"

At Pearl Harbor, the Japanese had made a treacherously smart first strike. It would take many months for the United States Navy to recover. Of course the Japanese realized that they had awakened a "sleeping dragon." At that moment, the Japanese equivalent of the "million-dollar question" was how much damage could they inflict in the time it would take for the dragon to shake out the sand in its eyes and fully awaken? If luck was on their side, perhaps they might even slay the dragon as it wobbled to its feet. Herein lies the reason for our Japanese mini-sub. It was prowling the West Coast on a most important secret mission.

Thousands of miles away, around a Japanese war table, a mind-boggling idea had arisen. Perhaps the mainland of the United States should be directly invaded. At first glance this idea seemed outlandish, but then the idea of attacking Pearl Harbor, at first glance, had also seemed outlandish. Keep in mind that a miniscule island called Britain had ruled half the world merely four decades earlier.

Yes, the United States was a mammoth country and Japan a tiny speck of an island. Yes, the United States had displayed great valor and strength in the first World War, and Japan would only be able to muster a tiny fraction of the armed services of this colossus from North America. But . . .

And, it was an important "but." There was one major factor in favor of a Japanese attack, the same advantage that they had held at Pearl Harbor — surprise. The idea of a land invasion of the United States mainland was so outrageous that the Americans would probably be unprepared.

In favor of this belief was the fact that the naive Americans clearly never felt that a land invasion would ever happen to them. There were no, and had never been, cannons protecting its borders with Canada or Mexico. It was a country with essentially no defenses. Ripe prey. Easy pickin's. Or so the

Japanese thought, which is why the Japanese officer peering through the telescope of our mini-sub in question could hardly believe his eyes.

He knew that the Americans were tenacious and innovative. He also knew that the American factories stood as the greatest pinnacle of manufacturing prowess and expertise in the entire world. Undoubtedly, this expertise would quickly be turned from automobiles and farm tractors to cannons and tanks. On the other hand, it would all take time. There was no magic switch that a factory manager could hit that would turn a production line for Ford sedans into a production line for Sherman M-4 tanks.

Because of this fact, our Japanese officer could not believe what he was seeing. For hours on end, as he peered at the highway snaking along the curves of the Portland coast, he could see the massive trucks. The rigs were rumbling up and down the coast at a furious pace. Upon their sprawling flatbeds, the Japanese officer looked at the endless stream of huge cannon barrels, as big as he had ever seen.

The frenzied pace of their deployment, if the activity of the trucks was an accurate reflection, suggested that, by the time the Japanese fleet could cross the Pacific to launch an amphibious assault, the West Coast of the United States would be bristling with walls and walls of deadly cannon. From the Japanese perspective, invasion was out.

Thank god, lumbering was still in as one of the major staples of the American economy. The Japanese officer was not seeing military trucks loaded with cannons, he was looking at lumber trucks packed with redwoods.

The accuracy of this delightfully intriguing anecdote is not entirely clear. If completely accurate, the historical importance of this error is obvious. But even confined to the category of an urban legend, it is an urban legend that provides a metaphorically critical lesson for us as we begin our search for a blueprint to our happiness machine.

Because the Japanese officer was unfamiliar with American logging practices, he misread what he saw. Had there been an American peering into the eyepiece of that telescope, he would have quickly seen logging trucks, not cannon caravans. Our lesson is simple: If we are not careful, the intellectual lenses that we use to ferret out the answer to the question, "What am I?" might lead us to see cannons when we are looking at red-woods. Intellectual lenses—such as the one used by Lucretius—can misin-terpret what is seen. We must move with caution.

But what of physical lenses themselves as opposed to the lenses in our heads? Do the lenses in our eyeballs have limitations as well? To answer this question, we must leave the Oregon coast and follow a yellow brick road to the Emerald City, where we have an appointment with the Wizard of Oz.

Let me openly and unabashedly admit that one of my all-time favorite movies is the 1939 MGM production of *The Wizard of Oz*. I'm not ashamed to say how many times I've watched *The Wizard of Oz*; I just can't remember. I do vividly recall as a child sitting in front of the television set once every year, in the late 1950s and early 1960s, to watch Dorothy, the Lion, the Tin Man and my personal favorite, the Scarecrow, skip their way to the Emerald City.

It will be the rare reader who hasn't seen the movie, but it will also probably be the rare reader who has read the book *The Wonderful Wizard of Oz* upon which it was based. Frank L. Baum's book came out right on time to turn the century in the year 1900. *The Wonderful Wizard of Oz* was the *Harry Potter* of its period. The book was bringing in big bucks long before the movie left the Hollywood lot in 1939.

If you haven't read the book, I heartily give it a thumbs up. I read it for the first time when I was about forty years old. What a shock. It is remark-ably similar to the movie and also remarkably different. It is the differences that are fascinating.

Let me share right from the beginning the big shocker. Dorothy's prized ruby-red slippers, are, in actuality, silver. Because the MGM movie was one of the first movies to ever employ Technicolor, they decided to jazz things up just a bit.

But this bit of movie trivia, which might score you some points during your next *Trivial Pursuit* game, is not the most interesting point for us as we try to understand the limitations of a mechanical lens, whether sitting in a telescope or in an eyeball.

The interesting point in that regard is that, in the book, the Emerald City is not emerald. When you pass through the outside gates of the city, you are commanded to don goggles, the lenses of which have been ground in an emerald color. Voila, the city is ablaze with emerald green. But it is all a fake.

If we were standing in the Emerald City as we began our search for the nature of man, we would be convinced his skin was green. Mechanical lenses—whether made of glass or eyeball—can make the world look marvelous by completely distorting what is real. The burning question for us is, "Should we, as we search for an answer to the question 'What am I?' be skeptical of our eyes that record the physical world and our brains that must interpret that world?" To answer this question we must look at the lenses that most of us have available to us.

In the last analysis, the quality of our answer—our blueprint of Homo sapiens—will depend entirely upon the quality of the lenses that we use to create it. It will depend on how our lenses determine what we see, distort what we see and alter what we see while we are looking.

We have in-born limitations. Our perceptual apparatus, our brains and our thoughts are all lenses. They are the lenses that we use to look at, and to define, ourselves. The question is, are they from Oz?

Vanishing Temples and Human Replicas

We are back in Japan. It is peacetime. We have just crossed the long wooden Uji Bridge that spans the Isuzu River. We are standing before the most sacred temple in all of Shinto, the mysterious religion that has shaped Japanese culture for several thousand years.

The Shrine at Ise is dedicated to the Sun Goddess, Amaterasu. Nearby, another shrine is dedicated to the Harvest Goddess, Toyouke. It is to the shrine of the Sun Goddess that we now turn our attention. It is rather modest in size but wonderfully graceful with its ancient timbers bedecked in muted colors.

Shinto reaches deep into the past. It is a religion steeped in respect for tradition, the spirits of the dead and the miracle of renewal. A reverence for the power of nature to bring forth fresh life and promise is at the very heart of Shinto. This respect for the promise of cleansing and renewal is reflected in everything from the mundane—removing shoes before entering a house—to the sacred—ritualistically washing one's hands and rinsing one's mouth before entering a temple.

As we stand before this lovely shrine, we can almost feel the power of Amaterasu rising like heat from a summer road arching over a hill. She is everywhere. The sun gives birth to all that grows and all that sees.

The ancient quality of the shrine is palpable. It would be easy for any visitor to come under the spell of this ancient structure, marveling at how well it has been maintained over the past 1,400 years. It is perhaps one of the most remarkable jobs of preservation known to contemporary times.

It is the perfect example of a "thing"—in this case a building—that does not change, that seems to weather the very ravages of time. If one possessed a photograph of this temple from 1860, it would appear almost identical to the image before us. Not a single wooden peg would look different.

Yet every single peg is different.

This apparently enduring "thing" is a replica. No, not just a replica, but a series of replicas—about seventy of them. Every twenty years, the last year being 1996, the Shrine at Ise is completely dismantled and a brand new shrine, identical in every plank and every wooden peg, is built in its place. It is a marvelous ritual capturing the very essence of renewal, a belief that there is always re-birth, always hope.

The details are intriguing. The standing temple is not torn down until its brand-new replacement has been built directly beside it. Every twenty years there is a time when the abode of the Sun Goddess stands as a twin. The priests of Ise then carefully and with great reverence transfer the sacred objects of Amaterasu, such as her mysterious mirror, from temple to temple, from what is about to die to what is about to be born. Once the transposition of the sacred objects is complete, the old temple is carefully torn down one plank at a time. The bits and pieces of the old temple are distributed to shrines around the island to be incorporated into their walls. Like the fingers and bones of the Christian saints that made the rounds as sacred relics to various medieval cathedrals, the planks and pegs of Amaterasu imbue each of the Shinto shrines with her grace and her quiet strength. I find this ritualistic rebuilding of the Shrine at Ise to be breath-taking in its ingenuity, symbolism and denouement.

But what does it have to do with answering the question, "What am I?"

The answer is, "You are a temple."

We humans are mirages of a sort. Like the "thing" called the Shrine at Ise, we are not as enduring as we may appear. Indeed, we are fake. We are human replicants.

Here is where the first of Sir Eddington's sciences—biology—shows us that things are not quite what they seem. Like the Shrine at Ise, we are rebuilt. But we are being rebuilt not every twenty years but every twenty seconds. In fact, we are under constant construction.

All of that hamburger, cheesecake and tofu is being eaten for a reason. A relatively small amount of it is used for energy purposes to drive our muscles and synapses. A goodly part of the cheesecake is used to build unwanted new things like extra chins and spare bellies. But a substantial chunk is used to replace what is already there. Cell membranes, Golgi bodies and mitochondria wear out. The interior masons of our bodies are constantly at work replacing, molecule by molecule, the "planks of Ise."

It is an extraordinary process when one comes to think about it. At one level it is obvious. We need only to contrast a picture of ourselves at a birthday party at four years old to a college graduation picture at twenty-one to recognize that we are constantly growing—changing. But it is yet another realization altogether to understand, in our gut, that every single molecule in my body is different than it was seven years ago. Quite literally, I am not the same "thing." This is not a clever use of words. It is the truth. Despite the fact that "I" feel the same, I am entirely different.

The image of a stable body is a red herring produced by a problem with a mechanical lens. Our eyes are not built to see microscopic "things," thus we are unaware that our cell walls and blood corpuscles are being constantly replaced. It is as if the masons of our innards were replacing a wall, brick by brick. But only one brick was replaced at a time, and it was only replaced at night under the veil of darkness. To us, as we awaken and look at the wall in our bathroom mirrors, the wall is always the same. In reality, it is always different.

For me, this obscure bit of biological information stirs up a little disquietude. Apparently, I'm not quite as much of a static "thing" as the "world as a thing" blueprint might suggest at first glance, a blueprint that I have been using since I was watching my first *Captain Kangaroo* episodes with Mr. Green Jeans and Bunny Rabbit over forty years ago. It bothers me that Captain Kangaroo might not have been a "thing." It just does. It's creepy.

But, rest assured, I don't really buy it. In the last analysis, the Captain and I are still "things." We just happen to be things that need to be rebuilt all the time. I can live with that realization, although it still feels a little creepy.

How do I know I'm a thing? I know I'm a "thing" because I am clearly a solid. I am obviously fleshy to both touch and sight. I am a thing as sure as my dog, Scout, is a thing—although not a particularly intelligent thing—when I scratch his ears. We are both solids—Scout and I. We are made of solid atoms, just as Lucretius said a couple of hundred years before the Shrine at Ise began its mysterious renewal rites.

It is at this juncture that a second science—quantum mechanics—carries on the task of Sir Eddington. If biology put some serious cracks into the "world as a thing" model, it was quantum mechanics, somewhere around the 1920s, that shattered this model forever as sure as if it were a fragile Ming vase dropped off the Sears Tower. It went kaput. Let us see what this "kaputness" means in everyday language.

Big Fans, Miniature Particles, Outrageous
Speeds and the Quantum Quaker

Before we can ascertain just how much our human lenses may be distorting how scientifically accurate our picture of a human being is—before we can answer the question "What am I?"—we first need to make a rather large digression that will rapidly become the focus of the rest of this chapter.

It is a critical digression and one filled with mystery. First we must see how much these lenses distort the blueprint of the universe in general. Only then will we have a clearer idea of how they can distort our blueprint of a specific chunk of that universe, a particularly favorite chunk—me. With the answers to these two questions, the answer to our big question, "What am I?" will be within our grasp.

As one could well imagine, to answer this little darling of a question it might be wise to bring along some friends with more than their fair share of smarts. It is at this moment that a Quaker and some of his buddies enter our picture. This isn't just some everyday Quaker hanging out at the old meeting hall. It is Sir Eddington who penned our opening epigraph. Sir Eddington was not only a Quaker, he happened to be a nuclear physicist. Now *that* is precisely the kind of Quaker that we need.

I might add that being a Quaker, Sir Eddington was a spiritual kind of guy. This trait would serve him well. It allowed Sir Eddington to open his mind to the surprising conclusions about the universe, the world and everything in it to which modern physics would point him, and to which we will now turn our attention.

The Age of Breakthroughs from 1900 to 2000 witnessed "breakthroughs" in knowledge of unheard of proportions in an unheard of number of fields embracing both the arts and the sciences. It is hard to believe that just one century could produce television, airplanes, space travel, the computer, the microchip and the Internet. Almost every major field was transformed, including dance, poetry, art, architecture, music, medicine, agriculture, transportation, genetics and biochemistry. But no field was more transformed than physics.

Jacob Bronowski's wonderful book *The Ascent of Man* includes a photograph of about thirty nuclear physicists sitting in three rows at the fifth Solvay Conference in 1927. The names included Albert Einstein, Marie Curie, Max Born, Louis de Broglie, Erwin Schrodinger, Niels Bohr, Max Planck and Werner Heisenberg. Not necessarily the best-looking group of guys, but if you had all of their brains sitting out in jars—wow!

But they weren't the end of it. A pack of other brilliant brains are not in the photograph including Enrico Fermi, Wolfgang Poli and Robert Oppenheimer. In my opinion, at no time in history have so many geniuses—true geniuses—within one field lived at the same moment. Each of these men and women, within the field of physics, is comparable to a Bach or a Beethoven in music. It is uncanny that they were all hanging out at the same bar working on the same symphony.

We know of them because they "cracked the atom" so precious to our good friend Lucretius. Sir Eddington, who was no intellectual slouch himself, knew them because they were his friends. What they uncovered when they cracked open this most marvelous of marbles was so startling that many of them were changed men—not just in the mind but in the soul. Inside the atom there is something pretty strange going down. This strangeness directly impacts how we answer the question, "What am I?"

The strangeness began when modern physicists started to unravel the nature of light. We all know that light is a cool thing, but as it would turn out it is also, as they say, wondrous strange. Apparently, light is composed of little packets of energy called "quanta."

But these little packets don't act like good little packets always should. Sometimes they act like particles, and sometimes they act like waves. When acting like particles, light gives off bursts of energy that can actually be quantified, like counting peas on a plate. On the other hand, light travels distances at speeds that could only be accomplished by waves, and indeed, like waves, light waves, can interfere with each other. Hence, light is simultaneously both a particle and a wave. This is strange stuff indeed, for a natural paradox of this magnitude had never been uncovered in the history of humankind.

I'm not kidding when I say that these physicists were shaken by this finding. It didn't make sense. And, up until this point in time, science always made sense. Science did not allow for paradox. Science did not allow for illogic. Yet here it was.

The field that evolved out of this study of light quanta became known appropriately enough as "quantum mechanics." Let us allow one of these physicists to describe his own encounter with what was wondrous strange:

> *The classical concepts, i.e., "wave" and "corpuscle" . . .*
> *do not fully describe the real world and are, moreover, complementary*
> *in part, and hence contradictory. . . . Nor can we avoid occasional*
> *contradictions; nevertheless, the images help us to draw*
> *nearer to the real facts. Their existence no one should deny.*
> *"Truth dwells in the deeps."*
>
> Niels Bohr

This last sentence of Bohr's, "Truth dwells in the deeps," is the tip that he and his fellow scientists were being touched to the depths of their souls. It is just not the way scientists are supposed to talk—like mystics. Something big was up.

What was big was the fact that these scientists had happened upon some mighty fine new lenses. With their use, Eddington and his friends could "see" inside the atom, and things weren't quite what they were supposed to be in there. The first thing that you will recall is that Lucretius, and just about everybody else, thought that atoms were the smallest marbles in the world and were, essentially, indivisible. We all know from high school physics that this "fact" is false. Each atom is composed of a nucleus that contains smaller marbles called protons and neutrons. Furthermore, around this nucleus, there swirls a cloud of electrons forming the shell of the atom.

Here is where it starts to get strange. Let us suppose, as Fritjof Capra proposes in his delightfully provocative classic *The Tao of Physics*, that we had a model of an atom that was the size of St. Peter's Cathedral in Rome. Big atom. The electrons are busy racing about the nucleus on the outside shell of St. Peter's dome. How big would the nucleus be in such an atom if our model is proportionately accurate? The answer always shocks me. It would be the size of a grain of salt! In short, there is a gigantic amount of space between the nucleus of an atom and its surrounding electrons.

This hard little marble of which all "things" are made, including yours truly, is basically a big hollow ball filled with next to nothing. If my body is composed entirely of hollow little nothings, then I should basically be a big hollow nothing, sort of a Macy's Thanksgiving Day Parade balloon on legs. But I know that is not true. I'm made of solid stuff. I can see it. I can poke at it.

Apparently, we have a lens problem here, because it is true that we are composed of atoms and that these atoms are primarily composed of space. In fact, if we could extract all of the nuclear matter—the nuclear "thing-ness"—in our bodies, we are a bit of a disappointment. Our whole body would be about the size of a pinhead. When I've been dieting, I only wish to god this were true.

But it is true. Our eyes just can't see it. How could a human body, that is primarily empty, look and feel so damn hard? How could something feel solid when it isn't?

The answer is speed. Outrageous amounts of speed.

Picture a big fan sitting in front of you. A really big fan. It is thirty feet across. It has four blades. The blades are perfectly flat and only about two feet wide. Our fan is currently turned off. At rest we can see through most of it, for the blades are relatively narrow and there is quite a bit of space between each blade. In fact, the "disc" formed by the blades is mostly space, just like our atom.

Suddenly, I turn the fan on. As it begins to pick up speed, a funny thing happens. The lenses of my eyes cannot keep pace with the speed of the blades. Soon enough my eyes see what is not really there—a solid disc. It doesn't matter if this happens with a fan or the spokes of a hubcap on a passing car, we experience this phenomena on a daily basis.

This example gives a perfectly good explanation of how our eyes could be fooled by objects moving at great speed into "seeing" a solid object when we know the object—a set of fan blades—is not solid. But it doesn't explain the simple fact that I know I'm a solid because when I push on myself, I feel flesh. Too much of it, I might add.

Keep looking at our gigantic fan. Crank it up. Make it rotate a thousand revolutions per minute. Fast. Very fast. It certainly appears as a pure solid disc now, but it is also starting to have some strange characteristics. The blades are moving so fast and replacing each others' positions so rapidly that it is getting hard to pass something through them unless you really shoot it through fast.

Crank it up some more, five thousand revolutions per minute. This big fan is humming. It is getting harder and harder to shoot something through the blades. They are beginning to function as if they really are a solid disc.

Let's really crank it. The blades are now rotating at six thousand revolutions per second. That's per second, not per minute. Our fan blade is now rotating at an astonishing 360,000 revolutions per minute. I dare say our hollow fan is now functioning like a brick wall. If you throw a Superball at it, you had better be ready to duck. That ball is gonna bounce right back at you. Speed has made something filled primarily with space as solid as a rock.

The speed of an electron as it whips about the nucleus of an atom is about six hundred miles per second! Within the nucleus itself, the speeds are even more outrageous, for the protons and neutrons in the nucleus are not just sitting there, they are moving too—at forty thousand miles per second!

It is "speed" that creates the illusion that we are solids. And it is just that, an illusion. Our actual subatomic mass is the size of a pinhead, but the speed of the particles creates the illusion of a hard object capable of riding a bike or making love. Thank goodness for illusions. Or as Mae West said, "Whenever I have to choose between two evils, I always like to try the one I haven't tried before." This "my body is a solid thing" illusion is a deliciously good one.

In actuality, we are a massive blur of sub-atomic particles whizzing about at speeds ranging from six hundred miles per second to forty thousand miles per second. We are high energy patterns that because of our outrageous speeds look and act as if we are solid. Nifty. Somebody up there is pretty clever.

Even as I write this sentence, I am amazed at the idea that, in reality, inside the hand that is typing these pages, there are neutrons and protons moving at forty thousand miles per second. I just don't have the perceptual lens to see it or feel it. It is not at all unlike a much better known strangeness that we all accept as an everyday given—we are standing on a globe, the earth, that is spinning at 1,036 miles per hour. Once again, we lack the perceptual apparatus to feel it. But it is so.

It is time to return to our big question—"What am I?"—for I feel we are close to an answer. Curiously, it is not a physicist but our old friend Alan Watts who seems to have phrased an answer that fits all the facts set forth by both our forays into biology and quantum mechanics. Let us allow Watts to speak for himself:

> *What is the body, for instance? The body is something that is recognizable. You recognize your friends when you meet them. Although every time you see them, they are absolutely different from what they were. They are not a constant, just as the flame of a candle is not constant.*
>
> *We know that a candle flame is a stream of hot gas, but still we say "the flame of the candle" as if it were a constant. And we do that because the flame has a constant, recognizable pattern. The spear-shaped outline of the flame and its coloration form a constant pattern. And in exactly the same way, we are all constant patterns. And that is all we are.*
>
> *You might be a vegetarian for several years, and then you might become a meat eater. In any case, your constitution changes all the time,*

but still your friends recognize you, because you are still putting on the same show, you are still the same pattern. And that is what makes you a recognizable individual.

At this juncture, it is interesting to note that the emerging view of the world—directly—and of a human being—indirectly—created by quantum mechanics has a curiously familiar ring to it. It is suspiciously similar to the view of the universe one sees when peering through the fourteenth-century window of Julian of Norwich. It is a world not so much filled with static "things" as it is teeming with constantly speeding things that form a large interlocking pattern. It is a world strikingly redolent of mysticism.

I am reminded of the saying by the enigmatic Greek philosopher Heraclitus of Ephesus, who seemed to get it right without the help of quantum mechanics when he simply commented, "Panta rhei"—everything flows. He meant just that—the world is in constant flux. Like all mystics, he felt there was a constant dynamic interplay between opposites so that he saw all opposites as reflecting a single unity. Light does not exist without darkness. They define each other not so much by their "thingness" but by their flow. Light flows into darkness. Darkness flows into light. They exist because of their movement and their relationship.

The parallels in wisdom garnered from quantum mechanics and from mystical traditions—both Western and Eastern—was a fact not lost on the nuclear physicists themselves as witnessed by these words from Julius Robert Oppenheimer:

The general notions about human understanding . . . which are illustrated by discoveries in atomic physics are not in the nature of things wholly unfamiliar, wholly unheard of, or new. Even in our own culture they have a history, and in Buddhist and Hindu thought a more considerable and central place. What we shall find is an exemplification, and encouragement, and a refinement of old wisdom.

Niels Bohr, always one for getting to the point without mincing words, put it succinctly. "I am now convinced that theoretical physics is actual philosophy."

Of course, we are still dealing with the idea that the world is ultimately made of things, they just happen to be things much smaller than the atom—neutrons, protons and electrons. Lucretius and his "world as a thing" model may still hold water, but it is just inaccurate as to scale. What happens if we go even deeper? If we go inside the protons and neutrons, will we still find "things?" Or is the stuff of the world something entirely different?

Truth Dwells in the Deeps

When we move deeper inside the atom, we find a world of even smaller particles with strange names such as neutrinos, muons, kaons and pions. They are subatomic particles. We have some rather remarkable lenses with which to study such miniature marbles. These machines, called particle accelerators, made to study miniscule bits of matter, are, paradoxically, rather mammoth in size. A cyclotron called the Tevatron Ring—a type of accelerator that is a tunnel made into the shape of a circle—sits outside of Batavia, Illinois. It has a circumference of three miles.

These big toys are designed to hurtle protons near the speed of light. Once at this speed, they are shot at other protons and neutrons to see what happens after the collision. Can you crack one of these babies open? The answer is yes.

The result of these ferocious high-speed collisions is the production of subatomic particles that last for only a millionth of a second, but in that time their pathways can be captured in so-called bubble chambers. They leave trails, graceful curves and intricate spirals, much like a plane leaving white tracks against a blue sky.

And here—within the deeps of the atom itself—is where the death blow to the "world as a thing" view occurs. For these subatomic particles aren't really marbles at all. They are fields of energy. Like the candle flame of Alan Watts, these subatomic particle are not particles, they are patterns. They do things that particles simply couldn't do. So puzzling is their behavior that it defies all use of language. It is quite literally so paradoxical and quizzical that Neils Bohr warns:

> We must be clear that, when it comes to atoms, language can be used only as in poetry.

These subatomic "particles" display all sorts of characteristics that a good ole "thing" just simply wouldn't do, including transforming into one another for no apparent reason, spinning in opposite directions at the same time and appearing in two places at once. The reason for these outlandish behaviors is so startling that it is worth repeating: The building blocks of all things in the universe are not "things," they are fields of constantly shifting energy.

One can picture the world of subatomic particles as being a world of ever-changing fields of potential. At points where the fields are particularly dense, "particles" appear and then disappear. All of the world is composed of these interlocking fields.

Einstein phrased it as follows:

> We could regard matter as the regions in space where the field is extremely strong. . . . There would be no place, in our new physics, for both field and matter, field being the only reality.

Werner Heisenberg, a noted physicist, put the final nail in the "world as a thing" model with these words:

> The atoms or the elementary particles . . . form a world of potentialities or possibilities rather than one of things or facts.

He later added even more succinctly:

> Atoms are not things.

Our bodies are not a pattern of "things" traveling at vast speeds. Our bodies and the rest of the "things" in the universe are made up of a complex web of energy fields that congeal to create "particles." The particles are, in essence, illusions created by the lens of the observer. Say it ain't so, Joe. Captain Kangaroo was a big fat congenial fake "particle."

If you use a big lens that can only see big things, like the human eye or the eye of my dog, Scout, you will see a world of "things" only, because you are incapable of seeing the energy patterns that actually make up the world. These things exist. We do have bodies. Scout has ears. But they exist because of the lens. The Emerald City is indeed emerald if you wear the Wizard's goggles.

If you had a different lens—a cyclotron for instance—then the world would look entirely different. What we see as "things" would completely disappear. Instead we would be "seeing" fields of fluctuating energy. All distinctions between "things" would disappear, for, at a subatomic level, there are no boundaries, just patterns of energy potential.

We quite literally create the world around us with our eyeballs and our brains. The false world of things is created out of the real world of fluctuating fields by the limitations of our perceptual abilities. What we see is not really the way it is anymore than the buildings of the Emerald City are green.

And the world of other creatures is not the same as ours, because they have different lenses, and their lenses distort the world differently than ours do. For instance, an animal that could see infrared would see different boundaries to the human body, boundaries that formed at the outer edges of the infrared emanating from our skins. To that creature that outer boundary is what would constitute a human "thing." They might not even be able to see our skin. Are they right or are we? The answer is, we are both right.

Each lens shows a different universe. Each universe is valid. Each lens has both its uses and its limitations. You build skyscrapers using the knowledge gained from "the world as a thing." You crack atoms using the knowledge gained from "the world as a process." You can't build a skyscraper with a cyclotron, and you can't crack an atom with a hammer. Both lenses are valid and useful. Both lenses are limited and useless—if applied to the wrong task.

Leave it to the Buddha to put the last thirty paragraphs into eight simple words. "For the wise, all 'things' are wiped away." And this guy didn't even have a cyclotron.

By the way, if for even a fleeting moment you are saying to yourself, "This stuff is fascinating, but its intellectual bullshit. It don't mean nothin' in da real world of finding a cold Budweiser," Please don't think that.

The world of quantum mechanics—the "world as process"—is the real McCoy. As Lucretius would say, this is "the way things are." If you want to see the world of quantum mechanics in action, think about this fact. Quantum mechanics is so real, that a product of its making (the atomic bomb) leveled 90 percent of the seventy thousand buildings of Hiroshima in ten seconds. On a much more positive side, another result of quantum mechanics (nuclear medicine) cures cancers. If you are diagnosed with cancer, it is the very real world of quantum mechanics that may add twenty years to your life—which is a hell of a lot of Budweisers.

It appears that we have finally found ourselves an answer to our question, "What am I?" We have discovered that the answer is a good deal more complicated than first appearances would suggest. We are what we are depending upon which lens one puts to the eye. Apparently, Popeye was not so far off when he said, "I yams what I yams." And I thought he was a moron.

Used alone, the traditional lens, "the world as a thing" lens seems to come up a bit short. The less-traditional "the world as a process" lens—the lens forged by quantum mechanics—presents quite a different picture. It is a picture that will prove to be of great use when creating our blueprint for the happiness machine.

On the Differences Between Skating Machines
and Happiness Machines

Let us return to the graceful figure of Michelle Kwan. In our prelude we stated that her skating machine may not be identical to her happiness machine. We now have a framework for why. Her skating machine is most usefully viewed through the lens of the "world as a thing," and her happiness machine is most usefully viewed through the lens of the "world as a process." As was the case with the model from which it was born—quantum mechanics—this new view of the structure of Homo sapiens may prove to be a bit startling and more than a bit useful.

Let's review what we have discovered so far.

1.) Things are not as they seem, for the world is in a constant state of flux.

2.) There are two equally useful ways to view the world using two different lenses.

3.) One way, the traditional way, views you, me, Scout and Michelle Kwan as separate entities (the world as a thing). The other way views you, me, Scout and Michelle Kwan as parts of one functioning whole (the world as a process).

4.) In this second view, the "things" in the world are viewed not as static entities but as dynamic creations that result from the interactions of various shifting fields or processes.

5.) With the second view, the "things" in the world do not have boundaries, for they are all part of one whole.

Using these principles, the distinctions between Michelle Kwan as a skating machine and Michelle Kwan as a happiness machine begin to emerge, for both models are illusions created by whichever lens we happen to be holding to our eye at the time of observation.

Her skating machine is a thing. It is composed of smaller things—muscles, tendons and neurons. All of these things are contained in another thing, a giant baggie thing called the skin. In the case of Michelle Kwan skating across the glistening ice, it is a delightful baggie thing to watch. But it is a baggie thing nevertheless. Michelle Kwan's skating machine is an easily identifiable thing that ends where her baggie thing ends. It has boundaries. Her skating machine is primarily dependent upon the resources within its own skin. It is an isolate.

But what of Michelle Kwan when she is viewed as a happiness machine? Where does she begin and end? More important for us, how does her structure, as conceptualized through the lens of quantum mechanics, determine how and to what extent she can feel happiness as we have defined it—an attitude of profound trust and a reassuring feeling of confidence?

To begin our search for these answers, imagine for a moment that Kwan's skating machine delivered the performance of its lifetime, and she won a gold medal. Would Michelle Kwan be immediately happy? And if so, would she remain happy over the next several weeks? Maybe yes . . . maybe no.

It is important to realize that although happiness can be nurtured by our thoughts into a surprisingly enduring attitude and feeling, as we saw with John Merrick, Julian of Norwich and Benny, it is not always easy to do so. Happiness fluctuates. Some life circumstances make it easier to nurture a sense of trust/confidence, and some circumstances make it harder. Uncovering, nurturing, and maintaining trust and confidence is an ongoing process. It requires work. The difficulty of this work is partially dependent upon circumstances that lie outside our skin.

Who could argue that John Merrick was able to more easily forge a powerful sense of forgiveness, trust and confidence after he encountered the revitalizing compassion of Sir Frederick and the relative comfort and safety of his two rooms in London Hospital? This does not diminish the remarkable efforts and impact of Merrick's attitudes towards life on his degree of happiness. It merely acknowledges the fact that these attitudes are not independent things disconnected from the rest of the universe.

We human beings like to think that we are in 100 percent control of our own attitudes and emotions, and hence can always directly control our extent of happiness, but I suspect that such a belief is a misguided illusion drawn from the "world as a thing" perspective.

The apparently isolated products of our psychological and spiritual processes, such as our attitudes and feelings, are also partially the products of factors interpenetrating from outside of our skins. At any given instant, our individual attitudes—such as trust—and our individual feelings—such as confidence—are partially shaped by factors such as culture, politics, and the influences of our gods and goddesses. Vice versa, individual attitudes and feelings, when massed together, tend to shape cultures. In a quantum model, everything interconnects. Everything effects everything else.

Part of Michelle Kwan's happiness machine is identical to her skating machine—muscles, tendons and neurons—but part of Michelle Kwan's happiness machine is made from the "bits of soul and belief, fragments of thought and dream, orchestrations of government and culture" mentioned in chapter 1. Many of these processes are not contained within her giant baggie thing, yet all of these processes play an organic role in the production of her trust and confidence at any given moment. Even within her skin, it is not just her psychological cognitions that determine her beliefs and emotions, for the molecules of her brain and the vicissitudes of her spirit play a pivotal role in their creation as well.

No matter what her psychological perspectives at the time of the judging of her skating performance, other factors—both internal and external—can, in a moment's notice, markedly change her attitudes and her confidence. In a quantum world, all is flux. To a skater, a single comment from a coach such as, "If we win this one, we've dodged a bullet, because you can skate much better than you just did," can dramatically impact how happy that particular skater will be upon immediately winning his or her gold medal. Two days later, a breakup with a potential spouse or the death of a beloved parent could dramatically change how easy or hard it is for this same skater to maintain an attitude of trust and a feeling of confidence over the ensuing weeks.

If we try to determine the extent of Michelle Kwan's happiness or understand how she achieved it by using the "world as a thing" model— did she win gold or not—we are using the wrong lens. We might as well try to crack an atom with a hammer. It isn't gonna work. Things do not explain happiness. Processes do.

Paradoxically, once formed, the process called happiness (our attitude of trust and our feeling of confidence) becomes the main tool with which we shape how we relate to the very processes of life from which it just emerged—the good times and the bad times. It is all a marvelously self-adjusting and transforming system. The world of the happiness machine is a world of process, interpenetration, and swirling quantum patterns.

To understand it one must come up with a blueprint that helps to explain how our happiness is partially shaped not only by the things such as bones, tendons and neurons that lie within our skins, but by the love affairs, family intrigues and political swayings that lie outside our skin. And, of course, our blueprint must also account for all those processes—our bits of soul, dream and belief—that may sit inside or outside of our skins or a little of both.

Fortunately, there is a model from the world of mathematics and quantum mechanics that is ready-made for designing a blueprint for a "thing that is not a thing." It is called a matrix. At its simplest level, the word matrix means "the stuff of which something is built."

From the more complex perspective of quantum mechanics, a matrix is defined as a myriad of interlacing processes all of which are in constant flux. Consequently, the "thing" a matrix defines is a constantly shifting, constantly transforming mystery. Werner Heisenberg captures its essence perfectly:

> *The world thus appears as a complicated tissue of events, in which connections of different kinds alternate or overlap or combine and thereby determine the texture of the whole.*

A happiness machine is just such a complicated tissue of events. It is a human matrix. The resulting happiness—as defined as the intensity of our trust and the depth of our confidence at any given moment—is "the texture of the whole" that it weaves. As the poet Paul Valery suggested, we are indeed infinitely more complicated than our thoughts.

In the next chapter we will see that, according to the human matrix blueprint, our happiness machine is composed of five constantly shifting and interacting processes—some contained within our skin, some not. These continuously morphing processes include our biology, our psychological perceptions and constructs, our interpersonal relationships, our relationship to our environments, and our spirituality.

One can determine the degree of happiness of a human being if one knows the net interaction of these five processes at any given moment. Moreover, by learning how to manipulate each wing of the matrix we can learn how to increase the likelihood that we successfully generate happiness on a moment by moment basis.

Bringing this chapter to a close, it is apparent that the quantum view of the universe as field—not matter—is a strange one indeed. Our good friend Niels Bohr put it bluntly. "Anyone who is not shocked by quantum theory has not understood it." Likewise, as derived from this quantum view of the universe, our new blueprint for man is strange and wondrous, for we have shed our skins. Hopefully it will prove to be equally powerful in helping us to uncover happiness. Toward this end, in our next chapter we will take a much more detailed look at exactly what makes up the human matrix.

As I contemplate the far-reaching intimations and exciting possibilities presented by our new model, I am reminded of one of my favorite writers, Arthur Machen. He was an Edwardian author who created those good old-fashioned horror stories that were filled with strange potions and "bumps in the night" as opposed to serial killers and chain-saw specialists. Machen was a lover of the mysterious, and his favorite phrase was a Latin one—"Omnia exuent in mysterium."—All ends in mystery. And so it does.

9 Far More Beautiful

"Going back to the idea that the living body is like the flame of a candle, we can say that the energies of life— in the forms of temperature, light, air, food, and so on— are streaming through us all at this moment in the most magnificently harmonious way. And all of us are far more beautiful than any candle flame."

ALAN WATTS
FROM *THE CULTURE OF COUNTER-CULTURE*

Gumby Imitations, Taoist Obsessions and Two-Legged Meeting Places

Our goal in this chapter is a simple one: Define concisely and clearly what we mean by the human matrix. Specifically, what are the roles of each of the five wings of the human matrix, and how does this fresh blueprint for the happiness machine help us to do just that—find happiness? Let's begin by examining the ramifications of borrowing an idea from quantum mechanics—the matrix—and applying it to the world of human psychology—you and me.

If you are under the age of forty and you hear the word matrix, you, more likely than not, are going to spontaneously see images of Keanu Reeves as Neo. On the screen of your mind Neo is bending over backwards, dodging thousands of bullets, while creating the best-known imitation of Gumby on methamphetamine ever put to film.

The Matrix is to *Star Wars* what *Star Wars* was to *Star Trek*—the next generation's exhilarating yet subtly subversive view of reality. It is a movie that has captured an entire generation's eye, and, whether one approves of its violence or not, who can deny that Trinity is this generation's Emma Peel—a passionate defender of what is good, a sensual and deadly packet of modern femininity that is just a tad naughty to boot. Sign me up.

I need to state right from the start that, for the most part, this book and that movie have next to nothing to do with each other. I've been using ideas based upon the human matrix model to help my patients since long before the Wachowski brothers were getting ready to play their first level of Doom II. And the matrix of the movie is make-believe—fabulously good fun, but make-believe nevertheless.

But *The Matrix* trilogy does have a few things in common with both quantum mechanics and our new blueprint for man. The movie, if you are not familiar with it, postulates that the world as we know it is not as it is. In the movie, the world as seen by everyday people is actually a computer program called "the matrix," created by malevolent machines more mad than ten Dr. Frankensteins.

We can immediately see a similarity with quantum mechanics, for Sir Eddington and his friends—although not mad scientists—also postulated that the world is not as it seems. Unlike the movie, this quantum world of illusion has absolutely nothing to do with computer programs and malevolent monsters, and everything to do with nuclear physics and a wondrously benevolent universe or God—take your pick.

As we move in this chapter from the generic world of the universe to the meat of the matter—the specific world of a single human being, the question becomes, "Can quantum mechanics give us a realistic blueprint for a human being, as a happiness machine, in the same fashion that it provided a valid blueprint for the universe?"

It is at this juncture that we need to be a tad careful. In my opinion, it is a bit of a stretch to claim that quantum mechanics can tell us exact specifics about the real nature of a human being, for it is a language developed to study protons not neurons.

But it is not a stretch to hope that the model of quantum mechanics—the world as a set of interlocking processes—can provide us with a rich metaphor. This metaphor may help us develop a fresh perspective from which to better understand ourselves psychologically and, more important, to guide us on our quest for happiness.

The "process lens" of quantum mechanics is not so much a new physical lens with which to see the image of our mugs in our mirrors as it is a new mental lens with which to interpret what we are seeing. Erwin Schrodinger sums it up rather nicely. "The task is . . . not so much to see what no one has yet seen; but to think what nobody has yet thought, about that which everybody sees."

And who better "to think what nobody has yet thought, about that which everybody sees" than our endearing wanderer and philosopher, Alan Watts. I am reminded of the opening epigraph of this chapter, where Watts already displayed some nice, crisp, new thinking about old mugs. Watts tells us that, as patterns of the greater pattern of the universe, we are far more beautiful than any candle flame, for with every single moment we define a remarkably complex and fleeting pattern that will never be seen again. Ever.

I believe Watts is already hinting at a metaphorical way of viewing man that is quite quantum mechanical in nature. Indeed, the Taoist and Zen monks, who so fascinated Watts, had a penchant for quantum thinking "way back when," both in their poetry and painting. I believe it is one of the reasons that beneath the strokes of their swift ink brushes, we humans are almost always portrayed as miniatures in the vastness of sprawling land-scapes. I'd swear that these Taoist monks and Zen artisans were absolutely obsessed with the need to paint tiny people.

My bet is that the old boys did this because they wanted to remind us that we are parts of a pattern, a matrix so to speak. It is important that we not get "too big for our britches." We need to be miniaturized in our thoughts. We humans are, after all, not magnificent so much for what we have made of our individual selves as for what God has made of us—intrinsic parts of a greater pattern, a pattern of awesome magnificence that we call the world. It is a world of constant mystery and from whose mystery we are unfolding constantly. It is most surely a quantum world even though it is being described by Taoist monks.

It is Watts who took this quantum world and really ran with it. In his book *The Meaning of Happiness*, he fleshes out this idea of man as an integral part of the process we call the universe. With his every word we uncover a more sophisticated meaning of the human matrix. And we can see that this matrix model seems to fit the characteristics of the happiness machine quite nicely:

> *Man is as much attached to nature as a tree, and though he walks freely on two legs and is not rooted in the soil, he is by no means a self-sufficient, self-moving, and self-directing entity. For his life he depends absolutely on the same factors as the tree, the worm, and the fly, on the universal powers of nature, life, God, or whatever may be. . . . For man is a meeting-place for the interplay of forces from all quarters of the universe, swept through him in a stream which is indeed more truly man's self than his body or mind, its instruments.*

Ironically, it is from the paintings of Taoist monks and the writings of Alan Watts that it has become clear that the happiness machine can be nicely described as an interacting set of processes, what in quantum mechanics would be called a matrix. I believe that our metaphor works. All that is left is to explore each of the wings of this human matrix and to grasp how they interact with one another to create happiness machines.

The Core of the Human Matrix:
Who Is This Ms. Randall Anyway?

How does all this stuff fit together into a practical blueprint that can help us find happiness in the real-world laboratory of daily life? Quantum mechanics has led to cures for various forms of cancer. Can the concept of the human matrix that we borrowed from it help bring relief from the various causes of unhappiness?

Fortunately, as a psychiatrist, I live and work in this everyday laboratory. Unhappy people always seem to be knocking at my door. Taking a gander at how my patients and I work together to transform their pain may more clearly show us the details of our new blueprint and how to use it most effectively. Let us take a closer look at what happens after that knock.

With every patient who walks into my office and snuggles uneasily into the comfy chair across from me, I must ask myself the following questions, "Who is this human being? Of what is he or she made? What can he or she become? What are the possibilities?" The philosopher—whether a Taoist monk or a quantum physicist—deals with the generic question, "Who is man?" but I, as a therapist, must deal with the much more specific question, "Who is *this* man?" Unlike the universe that doesn't much give a hoot about the philosopher's answer, my patients care a great deal about mine.

To start, I naturally think of each of my patients as a "thing" called a "self." In short, I use the everyday lens of the "world as a thing" just as we all do at work or at play. And I do everything I can to help my patient resolve his or her pain using this time-tested and well-proven lens. I even address this self with a greeting from one self to another self such as, "Good-morning, Mr. Tyndall," or, "Come on in, Ms. Randall." At such times, I am using the lens of Michelle Kwan's skating machine, and my patient has distinct boundaries.

I view my patients in the same manner that I view my everyday self. We are all "things" who sometimes through our own machinations and sometimes through the machinations of other "things"—partners, bosses, old-boy networks, natural disasters, creditors and microbes—encounter great pain. And, to some extent, new "things" can help us to transform these problems: new marriages with different spouses, new jobs with different bosses, and so on and so on—more money, safer homes, better medications.

But I also view my patient with our second lens, the world as a process lens. As mentioned at the end of our last chapter, from this quantum perspective Ms. Randall is the net interaction of five processes: her biology, her psychology, her interpersonal world, her environment and her spirituality. The patient, Ms. Randall, has no distinct boundaries.

Through this lens, a human being is less a thing and more a moment in time—a complicated tissue of events—determined by the activities of these five powerful forces. Each person is, moment by moment, a changing pattern—a flickering flame, as Watts would describe it.

As with any matrix, the human matrix is a set of systems whose ultimate composite functioning creates something new, something completely unique, a distinctive, one time only pattern with each passing second. The end result is a most wonderful two-legged meeting place for the interplay of forces coming from all quarters of the universe—you.

From our everyday experience we are all familiar with matrices of a sort. If you work for a company, you work inside a matrix. Your company is a collection of different systems. Each day your office is alive with the humming of the workings of your designers, the calculations of your research and developers, the bean countings of your financial department, the laborings of your factory workers, the tappings of your typists, the creations of your marketing department, and the musings of your administrative department.

Each system has its own rules, personalities, strengths and weaknesses. If you were limited to understanding only one of them, you wouldn't have the foggiest idea of what your company was, for your company is a matrix. Your company is the sum total of all of these systems at each sequential moment of time. In a split second the whole company can change.

If one system begins to fail—research and development has nothing in the pipeline—the company is immediately different, despite the fact that it bears the exact same name and is housed in the exact same building. "Things"—people, buildings, production lines—do not a company make. Processes, sets of systems, and interactions define a company. And that's the way it is. Period. If just one part does something stupid, the whole company pays the piper—just ask Martha Stewart.

And so it is with human beings. My patient, Ms. Randall, is not just a blonde-haired, middle-aged woman with depression. She is a happiness machine composed of a set of whizzing systems—some within her skin and some without—in which one or more of the systems is out of whack. Because they were out of whack ten minutes ago, there was a knock at my door. Because they are still out of whack ten minutes later, there is a tear forming in the eye of this particular happiness machine that happens to not be very happy at this particular moment in time.

The Lowdown on the Five Wings of the Human Matrix

We humans are miniature companies composed of the molecules racing about our brains, the thoughts banging about our craniums, the friends hanging out at our dining room tables, the weather systems moving over our wheat fields, and the angels and demons prowling about our souls.

We are indeed the meeting place of five very powerful forces in the universe that are constantly changing with each given second. Each of these systems forms a wing of our matrix. It is these wings that represent the departments of our company: our biological system, our psychological system, our interpersonal system, our environmental system and our spiritual system. Let's take a closer look at what can go well and what can go bad in each wing, for the trick to understanding happiness is to understand their interplay.

First, we are undoubtedly a product of our biological wing. All one has to do is note the ravages of a disorder, such as Alzheimer's disease, to recognize the pivotal role biology plays in maintaining our happiness or destroying it. In contrast, to see the positive impact of the biological wing, all we need note is the miraculous relief one can receive from an antidepressant if there is an imbalance in the molecules of the brain—a pinch too much dopamine here or a tad too little serotonin there. But an understanding of our biology alone would not be enough to tell us whether we are happy or not. Inside our skins, there is a second set of forces at work as well.

We are propelled, some would argue compelled, by the nuances and subtleties of our minds, the beliefs, biases and revelations that are so wonderfully unique to each of us and populate like flitting ghosts the psychological wing of the human matrix. All one has to do is note the ugliness and pain that erupts from a single destructive belief—such as revenge—to see the degree to which our happiness depends upon our psychological mindset. The power of the mind to do good is equally obvious in the wondrous calm that settles over us with the gentle phrasings of a mantra in meditation or the effortless musings that preoccupy us as we listen to a prelude by Debussy. But our degree of happiness is still incomplete. There are other factors that also must be considered before we can determine the immediate output of the happiness machine—factors that lie outside our skins.

For instance, our happiness is also impacted by the third wing of the matrix, for we are surprisingly at the mercy of our individual relationships and the skills we bring to each of them. You can have a sound brain and a bright optimistic perspective, but if you pick a spouse who is abusive, you are in deep trouble. On the plus side, I remember friends—Ed, Brian and Drew— who have carried me over torrents of pain, providing safe havens when I did not know such havens existed. Clearly, the happiness of each person cannot be determined until one has understood his or her abilities to pick, maintain and enhance relationships with individual friends, bosses and family members, or wisely end those relationships that prove to be damaging.

In the fourth wing of the matrix, environments factor into the equation.

Sometimes there are inanimate environmental factors—an automobile accident that kills one of our children, a stock market that crashes, a slum that fosters malnutrition, disease and inequality of opportunity—that drive us into the depths of human anguish. At other moments the factors and situations are all too animate—our social environments. It is collections of individuals, a family unit, a workplace culture, a political system that bristle with brutality, jealousies and even violence that must be factored into the equation.

A patient who enters my office in great pain could have perfectly normal biochemistry, a pleasant attitude towards life, excellent interpersonal skills with some powerful individual friendships, but if his or her family has become an abusive family, terrorized by a "control freak" in which the family members have become a bevy of enablers, then this patient's pain may be deep indeed, deep enough to kill—to lead to a suicide. On the positive side of this wing, I have seen the tenacious love of parents whose children are afflicted with schizophrenia or bipolar disorder provide healing homes of such unrelenting compassion that they beat death and their pained children choose life.

Fifth, we are undoubtedly creatures who hunger for meaning. We search for the spiritual, and it is often the spiritual wing of the matrix that brings brilliance to our lives—compassion, hope, courage and belief. Once again, the other four systems in the human matrix could be tip-top. But if the patient sitting in my office chair has fallen into the depths of a spiritual crisis, they may be in great pain indeed.

On the other hand, the human soul is a tough bird, and it is the soul that can keep a human alive in the horrors of a death camp. It is the soul that can lead a man or a woman to dedicate his or her life to helping the poor. Brains, minds, partners and families are powerful forces of the universe that meet inside my office, but I must never forget that one of the most powerful forces of nature is man's search for his soul, man's reach towards his God and man's use of his free will.

I believe we have accomplished a significant part of our goal for this chapter—to provide a concise, clear and crisp definition of the human matrix and its five wings. We have ourselves a sound new blueprint for the happiness machine. It is a blueprint quite consistent with what we know about the world from modern physics and what we feel about the world from daily religious experience. Our final task in this chapter is to ferret out the connection between the theory of the human matrix and the reality of using it to more effectively uncover happiness.

Chinese Herons, Treacherous Fields, Crocodile Hunters and the Nature of Stress

Let us return to an old friend, our perfectly poised and perfectly happy heron from chapter 7—lost forever in the eternity of the present moment, soon to be lost in the eternity of a most delicious gastronomic feast. Why was it so easy for this heron to move almost effortlessly from eternal moment to eternal moment, and why is it seemingly so hard for me to do so?

Now that we have achieved a clearer concept of the general structure of the human matrix and its basic functioning, we are better prepared to answer this question. To do so we must explore the exact relationship between the human matrix and happiness, for happiness, not a frog, is the goal of our quest. How can this human matrix model be used to impact on our attitude of trust and our feeling of confidence?

It can do so in two fashions, one direct and the other indirect. We will look at the direct method first.

The struggles and vicissitudes of everyday life tell us that trust and confidence can vary dramatically, on a moment by moment basis, in the ease with which they appear and in the degree of their strength and intensity. Two factors impacting on trust and confidence, in a practical and immediate sense, are the number and severity of the stressors that we are facing at any given moment, and the number and strengths of the resources and skills that we have available to cope with these stressors. A simple analogy clarifies this point.

Imagine that you have been asked to cross a two-acre field of tall grasses, sun-baked rock piles, and decaying logs on a hot summer day, with the buzzing of insects thick and loud. There are no paths. You have been told that the field has been liberally seeded with cobras, rattlesnakes, an assortment of pit vipers and an occasional fer-de-lance. I'll go out on a limb here and predict that you are probably not a particularly happy camper. You would have little trust that things would go well and almost no confidence to step into that field unless you are television's Crocodile Hunter, Steve Irwin, in which case, "Croiky, it doesn't get any better than this!"

Imagine now that I tell you that it will be two days before you have to cross the field, and that when you return we will have done our best to rid the field of every snake (removed the stressors) and, just in case we missed some of the little critters, we will provide you with vials of an antidote that is 100 percent effective and easily administered (enhanced your tools). I dare say that both your trust and your confidence of surviving the crossing would have greatly increased. In short, you are now happier—a great deal happier.

The human matrix model can help clear our fields of snakes (stressors) and, simultaneously, fill our packs with antidotes (skills for handling stressors). Specifically, there are methods of using the knowledge of the human matrix—which we will explore in subsequent chapters—that provide strategies for aggressively searching each wing of the matrix for problems while suggesting plans for addressing these problems.

Guided by this blueprint, we are less likely to miss the critical causes of our distress and more likely to uncover the potential tools for allaying this stress, for life is complicated and the stresses and solutions are often found intermixed. Once the problems are spotted they can be prospectively removed (good-bye, snakes). Similarly, on each wing of the matrix, we can methodically enrich our tools for coping with any of the problems that cannot easily be removed (hello, antidotes). The result is a human matrix that is less treacherous and a human being who is more capable of handling treachery.

Sometimes we can directly focus upon more effectively invoking happiness. This occurs when we try to develop our skills on the spiritual wing of the matrix by learning more about the nature and nurture of attitudes such as trust, acceptance, wonderment, hope and compassion. Indeed, part I of this book is an example of just such an endeavor. A weekend retreat on mindfulness or our attendance at a Sunday service are also excellent examples. Such direct approaches can yield invaluable tools for enhancing happiness directly.

But happiness is not so simple. Factors found on the different wings of the matrix interact with one another. Not understanding such distant matrix effects often makes the overall problems of daily living—picking friends, finding mates, choosing careers and making ends meet—look unexplainable and daunting. Understanding these matrix effects can help us cut through the clutter, and see what is really going on. In short, we might not be quite as "at the mercy" of the universe as we might first have supposed. Our trust increases. Our confidence grows. We are happier.

A strategy for directly nurturing happiness, when faced with specific difficulties, is beginning to emerge:

1.) View your immediate state of unhappiness as being a result of the net interactions of your matrix.
2.) Review what is happening in each wing of your matrix while looking for potential problems and enhancing potential skills for solving those problems.
3.) Recognize that both your problems and their solutions may come from the surprising interactions that occur among the wings of your matrix.

The fact is that as we learn more about each of the wings of our matrix, as we confront specific real world problems using the human matrix as a guide, we see new possibilities for real-world interventions. Each wing of the matrix posits its own unique and sometimes undreamed-of solutions.

As we shall soon see in upcoming chapters, the human matrix is a "possibility generator" par excellence. The unexpected answers that it supplies to our practical questions about navigating life are not cookbook responses or pre-ordained actions. They are ways of thinking, conceptualizing and designing that help us generate effective plans of action for coping with whatever life has brought us at that particular moment in time. The immediate practicality of these plans directly translates into an enhanced sense of trust and confidence.

And it is here that we have stumbled upon our more indirect link between the use of our knowledge of the human matrix and the development of happiness. Although this link may be indirect in nature, its resulting impact may be strikingly more enduring than the direct methods just described. Let's see how it comes about.

Once we have learned how to routinely use the human matrix effectively to maximize our happiness—a skill for both the good times and the bad times—a new and prospective trust begins to emerge. We begin to trust the matrix itself, or more explicitly, our approach to using the matrix model. We begin to realize that we don't have to worry so much about future obstacles, because we are armed with an extremely effective way of designing plans of action for navigating those obstacles no matter what they are. We gain the trust to have an ongoing and enduring confidence in our bodies, our minds, our friends, our families, our environments and our gods.

We begin to trust, deep in our gut, that there are endless permutations to our situations, endless solutions to our problems, endless answers to our fears. It is this trust, gained indirectly via our experience in using the matrix model itself, that allows us to better see the world with the eyes of Julian of Norwich—with the eyes of hope. When we move through her window of so long ago into the hectic yet endlessly fascinating world of today, we suddenly perceive a new world—dazzling in its complexities, wondrous in its strangeness and rich with its possibilities.

It is here—nestled in the palm of the present moment like one of

Julian's hazelnut things—that we find a world that is teeming with all of the attitudes we saw in part I that can enhance happiness: wonderment, gratitude, freedom, forgiveness, spontaneity, laughter and compassion. With our newfound sense of trust we paint, as if by magic (and I am not sure that there is not more than a touch of magic to it), a landscape colored by our creativity and framed by our moments of peak experience and peak performance.

For in the final analysis, stress is not so much composed of the many obstacles that life will undoubtedly present us; stress is composed of the fear that we will not be able to handle those obstacles.

Once we become adept at using the human matrix model to help solve immediate problems, we gain a new trust that we have the prerequisite methods to get rid of any nasty snakes that may cross our paths in future fields. We are confident that if a snake or two is missed we will have the ability to track down the antidote necessary to effectively cope with the stress in question. At such a point we don't have to worry so much. Like our heron friend, we can live within the present moment. Who knows, we might just find more frogs. Croiky, it doesn't get any better than this!

By the way, an understanding of how to work the human matrix can also provide us with something a little less tangible than a frog but a good deal more beneficial in the long run. It can also bring us luck.

This last statement may sound like a bit of a stretch, but it is not. I am reminded of one of the favorite sayings of Oprah Winfrey:

"Luck is a matter of preparation meeting opportunity."

Armed with our knowledge of the human matrix and the power of well-timed and well-planned matrix effects, we are prepared. It is now only a matter of opening our eyes to opportunity. And opportunity lies in the present moment. Just waiting.

10 Wondrous and Worthy of the Utmost Attention

"*But every man is more than just himself,*
he is also the unique, very special and in every case
significant and remarkable point at which the world's
manifestations intersect only once in this way and never again.
That is why every man's story is important, eternal, sacred;
that is why every man, just as long as he is in any way
alive and fulfills the will of nature, is wondrous
and worthy of the utmost attention."

HERMAN HESSE

Big Amplifiers, Small Gymnasiums and the Soft Folds of Everyday Moments

It is in everyday gestures, everyday conversations, everyday glances between an everyday Joe and an everyday Jane that the surprising powers of the universe intersect to meet once and only once. Within the soft folds of these everyday moments the secrets of the human matrix lay gently tucked away.

Our final task in part II is to take our matrix out of the world of theory, which we described in our last chapter, and put it into the world of everyday experience. We need a concrete example of whether the concept of the human matrix can explain how happiness can appear even during times of great pain and loss. We need our theory to be put to the acid test of real life. We want our example to come not from the solitary cells of saints and mystics, nor from the mathematical equations of quantum physicists, but from the furnaces and classrooms of steelworkers and teachers. Can our new blueprint uncover happiness in places where happiness seems least likely to be found and at times when it seems improbable to be encountered?

Our everyday Joe is named Bob. Our everyday Jane is named Judy. Their intersection with me occurred years ago. At the time, I had no idea that when I followed them through the back door into their kitchen, I was about to come upon a moment worthy of the utmost attention.

It all began on a hot summer night in July 1978. I had just returned home from my second year of medical school at the University of North Carolina at Chapel Hill, a wonderful place to learn the art of medicine. In North Carolina, we had been suffering through a severe drought.

I had been home for a day or two when I casually commented to my mother that I would love nothing better than to see a good old-fashioned thunderstorm. Somebody upstairs was listening. As the old saying goes, be careful for what you wish.

As I left shortly after dinner for an evening of adventure, the rains began gently enough. Within hours, they had undergone a change of temperament. By ten o'clock they were pounding with a torrential ferocity.

Later that night I was hanging out—as I still am thirty years later—with my great friend Brian, a gifted musician who was practicing with a local band for kicks. We were in the basement of the bandleader, Kendall, and his younger brother, who happened to be a wicked-good drummer named

Gary. Gary was pounding the skins inside with the same ferocity as the thunderstorm was pounding the streets outside.

Our basement hideout was packed with huge speakers and walls of electronic gadgetry. Guitars were tossed about with an almost artful nonchalance. Peels of laughter and bursts of guitar licks bounced off the walls.

Huge batches of wires were sprouting from the lips of the speakers and amplifiers. The wires mated with each other, forming thick cords of electrical mess that seemed to be writhing on the floor. I had never seen such a carpet of cables, connectors and wiring. The floor was an electrical hog heaven.

Perhaps this is why, when the smallish basement window burst open, when the torrents of rainwater came gushing through the resulting hole, that a unified "Holy shit!" leaped from the mouths of five late-adolescent males. In the ensuing moments the derrieres of the aforementioned males were moving faster than they had ever moved before. Very fast, indeed.

Inside the house of Kendall and Gary, the basement was flooding. Outside the house of Kendall and Gary, down over the steep hills that cradled Johnstown, down past the world's steepest inclined plane, the city of Johnstown was flooding.

From your history books, you might recall that this night was not the first night that Johnstown had ever flooded. It was actually the third. But the one that you might recall from your high school history books was the first one, in 1889. On that night the South Fork Dam burst. A wall of water raced through the snaking valley that funneled towards the downtown area of Johnstown nearly fifteen miles away.

It was the middle of the night. The hardworking steelworkers and their families, who were the mainstay of this little stepbrother of the steelmaking Goliath known as Pittsburgh, went to sleep to the pounding of raindrops on their rooftops. They were awakened by the roaring of a veritable wall of water (70 feet high in some places) from the burst dam. More than 2,200 people died that night in Johnstown—one of the worst natural disasters in U.S. history.

In the ensuing hundred years, riverbanks had been steepened, runoffs created, and flood walls constructed. There were no more faulty dams sitting above the city. The only water that could ever pose a threat to Johnstown was good old-fashioned rainwater. With all of the flood-proofing precautions, Johnstown was never supposed to flood again. Unfortunately, the engineers never imagined that on a night in July 1978, twelve inches of rain would fall in nine hours. This time the floodwaters managed to steal 78 lives, and the devastation to the city was, once again, extraordinary.

In the ensuing days people, supplies, roadgraders and plows of every imaginable kind poured into Johnstown. Everyone pitched in. Sometimes it seems that when we are forced to look squarely into the horrors of disaster, we also come face to face with the mirrors of compassion. No creatures on earth are as committed to strangers as human beings are to each other during the aftermath of a disaster.

Most of the town of Johnstown was evacuated. The houses, hospitals and shops were coated with muck and mud. The displaced families were housed in hastily prepared shelters, up top on the hills, away from the settling waters in makeshift shelters. Just about any building that contained a gym or an auditorium was put to use, and that was the case with the old Southmont School building.

They needed flood runners down there. At least that is what I called them. The displaced families who had been imagining what their houses now looked like—just how much damage had been done—would eventually need to be driven back to their homes and their mud-covered cars.

It was as a flood runner in the noisy gymnasium of the Southmont School that I met Bob and Judy. The gym was littered with lines and lines of cots. The cots were a jumble of pillows, crumpled sheets and anything the families had managed to bring with them as they had rushed out of the town—toothbrushes, a bag of dirty clothes, a cherished knickknack, an even more cherished doll or toy car. Pain was everywhere. Kids were crying and parents were comforting. No one knew exactly what had been lost.

Rumors raged through the rows of cots with the same viciousness as the floodwaters of several nights past had roared through the streets. Some heard that their houses had been destroyed, others that they had been spared, some that the waters had mangled all furniture, others that there were pockets of normalcy. One heard of heroics and also of looting and post-flood fires. Some wondered if a grandmother or dear friend had died.

All that one could do was sit and wait, sit and cry, sit and comfort. The unknowing was the worst of it now, two days after the flood. People were tired of sitting. People were tired of waiting. People were tired of the not knowing. It would be better to know the worst than to just keep on sitting. They needed to get back.

When Bob and Judy got the nod that their street had been cleared for return, their first question as they saw me was, "Are you the guy taking us back to our house?" I answered, "Yep, let's get the ball rolling." They nodded.

They were a curious-looking pair. Bob was short and heavy, not only with years, but with more than the necessary number of pounds around his pear shaped girth. This pear shape plumped down on a pair of legs that seemed just a bit too squat as they jutted out from a pair of dowdy shorts. The feet were stuck into a pair of white socks and black shoes. He was dirty and bedraggled, as all of us were, beneath thick-framed glasses and a thinly haired head.

"God bless you," he chirped with a matter-of-fact sincerity. There was no smile, just chirp. I could sense immediately that Bob was tough in an ordinary way. He had fought a grueling battle with life, as we all have to do one way or another. This "making a living" is not so easily made. But he was not about to quit just yet, flood or no flood.

Nor was Judy who I came upon as she was reattaching her leg. You see, Judy had severe diabetes. She had lost her leg to the disease several years ago. The prosthetic attachment was being a little bit ornery, but it finally snapped into place.

Judy was even stockier and squatter than her husband. The flowers on her patterned skirt had long since passed the stage of faded. What little blue was left, after years of wear, was wilted. Her face was puffy and weary.

But she also managed a "God bless you" in response to my appearance, and hers was accompanied by the faintest of smiles. She commented, "We're really worried about what we're gonna find."

I nodded and pulled my car keys out of my pocket as we headed towards the door of the Southmont School towards . . . we did not know what. But I remember hoping that their house would be okay.

I enjoyed this work, for it was the type of endeavor in which one can palpably feel that one is making a difference in the world. Flood runners were a curious combination of taxi driver, social worker, furniture mover and priest. Oftentimes, after finding the correct home, the flood runner would go inside and help with the earliest phases of "digging out." My first couple of runs had been to homes that, thank goodness had surprisingly little damage.

We pulled into one of the blue-collar areas of town. It was an area that was always kept up nicely but modestly, for no one made much money here. Bob did watch repairs for a living.

I was not sure what to expect as we pulled up in front of their house, walked back to their kitchen door, opened it and stepped inside.

Unexpected Boats, Plane Wrecks
and the Power of the Matrix

I remember hearing a gasp from Judy. When I crossed the threshold of the kitchen door behind her, I knew why. It looked like someone had taken the floor, picked it up like a tablecloth and tossed all of the kitchen furniture and appliances up into the air. Tables and chairs were upended and stacked like a pile of pick-up sticks. Spoons, forks and knives were strewn about with a devil-may-care flare. Then I saw it.

Right in the middle of the floor was a boat, only the boat was the yellow refrigerator, laying on its side, beached in a dune of mud. What I had not realized was the power of slowly but inexorably rising water. As more and more water fills a kitchen like a bathtub, it eventually reaches a level where things begin to float—big things—like refrigerators and kitchen cabinets. As these unexpected boats set sail, they dump their contents and then pitch anchor many feet away from their home ports in all imaginable positions.

As the water, brimming with mud, sewage, and debris settles, it dumps a thick carpet of mud, much like the Ice Age glaciers did thousands of years ago. Everything is carpeted in inches of mud. Thick. Slimy. Filthy.

I had not even begun to prepare myself for the stench—a rich blend of backed-up sewage, garbage-laden sediment and sopping-wet upholstery. One can imagine what such a carpet of water and mud could do to furniture such as sofas, beds and chairs. The entire first floor of Bob and Judy's house was completely destroyed.

It was then that I remember becoming aware of Bob's activities. He entered the room without comment, without gasp, without hesitancy. He quickly set to work. He began righting furniture, collecting eating utensils, unlocking knots of debris. His movements were a blur of steady, unswerving determination. With a hand on the toppled refrigerator, he called over to me, "Could you give me a hand with this?" Soon our boat had been dry docked and shoved back into its proper port.

There was no pause for self-pity, there were no complaints, there was no thought of surrender. His house was damaged. It was time to help it. I am reminded of Benny, our limo driver, and his often-ill wife back in Iowa. "When Patty is well, we rejoice. When Patty is sick, I try to help her. What else could I do?"

Here with Bob and the equally determined Judy, attacking what needed to be done with a simple determination, I was seeing something I had not really seen much of in my life—courage. It was not flashy like I had expected it to be. It was not dramatic like the war books always painted it. It was not bold, like an actor likes to portray it. It was mundane. It was quiet. It was almost shy. It was not Hollywood. It was Johnstown. It was magnificent.

And it was real. This was the real McCoy. People faced with terrible loss, knocked to the mat but back up on their feet. I am reminded of the phrase, "It is not how many times you are knocked down that counts, it is how many times you get up."

I watched this display of what it is to be a human being at its best with a quiet reverence of sorts, although I myself was busy pitching in a hand. It all seemed to pass seamlessly without a pause. Nothing was going to stop Bob from doing what needed to be done. Nothing. There was no time for pain.

Until he got sucker punched. It happened in the hallway from the kitchen to the living room. I saw this human dynamo come suddenly to a halt. I'm not sure but I think I heard a gasp. I saw Bob's shortish arms reach down into the mud and muck on the floor. He was picking something up, something small, something broken.

When I reached the hallway, I saw what had stopped Bob in his tracks. It was a plane wreck. Indeed, it was the site of many plane wrecks. Over the years Bob had not had much time for hobbies, but he had enjoyed one hobby, one activity that he had spent endless hours poring over with the meticulous care that only a watchmaker could bring. He built model airplanes.

Before him, in the mud and the muck, lay bits of propeller and wing, shards of fuselage and twigs of landing gear. I thought I heard him whisper, "They're all broken." As he stood up, he turned back towards the kitchen, toward myself and his wife.

Judy asked, "What is it?"

Before he even answered, she took one look at the hallway floor, and she got it. She knew. Their eyes met. His were moist.

It was at that exact moment that Bob smiled. Judy gently nodded and smiled back. Not a word passed between them.

With all the devastation about them, with a few nods of a head and a simple smile, the two fighters acknowledged to each other that one of them had taken a hit. One of them had been knocked to the mat. Life had landed a harsh and nasty sucker punch like a bully in a school yard. The planes had crashed to the ground, and for a brief moment Bob found himself knocked to the ground as well. But now, with a single look into the eyes of his wife, with a single smile, he was pulling himself up from the mat. The fight was not over by a long shot.

As he wiped his eyes, I asked Bob, "What are you going to do? I know it is all so much. How can I help?"

Bob shook his head. Then he said, once again with the same clarity Benny had displayed back in our limo on that Iowa interstate, "With God's help I'm going to rebuild my house. That's what I'm going do. I'm going to rebuild my house." There was a pause. He pointed down the narrow hall into the living room. "Give me a hand with this sofa?"

"Absolutely," I answered.

Here, in the mud and muck of a tiny flood-ravaged house, I had the luck to be at one of those moments when life confronts us and then transforms us. As we said earlier, apparently such moments have nothing to do with the extraordinary and everything to do with the ordinary—with moments as simple as two people exchanging a smile in a darkened hallway in a small town in western Pennsylvania.

Here, before us, is the raw power of the human matrix. Bob and Judy have just given us our first lesson. It is a simple lesson—no matter how punishing the hit on one wing of the matrix, the other four wings may provide enough strength to keep the human being upright.

We are a tenacious species. No matter how harsh the hits, we often come back with an even more ferocious determination. This resiliency is directly attributable to the fact that we are not just "things," we are processes when seen through a quantum lens. Things break, like the wings of plastic airplanes. Processes bend. They transform. They survive.

It is worth our time to briefly review each wing of Bob's matrix to more deeply understand the role that each contributed to his resiliency. On the environmental wing, Bob had taken a direct hit. A natural disaster, a flood, had devastated his home. It had destroyed what could eventually be replaced—a living room sofa—and had stolen what could never be replaced—a squadron of carefully painted dreams. Hundreds of hours of past pleasure were destroyed by a single minute or two of nature's ferocity. In the weeks to come, hundreds of hours would be needed to get his home and his life back to "point zero."

If one were to look only at this one wing of the human matrix, a smile would have been unimaginable. What is of immediate interest to us is the question, "How?" With all of this pain, *how* did this smile unfold instead of tears, instead of angry curses, instead of a startled wailing? It is with this question that we come upon our second lesson from Bob and Judy. The human matrix is not only powerful. It is fragile.

The existence of that smile (and the smile that Judy returned) was the result of thousands of interrelating processes. Change just one of those processes significantly and our smile might go "poof.'" It might never have happened.

The "thing" known as Bob is the net result not just of a flood meeting a human being, but of a flood intersecting with a unique biology, a unique psychology, a unique marital relationship and a unique framework for meaning. This smile was the confluence of a set of intricate balances and counterbalances that could occur only once in history. Period. Such moments in time, everyday moments—all moments—are magnificently fragile. Perhaps it is their fragility, the unlikelihood of their occurrence, that makes them sacred. To better understand the sacredness of this one singular moment in time, let us continue with our survey of each of Bob's wings in more detail, for it is the nature of these wings that will demonstrate the uncanny power of the human matrix to transform difficult times into times of opportunity.

Biologically, although Bob's pear-shaped body clearly had not been sculpted in a Gold's Gym, he was not critically ill. He was not wheezing from severe asthma. He was not fatigued by a cancer. He was not bedbound by a stroke. His biological matrix was in good enough shape to respond to the immediate crisis posed by the floodwaters.

Equally important, the complex chemistry of his brain seemed to be in reasonably good shape. I had seen no evidence of a biological depression in his activities. From all outward appearances, his brain chemistry was working normally. The one hundred billion neurons of his brain were firing on time and with precision, a fact of the utmost importance in the creation of this particular smile.

Imagine for a moment that they had not. Imagine that for months, because of a genetic process encoded in Bob's chromosomes and passed on from one generation to another generation for centuries as dependably as a family Christmas tradition, a small but pivotal section of Bob's billion brain cells were malfunctioning.

The result of the malfunction had been the loss of sound sleep, a marked reduction in energy, concentration and drive. On top of this huge biological deficit the malfunctioning cells were creating wave after wave of depressed feeling and spontaneous bouts of tearfulness.

Further imagine that this emotional storm—a biologically triggered depression—had been going on for months. Would we have seen a smile in that hallway? Would we have seen a man capable of even producing such a smile at such a moment? I rather doubt it. This moment was defined as much by the biochemistry of Bob's brain, by the genetics of his family, as it was by a summer flood.

But it was not only his body and biology that defined this intimate moment. On the psychological wing of his matrix, he appeared ready to pitch the fight against the flood. I saw no unusual propensities for self-denigrations, no out of control anxieties, no cognitive distortions telling him that his life was ruined or that all was lost. On the psychological wing, he was ready. Forces were surging towards the front lines, bayonets mounted to meet the struggles of the upcoming battle. We see again the power of one wing of the matrix to help carry the day when there is huge damage on another wing.

If any one of the above cognitions had been present—self-denigration, catastrophic thinking—all bets would have been off. Had Bob been struggling with low self-esteem, a self-denigration that could have been caused by any number of damaging matrix effects—beatings given by an alcoholic father during his childhood or a low intellectual functioning that had won him the taunts and denigrations of school yard bullies—there would have been no smile in that hallway. An extraordinary number of variables could have led to significant psychological damage. Any one of these events could have stopped our smile from ever unfolding.

We see with each wing of Bob's matrix—an everyday matrix in an everyday human being—that even the simplest of human gestures or behaviors is the product of a dazzling interplay. Our lesson is a simple one, yet an incredibly important one. To understand ourselves we must understand all five wings as they intersect at any specific moment in time.

How wonderfully evident this fact becomes when we look at the interpersonal wing of our watchmaker—Judy. Without a Judy, of course, there would not have been a smile no matter how sound his brain or his mind, for there would not have been anybody to trigger the smile. It was to her presence that he automatically turned, not mine.

Here, in Judy, was a most powerful ally. She had been a mate for decades, who needed only a single glance at broken propeller blades to know the pain in the soul of her husband, to know that no words were necessary—only a nod, a smile and a fleeting meeting of the eyes. Without a Judy, the moment that we witnessed would never have occurred.

But there was one more wing to this matrix, one more sculptor of this moment in time. For on the spiritual wing, a veritable army was waiting to surge forth to Bob's side. Bob had a supernatural ally. "With God's help, I'm going to rebuild my house." No doubts. No second guesses. Raw, unadulterated belief.

It was this strength surging from the spiritual wing of his matrix that pointed towards the hope that lies waiting for us even in the most mundane of tasks. It is the necessity of the moment that sometimes highlights the fact that we still have the ability to do what needs to be done. It proves to us that we still have strength. Hope, oftentimes, is sparked by the simple fact that we must do what the moment calls for us to do.

For Bob it was the hope that lay waiting in the living room, a sofa that needed to be tossed over a balcony. There was work to be done, and the fact that he could do it brought its own reassurance. God gives hope in some pretty unlikely places, exactly when it is most needed.

Apparently, Bob had found himself a seat beside Julian of Norwich. Through her window, through the trelliswork created by the intersection of all of the wings of his own matrix, Bob saw what Julian of Norwich had always found as she looked through her window on the plagues, wars and famines so common to her time and to her people. He found trust.

For Julian and Bob it was trust in a god. For others it might be the powerfully reassuring trust of the Tao, or a belief in their community and their mission. No matter what the source, it is the trust that brings hope. It is the trust that helped to trigger a smile during times of woe.

In 1374, Julian had held a fragile hazelnut thing in her palm. Six hundred years later Bob held a fragile propeller thing in his hand. Somehow as they both looked at what could so easily be chipped and broken—a world, a model airplane—they found the reassuring belief that it could also be fixed, and that something or someone outside of themselves would help do the fixing.

With Judy and Bob we have seen the human matrix as it was reflected in the actions of two ordinary people during some rather extraordinary times. We have seen that our theoretical matrix is actually quite tangible. Our blueprint is not an academic exercise. It can be used to explain everyday reality.

The human matrix itself also happens to have the knack of remaining surprisingly unobtrusive. It exists and functions without our conscious guidance. Bob and Judy were certainly not consciously aware of its presence, but it served them both well.

On the other hand, the unobtrusiveness of the human matrix does not mean that it cannot be consciously improved, maintained and employed. It can. Those who know how to do so are at a great advantage in the quest for happiness. Indeed, learning to do so effectively is one of the main goals of our book.

But before we look at the nuts and bolts of employing our knowledge of the human matrix, Bob and Judy have one last lesson to give us. It is a lesson that we have heard before in theory and I have seen in practice with my patients, one that is well worth emphasizing again as demonstrated in the real world of illnesses, deaths, taxes, layoffs and in this case, floodwaters.

As we already know, Bob cannot be understood as simply a "thing" encountering a flood. He is not just a skating machine hitting a patch of ice. He is also a happiness machine from the quantum perspective. As such, his happiness is a reflection of the intersection of many forces, some within his skin and some without, of which just one is a summer tempest and its resulting floodwaters. On another level the actual resources at hand—the support of Judy, the strength of his body, and even the presence of me—a flood runner—all play a role in his ever-transforming sense of trust and confidence.

Even more striking, it is his immediate attitudes, crystallizing on the psychological and spiritual wings of his matrix on a moment by moment basis, which ultimately determine the extent of his happiness. These ever-changing attitudes are being constantly created and recreated by the interactions of factors from all the wings of his matrix, from the swirling floodwaters outside his skin to the enduring attitudes toward life Bob carries inside his skin.

Floods alone do not cause unhappiness. How the five wings of the matrix interact to create an attitude towards a flood—now *that* determines happiness or unhappiness. As we said earlier, stress is not so much the obstacles that life throws our way but the fear that we will not be able to handle those obstacles.

Here we come upon a most wonderful truth. It is a truth to which we alluded in theory in our last chapter and which we now see in practice with Bob and Judy. Happiness begets happiness. If one brings to a crisis an enduring attitude of trust and a feeling of confidence, as we saw in John Merrick, Julian of Norwich and Benny, one more easily gains entrance to the present moment. Within that present moment one finds waiting the other attitudes—acceptance, wonderment, hope and compassion—that help one to successfully navigate the difficult time in hand. From each successful navigation we gain a deeper sense of trust and confidence. Therefore, armed with an even stronger sense of happiness, we are better prepared for the next crisis. It is one of life's most delightful positive feedback loops.

And it is a loop that, over the years, I have become convinced can be enhanced through a better understanding of how the five wings of the human matrix work and interact, for each wing has something special to offer. Each wing may house our downfall or our savior. Each wing may hold a new secret that leads to a deeper sense of trust.

Thus, we can see that from a practical standpoint, a better understanding of the human matrix can help us to nurture happiness in two ways. First, we can learn to optimize each wing so that we are more likely to encounter good fortune and better able to transform misfortune when it comes our way. Second, and perhaps more important we can learn how to use the matrix to shape the types of enduring attitudes—trust, acceptance, wonderment, hope and compassion—that allow us to maximize good fortune, when it is present, and gracefully navigate misfortune when it is inevitable—exactly as we just saw Bob and Judy do.

As we close, let us return one last time to the significance of the smile that passed between Bob and Judy so many years ago in that muddied hallway. It was a common hallway in a common house in a common neighborhood in Johnstown, Pennsylvania. It was a simple smile, a simple gesture between two simple people. It was a fleeting flash of human experience that undoubtedly occurs a million times across the world in the time that it is taking me to write this one sentence—so common that it could be easily viewed as insignificant. Twenty years ago, I was not certain what to make of it. Today, I'm still not certain, but I am more comfortable hazarding a guess.

For as I look back, I feel that the smile I stumbled upon in that seemingly inconsequential hallway was nothing less than a meeting place for the universe. As Hesse described it in our opening epigraph, it was a single brilliant moment in time, never to be repeated. It was a moment when a few tattered bits of plastic propeller and wing, two sets of human eyes, two beatings of human hearts and the touch of God all met at once, wondrous and worthy of the utmost attention.

Part III

The Rules of the Quest:
Inside the Human Matrix

*"The new view is entirely different.
The fundamental concepts are activity and
process. . . . Nature is a theatre for
the interrelations of activities."*

ALFRED NORTH WHITEHEAD
THEORETICAL PHYSICIST

*"Each time the wave breaks
The raven
Gives a little jump."*

NISSHA
(TRANSLATED BY R. H. BLYTH)

Blue Lakes, Unknown Hands and Dark Winters

11

"Each phenomenon is determining every other phenomenon and is simultaneously being determined by each and every phenomenon."

CHENG CHIEN
CHINESE MONK

The Wisdom of Watching Long Enough and the Return of Michelle Kwan: A Prelude for Part III

Now that we have a good understanding of the nature of our happiness machine, it is time to take it for a test drive. It is time to see how good it is at achieving an enduring sense of happiness.

Of course, it might be wise to read the owner's manual first, something I hardly ever do and inevitably regret not doing. It must be a male thing. Many stupid things are male things, according to my wife, Susan, and I have found her to be annoyingly correct on such matters.

If we are going to take our happiness vehicles out for a drive, we not only need to know the internal rules that determine how these happiness machines work but also the external "rules of the road" that determine their speed limits and their right of ways. I can assure you that finding happiness is sometimes a good deal more complicated than finding the local drugstore in a new car.

And, if you are like me, you have absolutely no desire to see a flashing pair of blue lights in the rearview mirror as you toodle toward Walgreens. Bottom line: Before we proceed with a spin in our happiness machine, it is prudent to review the rules in our owner's manual and come to an understanding of the principles that determine the "rules of the road" as well.

Consequently, we need answers to the following questions about the human matrix if we want any chance for success. What makes it tick? What rules govern how happiness machines can go about the business of finding happiness? How exactly is the game played? What are we allowed to do and what are the potential consequences of doing it? What is it sometimes best not to do?

Understanding the answers to these pivotal questions—the rules that govern the quest for happiness and the principles that follow from them—is the focus of part III. A knowledge of these rules will greatly enhance our ability to use the model of the human matrix to uncover an enduring sense of happiness.

I am reminded of an insight from a quantum physicist, the eloquent lecturer and writer Richard P. Feynman:

> *What do we mean by "understanding" something? We can imagine that this complicated array of moving things which constitutes "the world" is something like a great chess game being played by the gods, and we are observers of the game. We do not know what the rules of the game are; all we are allowed to do is to watch the playing. Of course, if we watch long enough, we may eventually catch on to a few of the rules.*

In part III we will attempt to "catch on to a few of the rules" of the happiness game. To do so, we must return to our ice arena, where we spot the graceful figure of our favorite skating machine, Michelle Kwan. Kwan has just finished a wonderfully executed triple salchow during her warmups. Our question is, what does this rule thing have to do with Michelle Kwan as her skating machine begins its quest for gold? The answer is . . . a great deal.

No matter how well-tuned, well-oiled and well-designed Kwan's skating machine may be, it will be doomed to failure unless Kwan understands the rules that govern both the internal workings of her skating machine and the external machinations of the world of competitive skating in which it must skate. Both worlds—internal workings and external machinations—have rules.

Although I don't know Ms. Kwan personally, I suspect that, like all great athletes, she knows this fact and accepts it. She understands that she cannot change the rules, nor is she above them. She realizes that they may not always seem fair. Undoubtedly, she has also learned, with the gracious practicality of Julian of Norwich, that it is wise to accept the good and the bad of the rulebook in her hands.

It is worth our while to examine in more detail what Kwan and other seasoned skaters actually "see" when they open the rulebook before hitting the ice for competition. We will discover that they do not just see the stated rules. They also see unstated principles. Each rule suggests specific creative principles for optimizing how to skate within its strictures. To a champion athlete, rules do not set limitations, they suggest possibilities.

One of the first concepts that any champion athlete must assimilate is an offshoot of the interdependence to which Cheng Chien hints in our opening epigraph and that echoes what we have already learned in part II of our book; every "thing" is a matrix if viewed through a quantum lens. For example, consider the skating machine of Michelle Kwan as it effortlessly glides by us. Her skating machine is an apparent isolate confined by the taut boundaries of her skin. But if we pop off our "world as thing" lens and pop on our quantum goggles—Poof!—Kwan, the skating machine, explodes into a starburst of interlocking fields and forces reaching far beyond the confines of her skin.

In this regard Kwan must understand that each phenomena that is impacting on her skating machine—everything that is contained within her delightfully graceful figure and without—may directly or indirectly interact with each other. Her conditioning, her nutrition, her muscle strength, her flexibility, her immune system, her appearance, her relationship with her coach, her relationship with the judges and the spectators, and even her attitude towards her competitors are each fashioning one another while simultaneously being shaped by what they fashion.

In short, Michelle Kwan's skating machine is not only a wonderful example of a "thing" as we first presented it in the prelude to part II. When viewed with a quantum lens—just as was the case with her happiness machine—it is a wonderful example of a matrix composed of many wings. And the matrix of her skating machine has much to teach us, that can be directly applied to the matrix of our happiness machines.

Its performance is determined by a myriad of interacting processes always on the go and always changing, their relationships ultimately determined by the following rules and principles:

1. All wings of her skating machine intersect and are interdependent upon one another. Consequently, because there is interdependence, a problem on one wing of her skating machine can cause problems on a different wing of her skating machine. (A hostile reception by fans could decrease performance.)

2. When a problem arises with her skating machine, the problem is not always on the wing that seems obvious, and it behooves her to always search for potential bugs in each wing of her skating matrix. (Her technical skills appear to be weak but, in reality, she has a severe anemia.)

3. In a similar fashion, sometimes a beneficial process on one wing can interpenetrate to the other wings and cause surprisingly powerful

beneficial effects on distant wings. (Her muscle strength appears greatly enhanced, but in reality, a new coach has inspired her to workout more.) Consequently, she must learn to seek out these beneficial interactions, and must always try to maximize the functioning of each and every wing of her skating machine.

4. Because of the interdependence of her skating matrix, if you change one wing of it, you potentially change all the wings of it. A tiny change can result in a huge change in the overall appearance or functioning of the entire machine. (Her artistry, technical performance, enthusiasm and fan response have all decreased; in fact, the changes are related to her dislike of her new dance program.) This generalized matrix effect can be good or bad, but at the very least Kwan must learn to make changes with caution, wisely recognizing that each change has many possible ramifications, some potentially unforeseeable.

So it is with happiness machines. As with skating machines, the most important rules for uncovering happiness appear to deal with how the wings of the human matrix interact with each other.

You will recall that in part II, as we explored the nature of the human matrix, some simple generalizations regarding its use as a tool for uncovering happiness began to emerge. We had agreed to view our immediate state of happiness or unhappiness as being the net result of the interactions of the five wings of the human matrix. We had further acknowledged that it would be wise to review what is happening in each wing of the human matrix while recognizing that both our problems and their solutions might come from some unexpected corners.

Let's take these generalizations and transform them into more immediately useful specifics. We will accomplish this transformation by dissecting these ideas, expanding them, applying them to real world situations, exploring their nuances and providing them with specific names to make them more user-friendly and concrete.

As a guiding model we will use what we have already learned about the rules and principles that govern the matrix of Michelle Kwan's skating machine. In one shape or another, we will find that all four of the rules and principles described above, which apply so nicely to skating machines, apply equally nicely to happiness machines.

Each of the four concepts will be expanded upon sequentially in the four chapters of part III. If we are successful, as we come to the close of these chapters, we will have the same expertise concerning the rules of the happiness game that Michelle Kwan has about the rules of the skating game. We will have ourselves a rulebook for questing beasts who are trying to uncover happiness. It will serve as our owner's manual for our happiness machines. If it serves us well, it will help us to understand exactly how happiness machines work as well as the rules of the road that govern them. Like Kwan, our goal is gold. Like Kwan, I believe that armed with our rulebook, we all have a reasonable chance to win it.

I don't know all the rules, effects and principles of the human matrix—no one does—but I have a pretty good idea of some of the key ones. And there is no better time than the present to look at one of the most important, if not *the* most important, of these rules. To find it, we are going to go to a place that is always brimming over with the magic, mystery and drama to be found inside the human matrix. Our first stop is a psychiatrist's office—my own.

The Woman Who Insisted That She Loved Her Baby

Whenever a patient first enters my office, I am keenly aware that I am in the presence of a happiness machine. My patient is one of those flames described by Alan Watts, whose pattern is the net result of the interactions of the five wings of its matrix.

This constantly changing interaction is encapsulated with an elegant simplicity in the "Interdependence Rule." As you read it, you will undoubtedly notice that the Interdependence Rule is a direct translation of the first concept we discussed concerning Michelle Kwan's skating machine:

> All wings of the human matrix intersect and are interdependent upon one another.

When one wing of the human matrix impacts on another wing, as per the Interdependence Rule, the result is called a "matrix effect." As with Kwan's skating machine, the Interdependence Rule suggests that two different types of effects may result from such interactions. An effect can be for the good (a healing matrix effect) or for the bad (a damaging matrix effect).

It is the latter effect that interests us the most as we begin our exploration of the rules and principles governing the human matrix, for I have become convinced that unhappiness is often the result of such damaging matrix effects.

These damaging matrix effects can directly cause unhappiness (a problem on the psychological wing—bitterness—can cause a problem on the interpersonal wing, such as physical abuse to a partner). They can also indirectly cause unhappiness through vicious feedback loops that undermine the attitude of trust and the feeling of confidence that we have found to be so critical for maintaining happiness (a psychological problem—insecurity—makes one act awkwardly with other people on the interpersonal wing; the resulting unpleasant social interactions destroy any remaining trust or confidence).

Indeed, almost every patient who enters my office is besieged by a bevy of damaging matrix effects. The resulting knot of combined effects frequently proves to be so puzzling that the patient often has no idea where one problem ends and another begins.

The existence and power of damaging matrix effects is concisely described by our second rule, the "Damaging Matrix Rule":

Because there is interdependence in the wings of the human matrix, a problem on one wing can directly cause damage on a different wing.

Simple enough. But don't be fooled. Beneath this simplicity lies a complexity of presentations. The Damaging Matrix Rule shows many faces. Developing a sophisticated understanding of how and why these different faces appear is a critical first step in learning how to effectively use the human matrix model in our quest for happiness.

Our goal in this chapter is to look at three specific examples of the Damaging Matrix Rule as it plays out in the real world of flesh and blood. It is here that the theoretical will become practical, that the abstract will become concrete, that our simplistic understanding will become the sophisticated knowledge that we need to secure an enduring sense of happiness.

Our initial example of the Damaging Matrix Rule as it appears in flesh and blood is named Maria. I remember vividly the day that she first walked into my office.

When Maria entered, it was like a sparrow had alighted upon my windowsill—small steps, small frame, small hopes, rapid breaths and darting movements. She perched upright in the chair. She looked about the room uneasily.

A highly competent office manager, Maria had been functioning quite well until she gave birth to her fourth child. During the days following the birth she had experienced the ups and downs so typical of the early postpartum period.

During the subsequent weeks, despite her delight at the presence of her new baby, she became disturbingly anxious with a dash of moodiness thrown in. With her first three children, she had had somewhat similar feelings, but they were more marked by depression than anxiety, what many women experience as normal postpartum blues.

This time it was different. This time it was not normal. The first anxiety storm hit several weeks after delivery. She was driving her car when, out of nowhere, she felt as if something terrible, something very terrible was about to unfold. Within minutes her face began streaming sweat, her breathing rate jumped. She began to shake almost uncontrollably. And then . . . it happened.

Her heart began to beat outrageously quickly. Within moments she was paralyzed with the fear that she was dying of a heart attack. She jerked the car over to the side of the road. While she sat trembling behind the wheel, over the next twenty minutes, it passed. Like a summer thunderstorm, it vanished, disappearing inexplicably in the same fashion as it had come.

Soon enough such storms became more and more common. Some attacks were just as bad. Most were not—more like nasty summer squalls. She began to be hesitant to leave her house or drive her car for fear that the attacks would incapacitate her. She was haunted by the impression that people could tell when she was losing control, that, at those moments, the whole world could intuit that she could not handle even the mundane stresses of life.

Questions plagued her. "What if this happens in the grocery store?" "What if I begin crying in the movie theater?" "What if I become so distracted that I hit somebody with my car?" But, in the last analysis, it all came down to one burning question: "What the hell is the matter with me?"

Maria was phenomenally embarrassed by her attacks, for she perceived them as childish. She adored her new baby, and she felt robbed that she could not enjoy the experience of his early months, for she was preoccupied with the answer to her question, and she was plagued by her belief that, "I must be a phenomenally weak person—no one else acts like this." Moreover, some people had hinted that perhaps Maria had ambivalent feelings toward her child—an insinuation that bothered her deeply.

Beneath the onslaught of such self-denigrating thoughts, Maria weakened. Soon enough, she became quite depressed. At that point, she did something very fortuitous. She knocked on my door.

For her part, Maria acknowledged that there were stresses, but she insisted that she adored the newest addition to her family. Of course there were ambivalent feelings as some "well-wishers" had been hinting. Who wouldn't be ambivalent about sleeping only two-hour stretches at a time, juggling the lives of three other children with half the time available to do the juggling, all on top of these anxiety episodes?

But Maria gamely held her ground. She quietly but firmly insisted that she loved her baby and that, whatever ambivalence she was experiencing, it was normal for any new mother. After about thirty minutes in my office, I knew she was right.

As Maria described her feelings about her child, it was very clear to me that she held a normal attitude toward her newest addition. She and her husband both agreed on this point. The problem was not on the psychological or interpersonal wing of her matrix, although at first glance it might have seemed so. Further questioning revealed what many of you have already guessed: Maria had a classic example of a panic disorder, a surprisingly common condition that afflicts about 2 to 3 percent of the U.S. population over the course of their lives.

Her psychological storms were panic attacks. Her symptoms were right out of a basic textbook of psychiatry. Panic attacks—despite their psychological symptoms—seldom have their origins in the psychological wing of the matrix. Panic attacks are the result of a most devious damaging matrix effect. Our question becomes, "If her psychological symptoms are not being primarily caused by problems on the psychological wing of her matrix, then which wing of her matrix is causing the problems?"

Finding this answer takes us to a most unexpected location. The key to Maria's mystery, her attacks and the answer to her pain appears to be related to a small, placid lake. Above this lake, there is a locale with a simple yet lovely name, the Blue Place. It is to the Blue Place that we must now venture.

Lest this sound like the key to Maria's problem lies in the environmental wing of the human matrix, I should mention a few things about the lake beneath the Blue Place. One, we won't be walking there. Two, the lake is not made of mountain water. Three, we are talking tiny lake here. I mean *tiny* lake.

The length of our lake is measured in millimeters not miles. Its banks are filled not with H_2O, but with a crystalline clear oil called cerebrospinal fluid. The lake actually lies within Maria's brain and bares the admittedly unromantic name, the fourth ventricle. These ventricles sit at various locations in our brain providing, among many other things, a sort of shock absorber system for the brain, for these bodies of fluid allow the brain to absorb hits and blows with a bit more resilience and adaptive "squishiness" than would otherwise be possible.

The Blue Place actually has a Latin name—locus coeruleus—sounding ever so much like it was named for a Roman emperor. It was not. It was named because of a geographic peculiarity. The locus coeruleus, of which there is one sitting on either side of the brain stem's midline, appears to have a bluish tinge to its grayness. Quite lovely, in fact.

Inside these little mounds, the brain packs a bunch of neurons that all use the same neurotransmitter called norepinephrine. These neurons shoot extensions into all sorts of exotic-sounding locales of the brain with names such as the raphe nuclei, the hippocampus and the pons.

The locus coeruleus, among other things, functions like a rheostat that tells the brain when it should be cool and calm, have fun, or become hot and frenzied, for there is imminent danger present. Sometimes the rheostat, for no good reason at all, is set too sensitively. It mistakes peacetime for wartime. Such was the case inside Maria's brain—the result is unexpected bursts of panic triggered by stress levels that would not normally trigger panic. It is not uncommon, during the raging hormonal turmoil following pregnancy and delivery, that this rheostat can get upset. More recent research has suggested that several other brain structures—including the amygdala—and other neurotransmitters such as serotonin, play a more central role in the development of panic attacks than even the locus coeruleus.

The fear experienced during a panic attack is of the same intensity as if the brain was convinced that a gun was pointed at its own skull inches away. Brains don't like this idea very much. The rheostat goes nutso, resulting in intense feelings that severe danger is nearby. The extreme intensity of the brain's response is why people with panic attacks are truly terrified, sometimes to the point of incapacitation, despite the absence of an external danger.

I once had a Vietnam vet who had been in numerous firefights in Nam tell me, "I'm not shitting you. When I'm having one of these damn attacks in the stupid supermarket, I'm more frightened than I ever was in Nam. No shit, doc. I mean it." And he did.

With regard to Maria, once we had the correct wing of the matrix identified—biological—we could effectively use medications to directly reset her locus coeruleus. In the meantime, I was able to teach her some psychological techniques to help her manage the panic once it was triggered by the biological storm in her locus coereleus.

Using these approaches, Maria's panic attacks had decreased a bit by two weeks—not a lot but a bit. By four weeks they were decreasing significantly. By six weeks, our sparrow entered the office with a smile on her beak, if you can imagine such a thing. The attacks were vanishing. There were still occasional squalls, but they were rare. Even the squalls were rapidly disappearing. By two months, the panic attacks were gone.

We will be hard-pressed to find a more compelling example of the Damaging Matrix Rule at work. In this instance, the damaging effect begins in the biological wing and then spreads to the psychological wing, creating intense fear, anxiety and self-doubt. Sometimes the often associated depression, coupled with the anxiety attacks, proves to be too much on the psychological level. The patient becomes a victim of suicide.

It is worth noting that if we had not solved this riddle through our knowledge of the Damaging Matrix Rule, the damage could have not only become more devastating but also more pervasive, spreading insidiously into other wings of the matrix.

For instance, if panic attacks become disabling, problems often arise on the interpersonal wing of the matrix. As more and more of the house hold labor shifts to just one partner, for the patient has developed a fear of going out of the house lest an attack is precipitated (a problem called agoraphobia), the baffled partner often begins to feel both resentment and demoralization. Such anger can reach such proportions over ensuing years that divorce results, a striking example of a damaging matrix effect starting on the biological wing and spreading into the social system of the environmental wing of the matrix.

More destruction waits on the societal wing, for even businesses can be effected by the huge number of sick days resulting from panic attacks. Indeed, when one looks at the costs to our economy of all the anxiety disorders combined (disorders such as panic disorder, obsessive-compulsive disorder, generalized anxiety disorder and post-traumatic stress disorder), it is a bit staggering—an estimated $42.3 billion per year!

If we had any doubts that damaging matrix effects exist, they are long gone. Maria's example has given us a much more sophisticated understanding of the power of damaging matrix effects to cause extensive unhappiness, ranging from the individual to the society at large.

But there is one thing that Maria can't show us—the great diversity of disguises in which the Damaging Matrix Rule can show itself. Damage can hop from one wing to another. Damaging matrix effects have a nasty penchant for spreading rapidly, like a wildfire raging across the dry hills of Southern California, ultimately engulfing all the wings of the human matrix.

To better understand such effects, it is worth our while to see a second example of the Damaging Matrix Rule at work. This example will solidify our understanding of how damaging matrix effects work, how devious they are, and how important it is to seek them out.

Moreover, the damaging matrix effect I have chosen is a most fascinating one and answers a pressing question, "We have seen how a problem beginning in the brain can cause problems on the psychological and social wings of the matrix—panic attacks—but what of the reverse? Can a problem originating in the psychological or social wing cause structural damage to the brain or the body?"

To find the answer, we must move far away from my psychiatric office in Keene, New Hampshire. We are heading to Haller Gate, which stands guard in the wall surrounding the city of Nuremberg, Germany. The year is 1828. John Merrick has not even been born yet, and Queen Victoria still has a svelte silhouette.

The Boy Who Did Not Know How to Grow

In 1828 a small boy, looking about the age of ten, was found abandoned outside one of the city gates of Nuremberg. Times were harsh. It was not uncommon to come upon abandoned children, yet there was something out of the ordinary about this particular abandoned boy, Kaspar Hauser. A cryptic note was found in one of his hands stating little other than the fact that he was about sixteen years old. On closer examination, this smallish lad—about four feet eight inches tall—did indeed show the faint shadowings of an impending beard and the mustache typical of an adolescent. Ten years old he was not. Small, he was. At the time, he was viewed as a dwarf.

Kaspar Hauser had very little to say for himself, for his language development was primitive. He was limited to a few words and grunting sounds. His story would never have been pieced together had it not been for the fact that once Kaspar Hauser reached a safe haven, he was patiently tutored by some caring mentors. Eventually, Kaspar Hauser was able to both speak and write in German, albeit in a simple fashion.

The story he told holds the secret for which we are looking. It involved a pair of unknown hands, an inconspicuous packet of cells in an inconspicuous part of Hauser's brain called the pituitary gland, and a bunch of disobedient bones.

According to Kaspar's writings, for as long as he could remember he had always lived in a small, dark room. His only roommates were two ragged toy horses. Throughout his life his keepers purposefully, for reasons forever unknown, kept the boy in isolation—almost total isolation. He did not even see the faces of the people who fed him. Instead, unknown hands would slip Kaspar Hauser whatever meager gruel would be his lot for the day.

Once Kaspar fell into the hands of caring people, his life was remarkably changed, a situation reminiscent of John Merrick once within the hospital lodgings of Sir Frederick. But Kaspar's story is even more bizarre than the story of John Merrick, for something quite odd happened to Kaspar Hauser shortly after entering his new home. He grew big.

At first glance one might suggest that this growth spurt is not so remarkable, for the poor boy was finally getting some decent food. But here is the catch. Kaspar Hauser had not appeared markedly undernourished when found outside Haller Gate, just short.

With the story of Kaspar Hauser, we have stumbled upon one of the most remarkable examples of a damaging matrix effect I have ever come across. Curiously, the answer to our mystery will come not from Kaspar himself but from about a hundred Kaspar Hausers. You see, Kaspar Hauser had a rare syndrome, seen in about a hundred subsequent children, called psychosocial dwarfism. It was in these other children, some of whom have been studied with state of the art medical technology, that the truth about Kaspar Hauser finally emerged.

Children with psychosocial dwarfism (which was first described as the Kaspar Hauser syndrome by the gifted neuropsychoendocrinologist John Money) all have one thing in common. They come from a family matrix in which there is marked social deprivation, sometimes accompanied by physical/sexual abuse. They are exceedingly short, usually in the bottom 1–3 percent of height for their age group, although they are not necessarily undernourished.

They often have a plethora of other problems, including hyperactivity, depression, stunted language and a low IQ. Other odd behaviors may emerge, such as a tendency to voraciously seek food and water long after plenty of food and water has been made available to them. They have been known to gulp water from toilet bowls. They also suffer from a peculiar inability to feel pain. But it is their problem with growth that most interests us in our search for another example of the Damaging Matrix Rule at work.

Normal human growth is controlled by a complex neuroendocrine system, of which the star player is the pituitary gland, attached to the base of the brain by a narrow stalk and looking ever so slightly like a piece of cauliflower. Under normal circumstances, the pituitary exudes a hormone, appropriately enough called growth hormone (GH), that stimulates the bones and muscles of the body to grow.

In some unfortunate children, the pituitary does not secrete enough GH, and, as one would expect, these children do not grow well despite good nourishment. Untreated, permanent dwarfism can result. Fortunately, if this disease process is caught early enough, cases of poor growth can be fixed by giving these children GH from an outside source.

But children with psychosocial dwarfism do not fit this pattern. Unlike children whose growth is being stunted by a malfunctioning pituitary gland, the pituitaries of psychosocial dwarfs, who happen to have a variant called type II psychosocial dwarfism, are capable of secreting healthy amounts of GH. They just do not do so.

Right off the bat, it is important to emphasize that these children are often adequately nourished when first found despite their small stature (a few psychosocial dwarfs have been found who are even slightly overweight for their size). Unlike children living in good homes, if given replacement GH while still in their abusive homes, they do not grow. Their bones and muscles refuse to obey the cues from the now adequate levels of GH despite the fact that they have plenty of food. Very weird indeed!

Even more startling, if you take them out of their abusive homes, they immediately begin to grow without any replacement GH being given. As stated earlier, apparently their pituitaries had been capable of producing GH all along, but would not do so while the child was being abused. As soon as they break free from their torturers, these wayward pituitaries begin to secrete GH, and the muscles of these children begin to obey it.

I don't think we will come across a much more striking illustration of the Damaging Matrix Rule. Here we have a damaging matrix effect which begins on the social wing of the matrix—extreme family neglect—and somehow manages to cause striking damage on the biological wing— markedly stunted growth.

It fascinates me that social mistreatment can make the pituitary gland malfunction with the result that it secretes inadequate amounts of GH. But it absolutely astounds me that, somehow or other, this same social abuse makes the bones of the child refuse to respond to GH even if it is injected directly into the child's bloodstream. Now *that's* a damaging matrix effect.

Before leaving the strange and sad tale of Kaspar Hauser, I should add one more detail that would qualify his story for inclusion in any contemporary soap opera. Five years after he was found alive, Kaspar Hauser was found to be quite dead—murdered. It was rumored, though not substantiated, that his brutal upbringing had been at the hands of nobility. It was further rumored that these nobles were not too keen on their identity being made known. What we do know is that Kaspar was murdered by someone who was promising to tell him the truth about his origins. Enough said.

For our third and final example of a damaging matrix effect, let's take a look at one that starts in the environmental wing of the matrix and once again causes damage to the biological wing. Only this time, instead of affecting one hundred people in four hundred years, it affects about ten million Americans every single year.

There is also something else different about this particular example of the Damaging Matrix Rule. It is not the human aspect of the environmental wing that causes the damage. It is the nonhuman part of the environmental wing that does the dirty deed. It is sunlight or, more correctly, a lack of it.

The Case of M, Strange Light Gizmos and Even Stranger Prescriptions

We don't have to travel far from the world of Kaspar Hauser in time nor place to meet our next patient. M, whose identity we know only by a single letter, is being treated for a psychiatric condition in nearby France. The year is 1825. M is in the care of one of the most illustrious early pioneers in the field of psychiatry named Esquirol.

M is going to provide us with our last look at the Damaging Matrix

Rule in action. I particularly like this example because it is so common and it is of immediate practicality in finding happiness. In fact, I have no doubt that what you are about to read will change the lives of some readers much for the better.

In many respects, M appears to be suffering from a garden variety depression. Previously, M looked like he had all the wings of his matrix in pretty good working order. He had a strong constitution and was a well-respected businessman. He loved his wife and had a happy home life. But for the last three years there has been a slight problem. Well . . . not so slight. We will let M describe it in his own words.

> It was at the beginning of autumn, and I became sad, gloomy and susceptible. By degrees I neglected my business and deserted my house to avoid my uneasiness. I felt feeble, and drank beer and liquors. Soon I became irritable. Everything opposed my wishes, disturbed me and rendered me insupportable, and even dangerous to my family. My affairs suffered from this state. I suffered also from insomnia and inappetence. Neither the advice nor tender counsels of my wife, nor that of my family, had any more influence over me. At length, I fell into a profound apathy, incapable of everything except drinking and grieving.

I think it is pretty safe to say that M was a mess. We are seeing a massive matrix meltdown. But the question is, "Why?" And even more to the point, "Which wing of the matrix is causing the meltdown, for they all appear to be affected?" The clue to the answer lies in his very next sentences:

> At the approach of spring I felt my affections revive. I recovered all my intellectual activity and all my ardor for business. I was very well all the ensuing summer, but from the commencement of the damp and cold weather of autumn, there was a return of sadness, uneasiness and a desire to drink to dissipate my sadness. There was also a return of irascibility and transports of passion.

One can only wonder what M means by "transports of passion." Nevertheless, the problems of M seemed to be distinctly triggered by the seasonal decrease in daylight seen in the autumn and winter months. Esquirol, who was an eminently practical man, had just the right prescription, strange as it might seem. He told M that at the first sign of autumn, he needed to get his butt out of Dodge, take a hike to the beaches on the South of France, and by the close of October he had better be sunning himself in Italy, not to return till the month of May.

If your doctor gives you that type of prescription, and you have enough money to fill it, you'd be crazy not to take your medicine. M did. He had a blast in Italy. And, as long as he followed the good doctor's orders every autumn, he never had any more trouble with depression.

M is one of the earliest and best documented cases of a specific form of depression called seasonal affective disorder (SAD for short). As mentioned earlier, SAD afflicts about ten million Americans every year in its full blown fury. Another twenty-five million Americans get a much milder form of seasonal depression that we sometimes call "the winter blues" or "winter blahs."

SAD is a marvelous example of a damaging matrix effect that begins on the environmental wing of the human matrix and interpenetrates into the biological wing with rather disastrous results. Let's take a closer look at the science behind this particular damaging matrix effect.

The science is not known for certain, but it seems very likely that SAD has to deal with our internal calendars. Many mammals and other vertebrates are exquisitely tuned to the turning of the seasons.

There is a time to mate, there is a time to plant wheat, there is a time to harvest wheat, there is a time to migrate. Our internal calendar also does double duty as a clock. There is a time to go to sleep. There is a time to wake up. There is a time to eat. There is a time to have sex, although most males of our species think the sex thing is just dandy all the time.

In any case, we seem to have a reasonable idea of the location of this internal calendar/clock. It is a tiny gland in the brain called the pineal gland that secretes a molecule called melatonin. When a bunch of melatonin squirts out at night, we tend to get sleepy.

Here is where the Damaging Matrix Rule enters the picture. Sunlight tends to decrease melatonin secretion and darkness seems to increase it. Prolonged darkness as occurs in autumn and winter may trigger unusual amounts of accumulated melatonin. Some susceptible people—like M— tend to develop depressive symptoms if there is too much melatonin onboard.

If you find yourself becoming significantly depressed in the autumn/ winter months with marked relief come summer, you may very well have SAD. Consult your doctor, and see what he or she thinks. Help may be right around the corner.

Concerning help, antidepressants often are of value, and some forms of psychotherapy can also be of benefit. But here is where a strange gizmo may be just what the doctor ordered, and it's a lot cheaper than a three month vacation in Italy. It's not as much fun though.

Sitting about thirty minutes a day beneath a specialized lightbox often does the trick with SAD. Such daily light showers can frequently keep seasonal depressions away. These lightboxes shine with about 10,000 lux. For the sake of comparison, normal indoor light is about 100 to 150 lux. It's a bit of a dirty trick on our pineal gland—faking summer—but it is for a good cause.

By the way, with the example of our lightbox, we are seeing a nice illustration of a healing matrix effect, a topic which will soon be a major focus of our attention. But let's first wrap up our discussion of damaging matrix effects.

With just two simple rules, the Interdependence Rule and its associated Damaging Matrix Rule, we have come upon some invaluable insights regarding our quest for happiness. Clearly, all is not as simple as it first seems once inside the human matrix. Because of interdependence, we have learned that damage on one wing can clearly cause severe damage on other wings.

If we find ourselves unhappy, not infrequently the most obvious solutions may prove to be the least effective, for they offer solutions to the wrong problems—the wrong wing of the matrix is being addressed. Someone is telling Maria to get rid of her ambivalent feelings toward her newborn, GH is being given to a kid who is still living in the abusive home that is stunting his growth, M is being told to get his spiritual and familial priorities in order. All of these "obvious" solutions are doomed to failure, for they are not addressing the core problem that lies hidden on a not-so-obvious wing of the matrix.

In fact, now that we have three vivid examples of the Damaging Matrix Rule under our belts, each one illustrating just how differently the rule can manifest itself, it is time to take both of our matrix rules one step further. As we mentioned earlier, the astounding quality of Michelle Kwan lies in her ability to creatively maximize her performance within the limitations of the rules that bind it. Her triumphs serve as a constant reminder that to a champion athlete, rules do not set limitations, they suggest possibilities.

To a champion player in the happiness game, both the Interdependence Rule and the Damaging Matrix Rule are filled with such possibilities. With the addition of just one more rule, these possibilities will coalesce into two strategic principles that will help to make us winners in the happiness game. That rule and the possibilities it unleashes are the business of our next chapter.

12

Slumber Parties
and Red Herrings

*"Things do not pass for what they are,
but for what they seem."*

BALTASAR GRACIAN
SPANISH PHILOSOPHER, CIRCA 1600s

A High School Fiasco, An Unexpected Knock
and Something Kinda Strange

In this chapter we will look at an enigmatic patient from my clinical practice of years ago. With this patient we will encounter an admittedly confusing mass of damaging matrix effects. Like a giant ball of tightly knotted and shredding twine, it will strain our understanding to sort it all out, which is good. It is from this complexity that the third rule governing the human matrix—the Red Herring Rule—will emerge. We will not define the Red Herring Rule just yet, for I feel it is more instructive to let our teacher do the defining for us.

Our teacher is a most unlikely candidate, a fifteen-year-old girl, in a most unlikely school, an emergency room. The girl's name is Sally. She awaits us in a small western Pennsylvanian town. The year is 1982.

At the time, I was a young psychiatric resident from Western Psychiatric Institute and Clinic in Pittsburgh who was moonlighting—making some extra bucks—in the emergency department (the ED) at a local hospital on weekends. I enjoyed the work immensely. The staff was excellent. We helped a lot of people. And the darndest stuff walked into that ED. I learned something every weekend that I was on-call there.

At about four one Saturday morning I got a wake-up call in my hotel room. "Dr. Shea, we have an emergency down here for you to see." I pulled on my pants, swished some mouthwash and drove down to the ED. What met me there were three sets of worried eyes. There were two sets of very worried parent eyes and one set of sort-of-worried adolescent eyes—Sally's.

Sally's parents were making their third trip seeking medical advice in the past two weeks. Nobody seemed to be able to help their daughter, and everybody had told them the same thing "Your daughter is hysterical. She needs to see a therapist." Mr. and Mrs. Thompson didn't know exactly what to make of that advice, because hysterical or not, there was something "not right—big time" with their daughter. And, according to her parents, the problems all began, innocently enough, with a slumber party.

If you will recall, the environmental wing of the human matrix is composed of two parts. The environment can consist of nonsocial elements—tornadoes, diseases and stock markets—or it can consist of social elements—families, business teams and friends at slumber parties.

Thus Sally's problems, if indeed they began with a slumber party, were a part of the social aspect of the environmental wing of her matrix. Let us see how the difficulties started on this wing and subsequently, illustrating both the Interdependence Rule and the Damaging Matrix Rule, caused big problems in other wings of Sally's matrix.

Sally was a somewhat awkward adolescent, sort of pretty but not pretty enough to be with the "in crowd"; a good cheerer, but not good enough to be a cheerleader; a good student, but not good enough to make the honor roll; a good time, but not a good enough time to be invited to the "right parties" in school.

The trouble erupted about two weeks ago, when Sally threw a slumber party. The only trouble with the party was that no one chose to slumber — no one came.

For an adolescent girl, there can't be a much bigger fiasco in the social wing of the matrix. Sally was crushed. She feigned sickness on Monday and Tuesday to avoid what she projected would be a round of brutal giggles and looks. I don't know about you, but at that age, I would probably have done the same thing.

It is here that the first leak occurred. Over the following days the Damaging Matrix Rule took hold, and the problem in her environmental wing began to spread into her interpersonal wing. Sally withdrew from each of her parents. For an outsider like Sally, her parents had always been her only "in crowd." Now, she could not even face them.

At nights, Sally's parents could sometimes hear Sally sobbing behind the door of her bedroom. Occasionally, much to their relief, they might hear a giggle or two or, perhaps, even a spontaneous laugh generated by a favorite TV show. Sally had quickly changed channels from the uncontrollable halls of her high school to whatever escape she could find while surfing the much more controllable channels of her television screen.

The insidious power of the Damaging Matrix Rule now began to show itself even more dramatically, for the problem on her social wing proceeded to infiltrate a third wing of her matrix—the psychological wing. Sally became atypically moody. Homework was left undone and her room was left cluttered. Her concentration was shot. She felt irritable and even angry at times.

We will now see one of those nasty feedback loops that we mentioned earlier, for the disruption on her psychological wing—her moodiness and irritability—reinfected the interpersonal wing from which it originated. Sally began to demonstrate behaviors that were unusual for her.

Her parents had a hard time describing them, but their daughter was somehow more provocative than normal. Sally Thompson had become just a bit of a "wise-ass." It made her parents uncomfortable, and such behaviors were surely what the previous clinicians had been alluding to when they had called her "hysterical."

Her parents defensively rationalized Sally's atypical behavior to themselves thinking, "If no one comes to your slumber party and you are a fifteen-year-old adolescent girl, it hurts bad . . . real bad. You get irritable. You get angry. You hysterically act out. That's just the way it is. She's in a lot of pain. We need to help her." They felt helpless to do so. Over the past two weeks, Sally was not the only one in the Thompson household who sometimes wept behind closed doors.

What a mess! It is about to get messier. Is the primary problem now psychological—her depression? Is it social—isolation? Is it interpersonal—angry outbursts with her dad or mom? Which really came first? Which is now worst? Where does one begin to transform this matrix gone awry? After an angry exchange with her mother, Sally now withdraws even more, an action that results in a deepening of her depression. Now what? As one can see, these damaging matrix effects have created an immensely confusing maelstrom. Sally and her parents are in the middle of it. It doesn't end here.

Like Sally, her parents are finding themselves to be both distraught and demoralized. To their own shock, they too have become irritable. They have begun arguing with each other. The slumber party problem has jumped matrices! It is now causing havoc in the interpersonal wings of both her parents. It even infiltrated the last medical clinic they attended, where Mr. Thompson had an angry exchange with a nurse after she said there was nothing "really wrong with your daughter that a therapist couldn't help."

To me, as I initially began unraveling the knot, it sounded like Sally was experiencing a depressive reaction to a very painful stressor on the social wing of her matrix, especially to an adolescent outsider like Sally, who was particularly vulnerable to such a wound. I felt very badly for Sally and for her distraught parents.

It was clear that, secondary to a bevy of damaging matrix effects, her pain was now invading all sorts of systems. By this point, there could even be a damaging matrix effect on the biological wing of her matrix. It is not uncommon for prolonged interpersonal or social stress to cause a disruption in the biochemistry of the brain that controls mood, not unlike the damaging matrix effect we have already seen with Kaspar Hauser and psychosocial dwarfism. Only this time, the result is not stunted growth, it is stunted mood.

These concurrent biological depressions can greatly complicate the already present reactive depression. Biological depressions, in addition to causing depressed mood, can wreak havoc with all sorts of physiological processes controlled by the brain. The resulting symptoms include disrupted sleep patterns, poor or increased appetite, low energy, poor concentration, lack of interest in doing activities and even disrupted sexual drive. Sally was clearly showing some of these. What was not clear was whether these symptoms were related to her reactive depression or were new symptoms caused by a new damaging matrix effect—a biological depression triggered by her social stress.

The bottom line in that ED in a sleepy town in western Pennsylvania was simple. The human matrix known as Sally Thompson was wildly awry. Before I made any treatment suggestions, I clearly needed more information. The first place to start was with her parents.

Sally's parents were examples of "the salt of the earth," hard-working, no-nonsense and in love with each other and with their only daughter. As our conversation warmed up, I intermittently asked the typical questions one asks in an ED. "Had their daughter used drugs?" "No." "Did she talk of suicide?" "No." "Had she been doing anything particularly strange such as hearing voices or describing delusions?" "No."

It was here that Mrs. Thompson glanced over at her husband, as if to inquire, "Should we mention it?"

I looked at Mr. Thompson, then back to Mrs. Thompson. She averted my gaze.

"Well?" I asked gently.

Mr. Thompson let out a sigh, "Well, she did do something kinda strange, but she's not crazy or something like that, doc."

I nodded my reassurance.

"No, she doesn't normally do strange things, I just think she was sleep-walking or something. People do strange things when they sleepwalk, don't they?"

I once again nodded in a comforting fashion.

"Well," Mr. Thompson continued, "Several nights ago she did do something kinda strange." He looked sheepishly towards his wife, "You tell him, dear."

Mrs. Thompson picked up the storyline. "It was about three in the morning. We had noticed that Sally had not been sleeping very well for several nights but just thought it was part of her depression."

I nodded, indicating it made sense to me.

"It really was sort of strange though, what happened, I mean. At three, Sally knocked softly on our door but loud enough that it woke us."

"That doesn't sound that strange," I said, trying to be reassuring.

Mr. Thompson chimed in, "It is, Doc, if when you open your door, your daughter is standing there topless."

"Topless?"

"Yup. Not a stitch on her top, and she just said, 'I need to talk to you guys.'"

"Yeah, that is kind of strange. I'm assuming that such behavior is way out of character for Sally?"

Both parents, scrunched their faces as in, "Way, way, way out of character."

To reassure them I commented, "Well, maybe she was sleepwalking," although this explanation seemed unlikely to me.

"Maybe." Mr. Thompson responded.

"What happened next?"

"She just said that she needed to talk." Mr. Thompson paused, "Then we just talked for about fifteen minutes."

"What did she talk about?"

"Lots of stuff. Sort of rambled on."

His wife quickly added, "But most of it was about the party and how miserable she felt, you know, how embarrassed and all."

"Was she making sense?"

"Oh yeah," Mr. Thompson chirped, "she was all upset about the party." I nodded. "Let me go talk to her. Maybe we might be able to help her."

Both Mr. and Mrs. Thompson looked at one another and gave a sigh of relief.

Devilish Eyes, Looking for Reality and a Ticket into the Hospital

When I entered the exam room, Sally was dressed in a hospital gown and sitting pertly upon the examining table. Her brownish hair, perhaps away from a shampoo bottle for a longer time than advisable, was hanging forlornly over her shoulders. Her hair was tired but not her brown eyes.

There was a bit more of a devilish look to them than I had expected from a girl who I knew to be quite depressed. Apparently, Sally was beaten down by the happenings on the social wing of her matrix, but she was still able to pick herself back up—a good sign.

When I raised the topic of the failed slumber party, she readily admitted her great disappointment and her social shame. "I guess I'm the class clown, and I don't want to be."

Apparently, one of her "friends" really gave her a ribbing in front of a group of fellow students, and the shrill cackles of the teasing still were bounding about the halls of the social wing of Sally's matrix. She was taking a serious pounding. Just as we had predicted, there was great leakage into the psychological and interpersonal wings of her matrix. Sally was a flame about to go out.

Sally described being quite sad and readily admitted that she had been having a hard time not crying. She didn't feel like calling her one best friend—another outsider who was big on braces and pimples. Sally complained that she wasn't sleeping well and that her concentration was shot.

I could attest to the latter fact, for Sally had an almost irritating way of not paying attention to me. Her eyes looked over my shoulders, down to the floor, and then almost directly into me, in a way that had an almost flirtatious feel to it. I could see how previous clinicians had accurately picked up on an "hysteric" quality to her, but I didn't see it as a very strong one. Until . . . until Sally Thompson looked up from the floor, looked me right in the eyes and with a tart smile asked, "What is reality, Dr. Shea?"

I was a bit caught off guard by the clearly wise-guy quality of the question. "I'm not entirely sure what you mean by the question, Sally, but we're trying to find out what your own reality is regarding some of the pain you've been feeling about the party, about school and how I might be able to help you tonight." Sally gave me a sideways glance, and then winked, as if to say, "Not bad, Dr. Shea, not bad at all." I must admit I found the exchange a bit unnerving. I thought I might be hearing the song "Tubular Bells" quietly playing in the back halls of my head.

At which point Sally sighed. The wise-guy smirk vanished, and she whispered softly, almost forlornly, "Yeah, I guess I do need some help. I don't know what's wrong with me." And then Sally Thompson began to weep.

I suddenly felt intensely sorry for Sally. Life was giving her a tremendous thrashing. I tried to comfort her and got her a box of Kleenex. As I handed her the Kleenex she smiled. Her pain had a relentless urgency. At that moment, her pain pushed its way into my own matrix. I sighed. It was a sad sigh. The rest of the interview was uneventful, although Sally continued to be mildly distracted.

I did a Folstein Mini-Mental Status on Sally, which is a specialized set of questions to pick up the presence of any problems with actual thinking process, concentration or memory that might suggest a delirium or street-drug use. Unsuspected drug use had crossed my mind. No problems. Her Folstein was as clean as a whistle; she was a bit slow on some answers but always correct. She denied any headaches, chills, nausea, muscle aches, stiffness or fever.

I decided that I should do a careful physical exam, with a particularly thorough neurological exam, because I was still nagged by the bits of oddness in her history that were not typical for a classic reactive depression. On the other hand, I had long since learned that each person's personality made "classic presentations" as atypical as a McDonald's on Rodeo Drive in Beverly Hills. Maybe there was just enough of a hysteric quality to Sally's personality that these defenses had been called into play to help protect her from the immense pain she was obviously experiencing.

I stepped out of the exam room for a moment to get my doctor's bag. When I returned, Sally was nowhere to be seen. I found her quickly enough. She was poking around behind a curtain that wound about an examination table down the hall.

"Sally, what are you doing?"

She dropped the curtain back, looking startled, and answered, "Oh, I'm sorry Dr. Shea, I got bored in there, and I was just curious what was behind all these curtains."

She was easily directed back to the exam room, and the physical examination was uneventful. The neurological exam was clean—no abnormalities.

Time to get back to her parents with a plan.

As soon as I approached them, Mrs. Thompson blurted, "Do you think she is hysterical?"

I shook my head sideways, "No. No, I really don't. There's a bit of that quality, but I don't think that's the real problem here."

They both looked relieved. Mrs. Thompson continued, an urgent plea to her voice, "She's depressed, isn't she?"

"Yes", I said. "Yes, she is. And I think we need to do something to help her. I agree with you, she's in a lot of pain."

Mrs. Thompson sighed with relief and glanced at her husband, "We knew there was something wrong. We knew she wasn't just hysterical. We knew she was depressed."

My next question caught them just a bit off guard. "Are you absolutely sure she is not using drugs?"

Mr. Thompson entered the conversation, "We don't think so." He glanced back to his wife. "I suppose a parent can't be absolutely sure of anything though these days, now can they, Doc?"

I gave a quick nod of agreement on that one.

"Are you suspicious she is?" he asked.

"Just sort of. There is something a bit unusual about her behavior, and we have that odd incident several nights ago with you all to explain. You sometimes can see that sort of unpredictable behavior with drugs or perhaps a seizure. I really don't know what to make of it just now."

Mrs. Thompson asked, "What should we do?"

I answered, "If it is okay with both of you, I would like to bring Sally into the hospital to observe her for awhile and see what we might be able to do to help her with her depression, and make sure there is nothing medically wrong with her."

It is hard to put into words the intensity of the looks of relief that flashed across both of their faces. "Oh, thank God! We knew there was something wrong, but nobody would do anything about it," Mrs. Thompson exclaimed.

I continued, "If there are drugs onboard, the effects will probably wear off pretty quickly, and if there is a problem with drugs we need to know about it. Naturally, we will help her to get some relief from her depression, and we will do a lot of talking with her about what happened with her party and her sense of isolation. We have some great therapists here. And if medications might help, we will consider using them too. Let's just see how she does first. I think she'll be just fine."

And that was it. I had ordered some blood work. Her blood count was normal and her vital signs—blood pressure, pulse and temperature—were fine. It was about six in the morning. It was time for me to go home to

Pittsburgh to start my regular work week.

One of my last suggestions before I left the ED was that the inpatient unit do a thorough medical workup, including an immediate neurological consult. A specialist could more ably rule out the distinct possibility of temporal lobe epilepsy, a disease that can make one show strange behaviors outside bedroom doors. The specialist could also check for things such as infections and endocrine disorders, although her lack of abnormal physical findings made such things seem less likely. I had already ordered a drug screen.

At this point we have accomplished our goal for this chapter. We have seen first hand a complex example of the Interdependence Rule and the damaging matrix effects that follow in its wake. We have a picture-perfect example of trauma on the social end of the environmental wing—the slumber party fiasco—quickly interacting with several other wings of the matrix. The trauma on Sally's social wing profoundly impacted on other wings, not only of her matrix, but of her parent's matrix, and even mine, an interpersonal jumping of matrices. We have also seen how ferociously quickly damaging matrix effects can spread across wings and how readily they can present a confusing picture as to where the core of the problem lies.

But there is one thing we haven't seen yet—the truth.

An Unpleasant Telephone Conversation and Red Herrings Galore

It was time for the two-hour drive back home. My work was done. But once I got back to the tiny apartment that Susan and I inhabited in Pittsburgh, which we affectionately called "the Small Place," I found myself intermittently thinking about Sally Thompson. I had really liked both Sally and her parents, and I prayed that everything was okay.

Several days later, I decided to see how she was doing. Perhaps she was even getting ready for discharge. I was also curious to see what the psychiatric unit had found. Had they discovered any missing puzzle pieces? I called the hospital's psychiatric unit to get an update. I wasn't prepared for what I heard.

Sally was no longer on the psychiatric unit. She had been transferred to the intensive care unit (ICU). She was unconscious. Sally Thompson was in danger of dying from viral encephalitis. An image of the faces of her parents flashed across the screen of my mind. I remembered saying to them, "I think she'll be just fine."

Over the receiver I heard a distant voice saying, "Doctor. . . . Doctor, are you still there?"

I said, "Yeah. Thanks. I'll give a call over to the ICU." There was a click. I gently put the receiver down.

It had all been a pack of red herrings. Don't get me wrong, the slumber party fiasco was quite damaging to Sally and had caused many damaging matrix effects. But it was a massive red herring. It had absolutely nothing to do with why Sally Thompson found herself in an ED on a hot summer night in July.

The main problem with Sally Thompson, and it was a life-threatening one, was not to be found on the social wing of her matrix or the interpersonal wing, or the psychological wing for that matter. It was hiding on her biological wing, where millions and millions of virions were busily at work.

And the core problem—a pack of virions attacking on her biological wing—had remained hidden for weeks because of the slumber party red herring and, in part, because of another set of red herrings: the remarkably striking problems the infection was causing on the other wings of Sally Thompson's matrix. These distant effects on the psychological, interpersonal and social wings of her matrix were so pronounced that they gave the erroneous impression that these wings were the main site of her problem.

It was the brain damage caused by the invading virions that explained the oddities of Sally's behavior on the interpersonal wing from her simple abnormalities—inattention and inappropriate wanderings in the ED—to her more complex enigmas—her playful "question on reality" and her inexplicable topless appearance at her parent's door at three in the morning.

Most likely this biological damage was also causing many of the symptoms on her psychological wing, including the disruptions in concentration, sleep, energy and even her depressive mood. The encephalitis was also busy casting red herrings on her interpersonal wing, for it probably had much to do with her irritability and "wise-guy" interactions. Moreover, although some of her need to isolate on the social wing of her matrix was probably related to a reactive depression caused by the slumber party fiasco, social withdrawal is often seen in encephalitis. Even her social wing could not escape the effects of the swarming virions.

The entire picture was confused by the coincidental damage on the social wing—the ill-fated slumber party—that seemed to so readily explain Sally's depression, coupled with the damaging matrix effects caused by the virions in her brain. All red herrings! As Sir Eddington discovered once he stepped inside the atom, and as Baltasar Gracian warned at the beginning of our chapter, things are not always what they seem once one steps inside the human matrix.

Sally Thompson has proven to be a better teacher than we could have ever expected. She has given us the crucial ingredients to understand the third rule of the human matrix in the sophisticated fashion it warrants. As mentioned earlier, this rule is aptly called the Red Herring Rule:

> Because of interdependence and damaging matrix effects, a problem on one wing of the matrix may cause such severe problems on a different wing that one is misled as to where the real problem lies.

Such misleading coincidences are all too common in human matrices. Indeed, all three of the examples of the damaging matrix effects from our last chapter—Maria's panic attacks, Kaspar Hauser's dwarfism and the seasonal affective disorder of M—were all examples of red herrings that could have all too easily tricked unseasoned participants in the happiness quest. Without a good rule book on hand, wrong turns can be common in the sometimes treacherous pathways of the human matrix.

Sally adds yet another level of complexity. She brilliantly shows the enormity of confusion that can be caused by the interdependence of the wings of the human matrix, the simultaneous appearance of multiple damaging matrix effects, and the resulting picture of a happiness machine plagued by red herrings galore.

As with our champion skaters, we can now look beyond the three rules of the human matrix to the principles of action that they imply. These strategic principles will prove to be quite handy at helping us to pick apart any complicated knots of unhappiness that happen to come our way in the future.

The first principle is called, with a tip of the hat to the vintage (never say "oldies") British rock group The Who, the Won't Get Fooled Again Principle:

> No matter how obvious it appears that one wing is the cause of the current state of unhappiness or disruption, search all other wings before deciding where the main problem lies.

If one follows the Won't Get Fooled Again Principle, it is much less likely that one will end up following a red herring as one tries to uncover happiness in a difficult situation. One can also move with a greater sense of trust and confidence, for one is less likely to fall into unexpected traps, all of which can make it much harder to find happiness and a few of which— as in the case of Sally Thompson—could lead to catastrophic results.

With Sally, my understanding of the rules and principles of the human matrix had kept me open to the idea that there might be potential hidden problems in the biological wing of her matrix. Consequently, she was admitted to the hospital and given the prompt and appropriate medical evaluation and interventions that would hopefully prove to be lifesaving.

The Won't Get Fooled Again Principle has a closely allied second principle that shows yet another good reason to always check all five wings of the human matrix for problems.

Even if one finds, as is often the case, that the originally suspected wing is the main problem (e.g., no red herrings), there may be problems on other wings that are still causing enough damaging matrix effects of a lesser nature that they warrant our attention. This realization leads to our second principle for effectively navigating the human matrix called the Cast a Wide Net Principle:

> No matter what the apparent cause of the immediate unhappiness, look at all wings of the matrix for contributing problems related to smaller yet still damaging matrix effects.

In short, when trying to deal with a problem that is causing us unhappiness, it is probably expedient to vigorously look at all wings, not just to prevent misadventures with red herrings, but also to clear out any problems that may be contributing ongoing damage to our happiness machine or causing it to function less than optionally. Sometimes a collection of small problems on multiple wings of the matrix can result in a composite picture of surprisingly major dysfunction and unhappiness.

Sally is a perfect example. If her clinicians eventually manage to save her life, she still has many problems with which to deal. She still underwent the social stigmatization caused by the slumber party fiasco. She will still feel isolated. She may still be quite depressed and be wracked with feelings of self-denigration and worthlessness. And there may still be problems with her relationships with her classmates and perhaps even her parents.

These problems on the different wings of her matrix have the potential to interact with each other, exacerbate one another and significantly interfere with her recovery from her encephalitis. Unchecked, they could even prove to be life threatening—suicide.

For Sally to develop an enduring sense of happiness, all of these problems will need to be addressed. Sally, and those people trying to help her, will have to cast a wide net indeed. But it will be a net well worth casting.

We have come to the end of our exploration of the Red Herring Rule, the Won't Get Fooled Again Principle, and the Cast a Wide Net Principle. We are starting to develop a pretty nice rule book concerning the human matrix and its intricacies.

As we conclude, it seems appropriate to end with a quotation by George L. Engel, who was one of the first physicians to think like a quantum mechanic:

> *Nothing exists in isolation. Whether a cell or a person, every system is influenced by the configuration of the systems of which each is a part, that is, by its environment.*

Engel's words point us in a new direction of inquiry, for one can sense a hint of promise in them. Thus far we have focused on the negative impact of matrix effects. If Engel is correct, there is every reason to believe that the influences "by the configurations of which we are all a part" could also be beneficial in nature.

In case of point, Engel was well known for his ability to help his patients by capitalizing on just such beneficial matrix interactions. We shall call these positive influences "healing matrix effects." Our next chapter is filled with examples of such effects and practical ways of using them.

13 The Woman Who Wanted God's Telephone Number

"Just a spoonful of sugar helps the medicine go down . . ."

MARY POPPINS

When Magic Bullets Fail

There are no magic bullets in medicine, but sometimes our medications are so effective that one suspects the presence of magic. This circumstance is particularly striking with medications that combat diseases caused by bacteria, such as pneumonia and strep throat. For instance, if the infection that was invading Sally's brain had been bacterial in nature, the potentially lifesaving result caused by the administration of an antibiotic could well have seemed magical in nature.

This "magic bullet" quality is also true when we are dealing with diseases caused by the body's inability to produce a substance that healthy bodies are supposed to produce, as is the case in diabetes, where there is a lack of insulin production. When we give insulin to such people the result is arguably magical. The medication saves their lives.

Similarly some mental disorders, not all, are primarily biological in nature, such as schizophrenia, bipolar disorder and dementia. As we saw with Maria and her panic attacks, it was a lack of certain neurotransmitters in her locus coeruleus and amygdala that was wreaking havoc upon her life. Indeed, just as one would when providing insulin to a person with diabetes, we returned her neurotransmitters to their normal state of balance through the use of an antidepressant. The result proved to be remarkably effective.

Sometimes, though, the magic bullets don't work. The bacteria have developed resistance, the body does not react normally to the additional insulin, the neurons stubbornly refuse to respond to the increases in neurotransmitters caused by the antidepressants. In other instances the medications work but the side effects prove to be too problematic to tolerate.

At first glance, in such situations physicians appear to be hopelessly stymied. The patient has a clear-cut disturbance on the biological wing of his or her matrix, and the physician has no method of directly altering the biological abnormality. No effective interventions appear to be at hand. No magic bullets await our touch. It is here that a second glance, a quantum glance taken from the perspective of the human matrix, offers the hint of hope.

From our understanding of damaging matrix effects we are aware that problems originating on a nonbiological wing of the matrix can directly cause great damage on the biological wing itself. The abusive environment on the social wing of Kaspar Hauser's matrix created pathophysiology on his biological wing. It decreased his production of growth hormone, changed how his bones responded to growth hormone and stunted his growth dramatically. Is the reverse possible?

The Interdependence Rule suggests that it might be. Because all the matrix wings interlace, theoretically, we should be able to do something on one wing of a matrix that creates a positive change on a distant wing, the so-called healing matrix effects described at the end of our last chapter.

More specifically to our current dilemma—what to do when our magic bullets fail—can an intervention on the psychological, interpersonal, environmental, or spiritual wings in the real world of everyday living cause lasting benefits on the biological wing? Can an intervention on a nonbiological wing of the matrix reverse pathophysiology on the biological wing? Can we heal flesh without magic bullets?

To find the answers we shall look into the blue eyes of a very troubled boy of eight. He has a secret. Nobody can know it, not his teacher, not his sister, not even his parents. But the secret is deeply disturbing to him. It keeps him awake at night. It gnaws at him almost every waking minute. And it makes him do something that he hates doing but he feels compelled to do.

What his secret is, what it makes him do and how he was helped to stop doing it will provide answers to the pressing questions posed above. I met Nick through an informal consultation. I soon found myself both fascinated and touched by his strength and his pain. His story will lead us to one of the most compelling examples of a healing matrix effect that I have ever come across. It made a believer of me. I think it will make a believer of you.

Nick, who was capped by a mop of delightfully untameable black hair, had always been precocious. He spoke early and, to his parent's delight, he spoke often. By eight he had the vocabulary of a twelve-year-old. He also had shown remarkable abilities at drawing. Sociable and unusually kind for a boy of eight, he was outgoing, hardworking and basically a good kid at school and at home. He also loved cats and snakes, several of which slithered about his house under his watchful eye.

His parents, both teachers, and younger sister, Becky, were friendly and warm. The home was abuse free and a frequent haven for laughter, feisty playfulness and lots of "wrestling" and hugging. Like all homes it certainly had its stresses and its moments of anger, but nothing out of the ordinary. Bad things, especially unusually bad things, were not supposed to happen in such homes. But in this home something unusually bad began to happen to Nick.

No one could quite figure out what it was. It seemed to unfold somewhere around his eighth birthday. It was insidious. In fact, no one noticed it at first. Nick slowly began to spend more time by himself, alone in his room. When he was with everybody else, at dinner, at the computer, in the TV room, he seemed vaguely distracted.

Soon enough, he began to act like a bit of a grouch. He began snapping at his sister, lost his temper much more often than normal, and even, to the surprise of his parents, began to mouth off. In response, Nick began to get more than his fair share of "time-outs" all of which were well-deserved.

Other than the moodiness and irritability, there was not much else new in his behavior, although there was one thing odd . . . he developed a rash on the backs of both of his hands. It was a tenacious little rash. His father, applied the age-old remedy, cortisone cream, but nothing seemed to help. The rash persisted. So did the tantrums. In fact, they escalated.

Curiously, there were no problems at school, although he had appeared more distracted to his teacher. His grades were fine. His temper at home was not. His parents were baffled, demoralized and genuinely puzzled. Were they doing something wrong? Was someone bullying him? Was this an early manifestation of dreaded adolescence? Everybody began walking on eggshells. They considered taking him to a psychologist as well as a dermatologist for his hands. Could the rash account for his irritability? It seemed highly unlikely. But it was time to grasp at straws.

There was one more thing. One more thing that seemed a bit odd. He seemed to be sneaking around a lot. Nick would look disturbed if anyone came upon him unexpectedly, as if they were interrupting him from doing something important. He also seemed to be spending a lot of time going to the bathroom.

All this behavior was reasonably explained by Nick, who was known to be both creative and quite logical, as part of a game he was playing. He was pretending that he was a robot on a secret mission. Fair enough. This also explained why he had been talking sort of funny, with his lips pursed, as if he was sucking in his breath. As he told his dad, "It's just the way robots talk, Dad." His father smiled and commented, "I hope your robot can knock it off sometimes, it's driving your mom and me nuts." They both laughed.

Then it happened. The anger increased significantly, the time-outs came more frequently, even Becky got tired of the tantrums and of her brother's funny way of talking. One day Nick exploded, yelling and swearing at his mom.

Off to the room he went for yet another time-out. His dad was furious and told him that under no circumstances was swearing going to be allowed. Nick was given a tougher time-out than normal. Normally during time-outs Nick was merely confined to his room. This time his dad told him to stand the whole fifteen minutes in place and "think about what you just said to your mom. There is just no excuse for it. After fifteen minutes if you have yourself under control you can come out, and please apologize to your mom. Same policy as always, no leaving the room until the time-out is over and you are under control." Nick nodded his head in agreement. He clearly was embarrassed by his own outburst.

About five minutes later, as his parents were animatedly discussing that something needed to be done, they heard them . . . footsteps across the hallway upstairs. Nick had left the room. "What is he doing?" his dad angrily asked in exasperation. "He knows we have to add to the time-out now. I just don't get it." His wife was equally baffled and upset. As he stomped up the stairs, fit to be tied, Nick's dad saw him race back into his bedroom, Kleenexes in hand.

When his dad asked what was going on, in a more angry tone than he wanted to be using, Nick commented, "I had to go to the bathroom." His dad replied, "You know the rule, Nick, if you need to go during a time-out, you just need to call out. Then you can go. But you didn't do that. Why didn't you do that?" His dad was fried. He yelled, "I just don't understand what you're doing!"

Nick shook his head forlornly, "I don't either, Dad." There were tears in his eyes. His dad's tone softened, "Look, Nick, you know the rules, if you leave the room during a time-out we automatically add ten minutes. That's the rule, so we just need to do it."

"I know, Dad." There was a pause, "I won't go anywhere, Dad. I promise."

His dad let out a sigh, a long and demoralized one, "Yeah, okay." He was about to start out the door, when the puddle caught his eye. There was a puddle in front of his son's feet.

"Nick, what is that?"

"What?" Nick's eyes widened.

"That." His dad pointed down.

There was a very long pause. Nick looked away as he mumbled, "It's my spit, Dad."

"Your spit?"

Nick began to shake, his eyes flooded with tears, "It's my spit, Dad. I have to spit. I think my saliva is poisoned. I can't swallow it." And he burst into tears. Sobbing and sobbing.

"Oh my God, Son. Is that why you have been talking so funny, you're holding in your spit because you're afraid it's poison?"

Nick nodded his head.

"I have to, Dad. I just have to. I know I shouldn't spit but I have to."

"It's okay, Son. It's okay. I had no idea." His dad knelt down and clutched Nick to his chest.

He pulled away a bit, looking his son in the eyes, softly asking, "My gosh, Nick, what do you do in school?"

"I just hold it in, Dad, and then I tell the teacher I got to go to the bathroom. . . . I think she is getting sort of mad."

Nick managed a smile between his sobs. His dad smiled back, shaking his head from side to side.

"Does this have anything to do with why you're going to the bathroom so often around here?" he asked gently.

"Yeah." Nick nodded. "Dad, I got another problem."

"What's that?"

"I got germs on my hands."

Oh my gosh, his father thought to himself, *the rash.*

"How often are you washing your hands?"

"I'm not sure, but a lot."

"How often is a lot?"

"I'm not sure, probably about every twenty minutes."

"Oh my gosh, Nick. How long has all this been going on?"

"A couple months." There was a pause. "I think about a year, Dad."

"Nick, listen to me. I think I know what is going on. You are totally safe. Your saliva is not poison. Your hands are just fine. You have a disorder that is common. I've seen it before. Some of my students have it. Your mind is playing a trick on you. It's called obsessive-compulsive disorder. I know somebody, a specialist, a friend of mine, who can help."

"Can he come right now, Dad, right now. Because I need help right now."

The father burst into tears.

"I doubt he can come right now, Nick, it's nine o'clock at night. But I'll give him a call." They sobbed together. There was nothing else to do.

As you can tell, OCD, as obsessive compulsive disorder is commonly abbreviated, is a great deal more painful and disabling than Hollywood or television renditions of the disorder would lead one to believe. It is often fictionally portrayed almost like an eccentricity. OCD is not an eccentricity. It often leads to a life of disabling pain, so unrelenting in nature, as with Nick, that it is estimated that about 12 percent of people with OCD attempt suicide. OCD clearly shows us the horrific pain that can result from unchecked damaging matrix effects, but we already knew about them from our last chapter.

OCD has something new to show us. Something that is filled with hope. Something that will prove to be eminently practical in our quest to intelligently use the human matrix to uncover happiness, especially in situations where happiness may be harder to come by, moments of disease, pain, loss and confusion. It will be one of our most memorable guides toward the development of the major goal of our quest—a tougher, more enduring sense of happiness—for OCD provides proof that our next rule, the Healing Matrix Rule, is valid, powerful and immediately useful:

Because there is interdependence in the wings of the human matrix, a beneficial effect on one wing can directly cause a beneficial effect on a different wing.

As you can see, the Healing Matrix Rule is essentially the opposite of the Damaging Matrix Rule. In the same fashion that Maria and Kaspar Hauser brought the Damaging Matrix rule to life, Nick is going to provide us with a prototypical illustration of the Healing Matrix Rule. His illustration will allow us to better appreciate it, understand its power to help us and more effectively use it to uncover happiness.

To do so we must first understand the virulent nature of OCD in a more sophisticated fashion, both its savage destructive effects and its origins. Only then will we be able to fully appreciate the immense power that can be unleashed through the use of healing matrix effects, power that can sometimes overcome obstacles as seemingly insurmountable as a major mental illness.

First things first. In OCD, patients have obsessions and/or compulsions. They usually have both. Obsessions are irrational fears, foreboding feelings, or images that patients can't seem to "get out of their head." Nick's belief that his saliva was poison or that his hands were teeming with bacteria are vivid examples. These obsessions repeatedly and intrusively enter the thoughts of people suffering from OCD, sometimes hundreds of times in a row, requiring minutes to hours to "work through."

When obsessions appear, the person intensely feels that he or she must deal with the obsessions immediately or something ominous, such as death or catastrophe, will happen. This was one of the major reasons that Nick was so irritable, for his family members were inadvertently stopping him from working through his obsessions.

Thus if a person were talking with a business partner and an obsession arose, he or she would feel an intense need to leave in order to find a quiet place where the obsession could be worked through. This intense drive to process the obsessions is why Nick was frequently withdrawing to his room and also explains why he so often looked distracted with family members or at school. Until this processing is done, concentrating on the conversation at hand is extremely difficult, if not impossible. Obsessions are generally accompanied by intense anxiety and sometimes frank fear.

Common obsessions include: fear of germs, fear of being poisoned or encountering toxins, fear that one has done something bad (e.g., hit or run over a person or a dog, left the stove or other electrical appliance on risking a house fire), fear that one is about to do something bad (e.g., fear that one is going to attack someone or perform an "immoral" behavior such as a sexual act).

Compulsions—Nick's need to spit or to wash his hands—are intense drives to perform specific behaviors or mental processes that relieve the anxiety caused by one's obsessions. For instance, if a patient has an intense fear of germs, as with Nick, the patient may feel a ferocious drive to get the germs off by washing his or her hands. At times compulsions can be independent of a specific obsession and, instead, are driven by an intense fear that something ominous will happen if the compulsive behavior is not done (e.g., someone will die if I don't say "Jesus loves me" a hundred times in a row).

Often, the compulsive behavior provides relief for only a few minutes. For instance, a patient's obsessive fear of germs may return with a vengeance only a few minutes after washing his or her hands, rekindling the compulsive drive to once again wash. Because the compulsion sharply decreases the patient's disabling anxiety, the patient becomes insidiously "hooked" into repeating the compulsion anytime the obsession appears. That's why Nick had to wash his hands about every twenty minutes.

Common compulsions include: frequent handwashing, repeatedly checking that electrical appliances are turned off, moving something or adjusting something until it is "just right," repeatedly asking someone to reassure oneself that a frightening obsession is not going to come true, repeated cleaning of surfaces, counting objects over and over, and massively hoarding material (including garbage) because one is afraid to throw it away.

As one can well imagine, in response to their symptoms these patients often have marked problems with functioning. This is compounded by a need to lie to hide their bizarre behaviors. Ritualistic compulsions may make them run late by hours (taking hours to shower or dress), be unable to finish tests, schoolwork or business reports (repeated erasing or answer checking), or unable to participate in social interactions (fear of contamination). They frequently do poorly at school or work, become chronically depressed and isolated, and have a high risk of substance abuse.

OCD is not the experience of everyday doubts that almost all of us have at times and that may increase a bit during times of stress. For instance, many of us have double- or triple-checked whether we locked up the house or double-checked our schedules to make sure we are not missing an important appointment. These are totally normal actions.

OCD is a massive onslaught of intense anxiety, which occupies at a bare minimum an hour a day of extremely unpleasant repeated worries about the same obsession or group of obsessions. It causes marked dysfunction.

I have no doubt that some readers are for the first time understanding that they have OCD. It is probably a tremendous relief to know what it is. It may also be a great relief to know that it is surprisingly common—about one in every one hundred Americans will have OCD at some point in their lives. Naturally, you never hear about it, because people are so embarrassed by its symptoms that they never tell anybody what is really going on. Instead they talk about being stressed, anxious or depressed. Like Nick, almost everyone with OCD has a secret that no one must know.

Here is where we get to the heart of our journey and the power of healing matrix effects. You see, despite the fact that OCD appears to be primarily a problem on the psychological wing of the matrix, this appearance is yet another red herring. OCD is primarily a biological disorder.

Don't get me wrong, elements from all of the wings of the human matrix may be involved in partially triggering or sustaining OCD, such as losses, generalized stresses and psychological reinforcers, but the current evidence strongly suggests that OCD is primarily biological in nature, caused by an imbalance in neurotransmitters, much as is seen in panic disorder but in a different part of the brain.

We even know what part of the brain is afflicted. Specialized scans, called PET scans, have demonstrated that the basal ganglia, a collection of complex balls and loops of neurons embedded deep inside the brain, is disrupted in OCD. The basal ganglia serve many functions. Of particular note to the symptoms of OCD, they seem to have a lot to do with how thoughts and motor movements start and stop. Nick also had developed motor tics—strange snouting movements of his lips.

Another important area involved is the part of the brain that sits on top of the bony orbits that house our eyes. This "orbital cortex" as it is called is also disrupted in OCD. When people have out of control OCD, if you study their brains with a PET scan you will usually find marked dysfunction in both the basal ganglia and the orbital cortex.

Some people with OCD, when given antidepressants that return the neurotransmitter balance back to normal in the basal ganglia, get wonderful relief without much psychotherapy and with minimal changes in their stresses or environment. This fact strongly supports the idea that the primary cause of OCD lies in the biological wing of the matrix. Even more fascinating, when such patients are rescanned with PET scans, their basal ganglia and orbital cortex have returned to normal.

Thus we do have some magic bullets for OCD. Some people do great with them. But there is a catch. Our antidepressants sometimes don't work as well with OCD as they do in biological depressions. They also seem to need higher doses to achieve relief, which means that side effects are more frequently problematic. Some people simply can't use them. Nick could not.

Nick had remarkable relief from his OCD with every single antidepressant used. Unfortunately, perhaps secondary to the immaturity of his brain, he would eventually develop quite severe side effects requiring the discontinuation of the meds. The OCD would return with a vengeance. After several years of this excruciatingly painful roller-coaster, a simple fact became painfully clear to all involved—there were no magic bullets for Nick. Medications were not an available option. Nick was at the mercy of his OCD.

Or was he? What do we do when the magic bullets fail? Nick had a severe biological disorder in which there was no direct way to make changes on the biological wing of his matrix. According to the Healing Matrix Rule, we might be able to concoct a way to impact on Nick's biological wing indirectly. But how?

For Nick, the answer lay in the skills of a gifted local therapist and the purchase of a book. The therapist was well trained in a specific type of psychotherapy called cognitive behavioral therapy (CBT). This therapy, which quite clearly represents an intervention on the psychological wing of the matrix, has proven to be quite effective at helping people with OCD. In fact, it has a higher rate of effectiveness than our magic bullets. Moreover, if OCD goes away with medications, one generally will need to stay on them indefinitely; with CBT, long-term remissions are common even without medications.

Now we come at last to the mindblower, the whole point of our chapter, the proof in the pudding that healing matrix effects are real and exquisitely powerful. In patients who never receive medications but do obtain relief of their OCD through the use of cognitive behavioral therapy, their PET scans return to normal. Somehow or other, the psychotherapy literally changes the biochemistry of the brain in both the basal ganglia and the orbital cortex. The psychotherapy reverses the wayward biochemistry. No magic bullets, just results.

This finding represents some of the most compelling evidence of a healing matrix effect in the history of humankind. It is tremendously exciting from a philosophical view, and even more importantly it brought great relief to Nick. Within six months the smiles were back, the snakes were out, the robot was gone, and I don't think Nick ever got another time-out.

In my own patients with OCD, I routinely use CBT if possible, sometimes in conjunction with an antidepressant, which may speed up the recovery process. As with Nick, I have found CBT to have a potent healing matrix effect.

Oh . . . the book. The book is called *Brain Lock* by Jeffrey Schwartz, and if you or someone you know has OCD, it is a must read. Schwartz is a psychiatrist who has been a pioneer in treating OCD with CBT. *Brain Lock* is a self-help book that has a rare distinction for a self-help book: It helps. Nick loved it.

If you have OCD, I also urge you to seek help from a competent psychiatrist or therapist. OCD can be treated. There is no need to suffer in silence. No need to keep your secret. There is help directly on the biological wing with medications and indirectly via a healing matrix effect, with CBT.

How does this healing matrix effect occur? We aren't certain. But it appears that the brain's circuits can be consciously trained to fire more or less frequently. In a highly simplified explanation, the CBT helps one to train the bad circuits that cause the obsessions and compulsions to fire less frequently and the good circuits to fire more frequently. Once the firing is increased or decreased on a repeated basis, the brain structurally tears down unwanted connections and builds up wanted connections. It's a tad like reprogramming buggy software.

The science behind it is described elegantly, and with a fiery intensity, in a book called *The Mind and the Brain* by Schwartz and his coauthor Sharon Begley. The book does a stunning job of showing some direct correlations between the power of CBT to help with OCD and with a world view that is dear to our own hearts—quantum mechanics.

With Nick we now have compelling evidence of the reality of healing matrix effects. He has brought the Healing Matrix Rule to life as promised. Such healing effects abound, and they seem to be able to crisscross between and among any number of different wings of our matrix. A change in the interpersonal wing may have a healing effect on the spiritual wing. A change in the environmental wing may have pronounced healing effects on the biological and psychological wings. And the effects can be simple, complex, gentle or powerful.

Their importance brings us to a new strategic principle. It is a principle that I cannot emphasize enough whether one is trying to uncover happiness hidden by small everyday problems (a terse exchange with a boss), to fairly big ones (financial or marital problems) to severe ones (death of a partner, a major mental illness).

Something Important Hiding Beneath the Bric-a-Brac in Room #903

Once again, like Kwan and her skating colleagues, we will now aggressively ferret out the possibilities that lay embedded within the nuances of the Healing Matrix Rule. The first strategy to address is the Distant Healing Principle. Its pivotal role for achieving our quest to forge a more enduring sense of happiness cannot be overstated:

> When problems arise in the matrix, look for healing matrix effects that can help a single distant wing—where the primary problem is originating—or other distant wings—where secondary problems exist.

Let us carefully tease apart an example of the Distant Healing Principle put to practical use in a difficult situation. I have chosen to use one of my first applications of this principle, for the lessons I gained from it still resonate in my daily clinical practice. It occurred when I was a second year psychiatric resident, more years ago than I would care to acknowledge. I was working on an inpatient unit with a gifted psychiatrist. We will call him Mack. Mack was a veritable wizard in matrix work.

To this day he is one of the psychiatrists that I most admire and have most tried to model. He was young, dedicated, compassionate and funny. He was often the last physician to leave the unit at night. And he was not afraid to cry with a patient when crying with a patient was what was needed. He was what we call in the business, "a clinician's clinician"—a clinician that other clinicians wanted to be. But he had one flaw. One blind spot.

I was working with a severely depressed woman in her mid-fifties. There was no doubt that the primary sources of her pain were on her interpersonal wing—an ugly divorce. The pain of the divorce quickly flamed severe problems on her psychological wing as manifested by a plethora of depressive symptoms—self-denigration, guilt, anger, depressed mood and suicidal ideation. As one would expect from the Damaging Matrix Rule, these problems further leaked into other wings of her matrix. In fact, the prolonged stress and pain on her psychological wing seemed to trigger a biological depression highlighted by problems with sleep, energy, concentration, appetite and a profound inability to enjoy anything. Put bluntly, Mrs. Perkins was a mess, a human matrix gone dangerously awry in Room #903.

It was a particularly heavy depression. It fell over Mrs. Perkins like a depressive shawl that not only covered her own shoulders but spread throughout the room. All was black. All was painful. When Mrs. Perkins sighed, it felt like the whole room sighed with her.

But Mrs. Perkins was a fighter. I could tell that fact by the spunk with which she still managed to answer some of my questions. And, despite her intense weariness, she always made the effort—and it was a real effort—to smile when I walked into the door. She had been in the hospital for quite some time. Several different antidepressants had been tried—interventions on the biological wing—but each had failed.

I had made good contact with her in therapy—a psychological intervention—but it too seemed to be going nowhere fast. I felt frustrated. And I felt bad for her. Mack felt bad for her. The whole staff felt bad for her. We feared suicide.

One afternoon, I noticed something sitting on her bedside table that I had never noticed before, for it had been covered by magazines and other hospital room bric-a-brac. It was a Catholic missal. I asked her if she had been praying. She sighed and shook her head from side to side.

"No. I have not." She sighed again. "I used to pray a lot. But it just doesn't do anything for me now. I used to be a good Catholic."

"Would you like to be able to pray again?"

"Of course I would. But I can't. I think I've let God down one too many times, but I keep it out there," she nodded towards the missal, "just in case."

"Maybe you should call Him up?"

She smiled.

"Not so sure I know his number anymore."

I smiled, "I doubt it is unlisted."

She smiled more widely.

My next question seemed a logical one. "Would you like it if I could arrange to get a priest to visit you?"

Mrs. Perkins mulled the question over for a second or two. "Couldn't hurt."

I told her I would look into it.

That evening, Mack was hanging out late as usual. It was about eight o'clock. Most faculty physicians had left by five or six. Not Mack. He was worried about a young boy who was being plagued by some really hideous hallucinations. Mack was racking his brain trying to figure out how to get him some faster relief. We'd taken a break and were joking around in the staff room, when I suddenly remembered.

"Hey, Mack, I meant to tell you earlier. I think I got a great idea for helping Mrs. Perkins, but I'm not sure of the logistics of how to get it done."

He looked genuinely interested.

"Well, I noticed that she had a missal beside her bed, and when I asked her about it she related that she was a Catholic but had stopped praying. So I asked her if she'd like me to get a priest for her. She would. I don't know how to do that. Do you?"

Mack didn't smile or nod. He usually did both when I made treatment suggestions.

"Shawn, I think you might be missing the point here."

"How do you mean?"

He paused and then smiled a different kind of smile than I usually saw from Mack. "You're a great young psychiatrist, but you still have some things to learn that only experience can teach you." Mack took a sip of coffee—very stale coffee. "No priest is going to help Mrs. Perkins. God ain't the answer. Imipramine (an antidepressant common back then) and some compassionate listening are. Trust me on this one."

I was shocked. My hero had a matrix defect. Because Mack did not believe in God, he had ruled out the spiritual wing of the matrix as a mode of either assessment or intervention. Now don't get me wrong. I don't believe the main problem for Mrs. Perkins was a spiritual crisis. Her divorce and biological depression had long predated her religious doubts. But I did think there was an accompanying disruption on this wing of the matrix, and I had a hunch.

I had a hunch that here was an inviting opportunity to put the Distant Healing Principle to the test. If we could reconnect Mrs. Perkins with her God, maybe her belief would bring forth some much needed reinforcements. She just needed to ring Him up. Like a pool shark calling up a combination shot—six ball, ten ball . . . side pocket—I was a matrix healer conjuring up a healing matrix effect—spiritual wing, psychological wing. . . . improved mood.

"Look, Mack, do you mind if I try to get a priest up here anyway? I don't see how it could hurt, and I just got a feeling on this one."

"Not at all. She's your patient. You do what you think is best."

So I did.

Several days after the priest had visited I noticed the rosary beads. They lay gently about the missal on her bedstead. I also noticed the missal had been moved.

"Hey, those are rosary beads, aren't they?"

She smiled, "Yep. I made the call to you know who after Father Garnier stopped by."

"I take it you're praying again."

"Yeah . . . . yeah, I am. Feels sort of good. I don't know if anything will come of it, but who knows."

What she didn't know, what Mrs. Perkins was too close to the situation to see, was that it already had. There was a sparkle—not a very big one, mind you—but a sparkle to her eye that we hadn't seen before.

As the next couple of weeks unfolded, the imipramine "kicked in." When these medications kick in, it is always such a delight to see. It is almost like a miracle because you can tangibly see the biological aspects of the depression heal, sometimes surprisingly quickly. The parts of the brain that deal with energy, drive, interest, motivation, appetite, sleep and concentration wake up and return to healthy functioning. As the chemistry of the patient's brain returns to his or her normal baseline, the brain has a fighting chance to regain its spunk. It is always such a pleasure to see, one of the greatest gifts that science has ever given to humankind.

And, to this day, I believe I saw a matrix effect. It is not at all clear why medication sometimes work and sometimes doesn't. But I am convinced that on some occasions it seems almost as if the medications need the mind of the patient to be ready before they can do their magic on the brain of the patient. It's like the brain has to be at the tipping point—call it hope. One thing is clear. Her spiritual awakening seemed to kindle hope on her psychological wing—a healing matrix effect if there ever was one. In this case, it was the spiritual wing creating a healing matrix effect on the psychological wing that seemed to have tipped the balance.

Whether you believe it was her new hope that tipped the balance or that God directly intervened and answered the prayers of Mrs. Perkins, it makes no difference to me, for they are both wonderful examples of a healing matrix effect. It also made no difference to Mrs. Perkins. Either way, she went home three weeks later, a new person. We had optimized all five wings of her matrix.

By the way, I do know somebody that it did make a difference to— Mack. As one would expect from such a gifted clinician, he was impressed with my pool shooting. He was impressed with the power of the fifth wing of the matrix to create a healing matrix effect on the psychological wing of a patient. And he subsequently used the Healing Matrix Principle to great effect with his future patients.

But there is something else waiting beneath all that bric-a-brac in Room #903. Something mysterious—a rather remarkable example of another healing matrix effect that will further dissolve the boundaries between our spirits, our minds and our bodies. To uncover it, we shall beg the attention of a well-known expert on mysterious things—Mary Poppins.

Just a Spoonful of Sugar

In our above example we focused upon the healing matrix effect that occurred when the spiritual wing of Mrs. Perkins crisscrossed with her psychological wing. But there may have been yet another healing matrix effect in action with Mrs. Perkins, which is where Mary Poppins enters the picture.

As you will recall, Mary Poppins was always running about singing with the contagious cheerfulness that only Mary Poppins seems capable of producing. "Just a spoonful of sugar helps the medicine go down, the medicine go down, the medicine go down." I believed her as a wide-eyed child of five. I believe her even more as a wide-eyed physician of fifty.

Mary Poppins had it right. But what she didn't know, or perhaps she knew but wasn't telling, was the fact that the sugar not only helped the medicine go down. Sometimes, it was the medicine.

We have all heard of placebo effects, but I believe the significance of placebo effects is often greatly misunderstood. Placebo effects (caused by sugar pills) are often treated as if they represent treatment failure, an indication that "a medication doesn't work any better than a placebo." What's often overlooked is the fact that placebos sometimes work quite well. They cure diseases, not placate them.

For instance, in major depressive disorders, placebos significantly improve the depression in roughly 40 percent of patients and sometimes produce higher rates of relief. This rate of success is a routine finding that has been documented over and over again in thousands of patients. Forty percent—that's a pretty good success rate for any medication! Imagine if you had cancer and a doctor said, "I have a medication that cures your kind of cancer 40 percent of the time." There would be a long line outside that physician's door.

Moreover, when one looks at what this statistic is really saying—a sugar pill (that is supposed to lack any biological effect) is reversing the patho-physiology of a major depressive disorder—one cannot help but think . . . healing matrix effect.

Some believe that this healing matrix effect occurs between the inter-personal wing and the psychological wing. The therapeutic alliance with the clinicians who are providing the sugar pills, instills hope, much as Mrs. Perkins' hope was instilled by her rekindled belief in God. I believe that such a healing matrix effect does indeed happen when using placebos in depression studies.

But I believe that in some instances, something else may be happen-ing. Something much more remarkable. Indeed, I believe it is possible that the change we engendered in the spiritual wing of Mrs. Perkins may have directly knocked about the neurotransmitters in her brain.

In short, the placebo effect may be real. The somewhat pejorative term "placebo" may be nothing more than a misnomer for the much more elegant concept "hope." There is mounting evidence that hope, and its re-flections—belief, conviction, motivation—may be able to change bio-chemistry. In fact, in the January 2002 issue of the *American Journal of Psychiatry*, Andrew Leuchter and a group of colleagues published a most unusual article, "Changes in Brain Function of Depressed Subjects During Treatment with Placebo" that addressed just this phenomena.

Using an ultra-sophisticated form of EEG that measures the electrical functioning of different parts of the brain sequentially over time, the researchers placed thirty-five electrodes on the scalps of their patients. Using computers they were able to detect EEG changes that reflected how much blood flow was occurring in specific parts of the brain. Blood flow is an indicator of brain activity.

Patients who responded well to medications showed changes in the parts of the brain felt to help modulate mood. Some patients did not respond to either medications or placebo and, as one would expect, their EEGs showed absolutely no changes. Not expected was the fact that patients whose depressions improved when given just the placebo also showed changes in their brains! Somehow the Mary Poppins treatment was actually changing the brain's metabolism.

This change tended to occur some weeks later in time than the changes caused by the antidepressant, but in the exact same area of the brain—only this time the blood flow to the prefrontal cortex increased, whereas it had decreased when there was a good response to the antidepressants. Curious. But the most important fact is a simple one. Sugar pills, which should not change brain activity at all, did. And when they did, they somehow helped the brain to shake off its depression. We just don't know how. If further studies back up such findings, we may have finally explained the placebo effect, but its power will now be recognized as a reality—pathophysiology reversed by hope.

Such findings would represent a remarkable example of a spiritual/psychological intervention creating a healing matrix effect directly on the brain. I am convinced that part of the magic of our magic bullets—our antidepressants—is that they create hope. The resulting hope then directly impacts the chemistry of the brain. This phenomena may explain the "tipping effect" I was describing with Mrs. Perkins.

By the way, there is more to the power of antidepressants than their wondrous placebo effect. They seem to work more reliably and frequently than sugar pills with about a 20 percent difference in effect between medications and placebos. They also may give more lasting relief than placebos, and this relief may last longer than with placebos, especially with severe depressions.

Several months after Leuchter's article appeared, a second provocative article written by Helen Mayberg and her colleagues appeared in the May issue of the *American Journal of Psychiatry*. Using PET scans to monitor brain activity, Mayberg and company demonstrated that as with Leuchter's EEGs, when placebos relieved depression, there were actual changes in the brain metabolism. But they also found that when antidepressants relieved depression there were similar changes as with the placebos, but there were also other changes not seen with the effective placebos below the cortex, deep within the brain and in the brain stem. This may explain why antidepressants are about 20 percent more reliable and effective than placebos.

All of this research is quite exciting, for now that we realize that hope may actually help to transform biological dysfunction, we may be able to learn better ways to maximize it and focus it as we battle a myriad of diseases. We are still at the very beginning of this scientific exploration of the biological nature of placebo effects, and much caution is in order. Perhaps future research will not support our current findings, but there certainly are some indications that we are onto something big. Not all of which deals with mental disorders.

For instance, researchers at the University of Michigan and at Princeton University saw similar results when studying pain. The researchers spread some ointment onto volunteers and told them it was a "special" pain blocker. In reality, it was merely regular skin lotion, a Mary Poppins' treatment. In many instances, when pain was subsequently administered to these "sugarized" volunteers, they rated their pain as significantly less intense. More remarkably the pain circuits of their brains showed less activity—a direct example of a healing matrix effect.

It should be noted that the pain circuits of the volunteers not fooled by the Mary Poppins approach showed normal pain activity. They also yelled a lot. It is my guess that it marked the end of their volunteering days.

If volunteers were smeared with placebo cream and were told that it was placebo, they felt normal pain and their pain circuits were appropriately active. The above research gives further support to the idea that belief and hope do indeed, in some instances, directly cross the wings of the matrix to change biochemistry directly.

Perhaps one of the most surprising examples of a well documented healing matrix effect comes from an unexpected place, the treatment of people suffering from Parkinson's disease. Parkinson's disease, which is caused by the underproduction of the neurotransmitter dopamine, can result in devastating neurological problems, including incapacitating stiffness and tremors. It is the illness with which the popular actor Michael J. Fox is doing battle.

Researchers at the University of British Columbia inadvertently stumbled upon a healing matrix effect while trying to discover a new Parkinson's treatment. They were testing whether a promising new medication might help increase dopamine in the brains of patients with Parkinson's. They needed to compare the new medication to a placebo. Once again, just a spoonful of sugar came into play. These sugar pills produced some very unexpected results: They increased the brain's dopamine release almost as much as the experimental drug. Curiouser and curiouser.

By now it is obvious why I have a lot of respect for Mary Poppins and her spoonful of sugar spiel. It is also time to wrap up our chapter on healing matrix effects with two final principles. Each principle stems directly from a deeper understanding of the nuances of the Healing Matrix Rule.

A rather unusual character will be our guide as we study these nuances. He is one of my favorite people and is without doubt one of the most special examples of a human matrix I've had the good fortune to meet in my life. Susan adores him too. We most recently had the delight of his company in the back seat of our car, where he was animatedly spewing bits of wacky humor and double-edged wisdom, somewhere in the frigidly cold winter of 2004.

We hadn't seen Paul for about seven years. I had forgotten how much his long and rather pointed nose looks rather like a bird's beak if caught at just the right angle. But Paul is not a bird. He is an errant anthropologist, who somewhere along the path of studying people and their standards of living became more interested in helping people and improving their standards of living.

From the moment Paul set foot in Haiti as a college student interested in cultural anthropology, he was destined to become an errant anthropologist—to focus more on helping than studying. Don't get me wrong, I'm sure he is still an outstanding anthropologist, he just happens to be an even more outstanding doctor and humanitarian. I like that about Paul. I always have.

A Matrix Wizard in Haiti and the Return of the Heron

Let us begin our final exploration of healing matrix effects by defining the two principles suggested by the nuances of the Healing Matrix Rule. The first one—the Maximized Matrix Principle—is the opposite of the Cast a Wide Net Principle, where we were reminded to search each wing of the matrix for possible contributing problems. In the Maximized Matrix Principle, we reverse this idea. The emphasis is now upon scanning each wing in the hope of uncovering hidden solutions, not problems:

No matter what the apparent cause of the immediate unhappiness, look at all wings of the matrix for possible healing matrix effects. Maximize all possible healing matrix effects and the functioning of all the wings in a general sense. The more healing matrix effects that one can muster and the higher the general functioning of all the wings, the higher the likelihood of relief.

Mrs. Perkins was a perfect example of the implementation of this rule. With her I was consciously using a healing matrix effect—re-establishing her relationship with God—to help a distant wing of her matrix. Our spiritual intervention clearly had a positive impact on her psychological wing. It may have even impacted directly on her biological wing.

Note though that the Maximized Matrix Principle also emphasizes that, even if there is not a direct healing matrix effect available, it is still wise to maximize the functioning of all wings of the happiness machine whenever possible. Optimizing functioning on each wing can potentially make it easier for healing efforts to be more easily achieved on the most troubled wings—sort of an indirect healing matrix effect.

With Mrs. Perkins, we were trying to maximize all of her wings: the biological wing with antidepressants, the psychological wing with therapy, the interpersonal wing with group therapy, the environmental wing by providing a safe haven in the hospital, and her spiritual wing through contacting a priest. Together, these changes across all the wings of her matrix contributed to a striking clinical outcome—an exquisitely unhappy happiness machine became a remarkably happier happiness machine. We done good.

Let's take another look at the practical utility of maximizing all wings of the matrix from an everyday example that may arise in any therapist's office. For instance, perhaps we have a couple with very severe problems on the interpersonal wing of their matrix—a failing marriage. Let us further suppose that both members of the couple are doing their best to work things out in couple counseling. Couple counseling is tough work. It's tiring. It requires sustained effort and commitment.

Of course our immediate focus is right where the problem lies: the interpersonal wing of their respective matrices. We will try to enhance their abilities to communicate clearly, to express needs effectively, to share anger reasonably and to compromise genuinely.

But there is something else we can do, something more subtle but potentially surprisingly helpful. It is always best to remember that magic—whether on stage or in a clinical office—is often at its best when it is subtle.

Let us take a look at Partner A. We will call him Robert. As we apply the Maximized Matrix Principle, we will examine and, if possible, try to maximize all the matrix wings for Robert. We will discover, upon examining his biological wing, that Robert is very much out of shape physically but would like to get into better physical condition.

We try to help Robert to maximize his biological wing by setting up a reasonable exercise routine, which he takes to like a duck to water. Suddenly, Robert has more energy. Robert has more to give to the couples therapy and to his spouse, whom we shall call Elizabeth. His increased sense of well-being and his increased energy indirectly energize the couple therapy itself—the Maximized Matrix Principle at work in the real world.

Furthermore, the change initiated on Robert's biological wing—an exercise program—may generate a healing matrix effect on his psychological wing—improved self-esteem. If Robert begins to have an improved self-image, this beneficial change on his psychological wing may trigger yet another healing matrix effect. In a delicious twist of circumstances, the resulting change on his psychological wing may create new beneficial changes right where the action is—the interpersonal wings of both Robert and Elizabeth. Partner A may be more willing to give emotionally to Partner B. It could even impact on sexual interest and responsivity, two areas that may have been contributing problems to the marital discord in the first place. In any case, I think you get the idea.

In my practice and, quite frankly, in the messes that I periodically get myself into in my own life, I am consistently amazed at how valuable it is to employ the Maximized Matrix Principle. I believe you will be pleased by its impact as well. It's a particularly great tool to have at one's disposal when there is interpersonal tension lingering in the dining room, the bedroom or the boardroom.

By this time, you may be catching on to something akin to a "bonus benefit" to our book on happiness machines. This bonus benefit even has a name, the Universal Applicability Principle:

> Since every thing can be viewed from a quantum perspective as a matrix, all of the principles that help to uncover happiness in the human matrix may be applicable to transforming dysfunction in other matrices: business problems, financial problems, community problems, even, at times, serious social problems (including crime, racism, poverty and political discord). Matrix problem solving has the potential to be a "possibility generator" in a surprisingly broad range of situations.

Time to return to our errant anthropologist. He is currently sitting in the back of our car as Susan and I are returning him and a young colleague of his, Deo, back to Cambridge from the Dartmouth Medical Center. At Dartmouth, Paul has given a series of exciting talks. Earlier in the afternoon he mesmerized an auditorium full of medical students with his unique combination of informality, sense of mission and zany wit.

At the present moment he is not mesmerizing anyone. He and Susan are terrorizing Deo and me, for the two of them are singing, at least I believe it is best categorized as singing, at the top of their lungs. They have joined forces with the unforgettable Tommy Tutone as his memorable chorus to that classic hit of the 1980s "867-5309/Jenny" blares out wildly on our car's quivering speakers. I'm joining in as well, of course, but with less gusto, because I sing like crap.

Dear dear Deo, who has never heard the song, is smiling at these old people. He knows that they are clearly not sane. He likes us though, because, being a kind person, he knows that we need help. He also smiles at us because he knows that his life depends upon my driving safely, and he believes it is best for him to just keep smiling.

Even as I write these words I can hear our joyous cacophony as we all belt out the numbers 8–6–7–5–3–0–nii . . . ii . . . ii . . . iinne. Giggles and laughter overflow the back seat as Susan and Paul relive our dear-old times at Duke. If you will recall, these are the same dear old times that I mentioned earlier in the book—when a kid who looked like SpongeBob SquarePants was wiping my butt all over the walls of the handball court known as the Torture Chamber. Ah . . . sweet memories.

In any case, this giggling, uninhibited maniac with the bird beak for a nose is not just an errant anthropologist. He is a very well-known errant anthropologist. You may be familiar with him as the humanitarian and physician who is the focus of Tracy Kidder's exquisite new biography, *Mountains Beyond Mountains*—Paul Farmer.

Paul comes to mind because he is one of the best examples of someone who knows how to effectively, and I mean *effectively*, implement our two new strategic principles. Indeed, Paul Farmer is a matrix wizard who can usually be found working his magic somewhere in Haiti.

It is my hope that the work of Paul Farmer will convincingly demonstrate that the healing matrix effects described in this chapter can help all of us to overcome remarkable obstacles (some of which may, at times, appear insurmountable). The best way to make this point is to take us to a place where remarkable obstacles are not remarkable. They are everyday occurrences.

Let us see what an understanding of the human matrix can do in a place like Haiti, especially the Maximized Matrix Principle and the Universal Applicability Principle.

Haiti is the poorest nation in our hemisphere. Seventy percent of the population lives on about $400 per year. The average Haitian is dead by his or her mid-forties. The country is wracked, especially its central plains and rural areas, by savage poverty, malnutrition and disease. TB, relatively rare in the United States, is common in Haiti. Even more unfortunate was the arrival of the AIDS virus, which was brought to its shores somewhere in the 1980s.

The AIDS virus likes places where there is poverty, poor education and compromised immune systems secondary to lack of water and food. The AIDS virus took to Haiti like a shark to a seal. There are currently about 300,000 adults and children with AIDS in Haiti. Five thousand babies will die from AIDS next year. So many people, most of whom are heterosexual, have died from AIDS in this tiny Caribbean Island that about 5 to 7 percent of children have lost one or both parents to the scourge.

And, as recent news headlines have proclaimed, Haiti is also a place of violence. The hideous reign of the Duvaliers and their notorious thugs the Tontons Macoutes still leave echoes of human wailing on the walls of the dilapidated jail walls where thousands were tortured. If one were deciding where to build a Hall of Fame for coups d'état, such as the one in 2004, one could make a solid argument that Haiti should house it.

Bottom line: There are few places where it is harder to have an enduring sense of happiness. In fact, there are fewer places in the world where it is harder to stay alive, if that is what one wants to do.

Enter Paul Farmer with his twinkling yet determined eyes perched intelligently above that beak of his. Those eyes, wise much beyond their years, saw a lot in Haiti. They saw immense pain, and from the pain they gained an even more steely unwinking determination.

Being a physician I can tell you that it is very difficult to lose a patient. But being a physician in Haiti, there is a deeper pain that I do not even pretend to know, for I have not been to the island. But I have seen it in Paul's soul.

You see, it is one thing to lose a patient to a disease when one has done all that can be done. It is yet another thing altogether to watch a man die in front of you, holding your hand, when you know for a fact that he would be alive if he was given a medication that is readily available just a thousand miles away—a medicine that no one is willing to give the man. This type of senseless death changes a physician. It changes a man or a woman or a child who witnesses it. I am convinced that it forever changed Paul Farmer.

The question that became the focal point of the man with the beak and the determined eyes was "How can we get these medicines to these impoverished people so that we can treat their AIDS and the other string of killers following in its wake such as TB?" The answer, according to just about everybody in the world, was simple—"You can't." Some even intimated, "Why bother? AIDS drugs are ridiculously expensive, and these people are horrifically poor."

Farmer did not like either of these answers. The second one really got his goat. To Farmer, everyone deserves good medical care. Period. It is, as he is fond of saying, a moral imperative.

As a result, Farmer, then a mere medical student, and a collection of his friends formed a group called Partners in Health (PIH) back in 1987. A band of dedicated people such as Thomas White, Todd McCormack, Ophelia Dahl, Jim Yong Kim and their many Haitian colleagues decided to tackle this problem head-on.

How Farmer and his friends transformed this AIDS matrix is an extraordinary example of the power of the Generalized Matrix Principle and of the Universal Applicability Principle. Let me emphasize that Farmer and his friends were in no sense consciously using the human matrix model and its principles, they just happen to be wonderful examples of how it all works! They are natural-born matrix healers.

According to the Universal Applicability Principle, we ought to be able to translate many of our strategies for helping a single human matrix to this overwhelming dilemma—the Haitian AIDS matrix. We will start with the Red Herring Principle. At first glance, the problem looks clearly biological in nature, but is it? Undoubtedly, the virus is real and destroying it is clearly one of the key obstacles to saving the lives of these Haitian patients, but is the biological wing the main problem? Possibly, but not necessarily.

Besides the biological disruption there is definitely a maelstrom brewing on the environmental wing of this AIDS matrix; specifically, there is a problem on the social wing of the matrix. To save these people, one needs to get to them the state-of-the-art AIDS medications called antiretroviral (ARV) therapies. These ARVs are saving thousands of lives in the United States, but not in Haiti, because such drugs cost a small fortune per patient, per year. The death of these patients is not solely the result of a virion, it is also the result of a significant and real obstacle on the social wing of the matrix—not enough money.

According to the Generalized Matrix Principle this biological/social problem may best be resolved by ultimately involving all wings of the AIDS matrix. The goal for Farmer and his colleagues was to look for healing matrix effects on each of the wings that might impact on the biological/social wings as well as maximizing all available resources on each wing.

First, on the societal wing of the matrix, money would have to start to flow. Pharmaceutical houses would have to be convinced to lower prices to the poor, and charitable outside sources would need to donate large amounts of cash to purchase these meds at the lowered prices.

But there was a nasty catch-22 waiting on the social wing of the AIDS matrix. AIDS drugs demand complicated dosing schedules and often require multiple doses per day. Taken improperly, the medications can be dangerous. If doses are missed, the drug regimens quickly become ineffective.

Thus, both drug companies and charitable donors, with reasonable caution, might be hesitant to "throw money away" if noncompliance was going to be commonplace. And truth be told, the clinics in Haiti were often empty, veritable bastions of noncompliance. Noncompliance would be a huge problem. Nobody, charitable organizations or pharmaceutical houses, was about to throw good money after bad.

But what caused the noncompliance? Was this a problem on the psychological wing of the matrix? Were the Haitian patients just unwilling to take the medications as indicated? Red Herring.

The noncompliance problems, although partially psychological in nature (for many patients felt stigmatized admitting to AIDS and thus were hesitant to go to the clinics), were more often a problem originating on the other wings of the AIDS matrix. There were good reasons not to comply: Transportation to the clinics was arduous on inadequate roads (environmental wing), transportation was literally dangerous because of thugs (social wing), patients were bedridden by the horrors of the disease (biological wing), patients were weakened by malnutrition and lack of water supplies (environmental/political wing), transportation was not available (environmental/political wing), and people did not want to help with transportation secondary to stigma (social wing). No compliance. No money.

With seemingly insurmountable roadblocks existing on the societal and biological wings, it was time to maximize all other wings in an effort to use healing matrix effects to transform the roadblocks. And here, in my opinion, is where the miracle began, where an understanding of the rules and principles of the human matrix were brilliantly put to use.

To begin with, Paul Farmer and the dedicated people by his side had an inside track on the spiritual wing of the AIDS matrix. These people believed. They would use their belief to make others believe. And they believed with every ounce of their hearts that all people should have equal health care, rich/poor, good/bad, famous/unknown. And people—the patients they touched, the family members they cried with, the financiers they lobbied, the pharmaceutical executives they enjoined—all could sense it. Something was up in the spiritual wing of the matrix. Somebody was ready to pitch the fight.

But more than just dedication and mission on the spiritual wing was needed. Results were needed. You still needed to convince people that the medications could get where they needed to get and that the patients would take them once they got there.

Here we come across one of the more amazing healing matrix effects I have ever seen. As the Maximized Matrix Principle would suggest, all wings should be maximized and all healing matrix shifts optimized. Consequently, the energy from the spiritual wing was directed not at the biological wings or the social, but to a most unusual place to attack the AIDS virus—the interpersonal wing.

If the patients couldn't come to the clinics, the clinics would come to the patients. Home visits. Casemanagers would transport the meds to the patients' homes and make sure the complicated drug dosings actually happened, because they would stand there as the patient took the meds.

"Impossible," critics cried. The cost to get trained nurses or professional casemanagers who could transport and handle the meds effectively was as financially prohibitive as the medications themselves.

The answer to Farmer and his colleagues was obvious: We will convince the town's people to volunteer to do the work and we will train them to do it well. Through immense efforts at communication on the psychological, interpersonal, social and spiritual wings of the matrix, Farmer and his colleagues broke through the stigma.

Some of the early patients who were healed by home interventions eagerly signed up to become community health workers for others. As death rates changed, entire communities took pride in their resilience, and more and more volunteers appeared. Some of these community health workers were eventually paid, causing improvement on the social wing (fighting poverty), the psychological wing (creating a sense of dignity and self-worth) and the spiritual wing (the birth of mission and compassion). The clinics began to fill.

Other diseases were being attacked. Trust had entered the picture. Even a gentle confidence, a confidence that change might occur, began to appear in the eyes of those who lived in Haiti and had forgotten the meaning of hope. Paul Farmer, Ophelia Dahl, Jim Yong Kim and many others had done what some would say was impossible. They had sowed the seeds—trust and confidence—for the type of enduring happiness that we all seek.

Some of this power, inherent in the human matrix is refreshingly captured in the words of the "accompagnateurs" as the community-based case managers are called. These are the words of people who at one time were beaten by life, but today embrace it: "We won't ever stop giving patients their meds." "Of course they are sick, so they need us, their accompagnateurs, throughout their lives." "We don't just give them medicines, we joke with them, we pray with them, we have them to our houses, we watch their children." "We know, that having this disease is a burden, and we help them with the burden."

Communities and local governments, as best they could, began to maximize other wings of the matrix. Rudimentary housing, electricity and water supplies were forged. Indeed, there were so many crisscrossing healing matrix effects that one could probably not account for all of them. Taken together, these constantly interacting matrix effects had kick-started a healing social cycle.

But the most important matrix effect finally hit home—money. Compliance was happening. It could be proved. Indeed, some of the TB clinics set up by Partners in Health had better compliance rates than similar clinics in the United States! Pharmaceutical companies lowered prices. Charitable organizations raised donations. At present, over 1,500 Haitians a year receive medications that save their lives.

Don't get me wrong, life is still horrific in much of Haiti. Thousands still needlessly die, and Partners in Health will always be in urgent need of funding to help them. And although Farmer and his friends have made a significant impact, it is still a small dent in the massive horrors of Haiti. But it is a dent, and it is a dent many felt was impossible to make.

It also highlights an important point. Many people have wanted to help the poor fight AIDS. Almost all have failed, because they could not get the drugs to the poor. Paul Farmer and company did not fail. Why?

The lesson is simple. Compassion is good, but compassion with skill is better. And I believe that it is a sophisticated understanding of how the human matrix works that can often provide us with the skills that we need to guide compassion to its greatest successes.

Paul Farmer and his colleagues are examples of people who understand how to make the matrix work. Although they were not consciously using this model, they are, nevertheless, brilliant examples of how the model can be used. We can see from their work that the strategic principles of the human matrix can be, in some instances, successfully translated to other matrices, as the Universal Applicability Principle predicted.

As we wrap up this chapter on healing matrix effects, I can't help but think back to Paul, Susan, Deo and me laughing merrily away in that car careening back towards Boston. I think back again to Paul's beak. Perhaps that nose really is a beak after all. Perhaps Paul Farmer is that heron we so respected back in chapter 7. I must add that he does have gangly arms and legs that seem to be gracefully uncoordinated at times, much like the legs that one sees on a heron as it gingerly walks across an inlet of water.

In this instance, the heron's eyes are not fixed and unwinking on getting a frog to feed its life. This heron's eyes are fixed, unwinking, on getting medications to save other people's lives. Like our heron friend, Paul Farmer lives in the moment at hand. The intensity of his compassion places him there. It just so happens that the "there" is Haiti. And Haiti is a better place for it.

14

The Three Paradoxes
of the Magic Theater

"A Steppenwolf must once have a good look at himself. . . .
It is possible that he will learn one day to know himself.
He may get hold of one of our little mirrors. . . .
He may find in one of our magic theaters the very
thing that is needed to free his neglected soul.
A thousand possibilities await him."

HERMAN HESSE
FROM *STEPPENWOLF*

Great Books, Mist-Enshrouded Alleyways
and Magic Theaters

We are almost done perusing the pages of our owner's manual for the happiness machine. In retrospect, it looks like it was a mighty good idea to take a peek at it. Susan was right. It's a complicated little dickens.

It is also readily apparent from our last chapter, highlighted by the accomplishments of Paul Farmer and company, that happiness machines, when guided by the intelligent use of the human matrix model, are not only complicated, they are marvelously powerful. It is difficult not to be excited about taking one out for a test drive. Soon enough, we will. And the ride will be a splendid one, I assure you. But first there are three strategic principles left to review—important ones—all of which are cautionary in nature.

I like to refer to them as the Three Paradoxes of the Magic Theater. They alert us to possible pitfalls when using the human matrix model. A wizened monk in the novel *The Name of the Rose*, written by Umberto Eco, put it most elegantly. "Learning does not consist only of what we must do or we can do, but also of knowing what we could do and perhaps should not do." We have mastered what we could do and can do to uncover happiness. It is now time to learn what we could do and perhaps should not do while attempting this quest.

To accomplish this task, we will enter a magic theater, actually two of them. The first one, described by Herman Hesse above, is a make-believe building, but it will have much to teach us by way of metaphor. The second one is a very real building in the very real world of a bustling small New England town. I rather enjoy both of these theaters, the make-believe one and the real-world one, and I hope that you will too. Inside them we will find the much needed answers to our paradoxical principles.

The opening quotation of our chapter is taken from Herman Hesse's delightfully decadent and philosophically provocative novel, *Steppenwolf*. It is the book that will transport us to our first magic theater and put us hot on the trail of our first paradox.

I don't like to pick favorites, but this book is near the top of my list. It has that rare ability, characteristic of most great novels, to change plots over the years even though there is not a single change in a word of their print. Good books change dust jackets over the decades. Great books change meanings. This shape-shifting quality is why great books never become outdated.

I've read *Steppenwolf* about seven times over the course of four different decades. Each time I have read it, I have been equally fascinated. But each time I have read it, it fascinated me in a different fashion. The lens of whatever wisdom my intervening years of experience had provided me colored the reading of the book differently with each passing year. The genius of Hesse is a simple one: How did he know how the book would read with each of my lenses so that with each reading the book made perfect sense to me—a nineteen-year-old, a thirty-year-old, a fifty-year-old?

I am convinced that each decade of life has its own packets of wisdom to offer us. We voraciously gather these packets—sometimes with laughter and sometimes with tears, but always with surprisingly great dexterity. But no one has the dexterity, the luck nor the time to gather all the packets of wisdom that are available at each stage of life. We all exit each stage missing a packet or two, unaware of what we are missing.

It is for this reason that I have found it beneficial over the years to listen very carefully to children and teenagers, for they display new wisdom that, by my very age, is now forbidden me. Without their words, I could never capture it for myself. It is true that one gets wiser with age. It is not true that the young do not sometimes speak with words of wisdom.

One of the wonderful things about Hesse is that his books seem to sparkle with this youthful wisdom. Perhaps this fact is one of the explanations of why so many people first read Hesse during their college years. The other reason is that, let's face it, *Steppenwolf* has everything that a maturing late adolescent is looking for in a good book—or a "bad" book, depending upon your perspective. The pages are teeming with good times, bad times, sex, drugs, jazz, secret assignations, curious characters, a rebellious attitude and, ultimately, a gentle but profound wisdom.

If you are unfamiliar with it, *Steppenwolf* takes place in a fictional and nameless city, a curious admixture of Berlin and Zurich during the pre-war rise of Nazi Germany. The book's protagonist, Harry Haller, is a middle-aged man in a middle-aged identity crisis. The book follows Harry's wanderings through the mist-enshrouded streets of the jazz-club scene and the mist-enshrouded back alleys of Harry's soul. During one particularly fateful night, in one particularly mysterious back alley, Harry stops before a large stone wall.

As a bewildered Harry looks on, the mists of the dark street begin to swirl about him climbing up and over the wall. Suddenly, a door appears in the previously doorless wall. Above the door, a sign reads:

Magic Theater
Entrance Not for Everybody
For Madmen Only!

As anyone would, Harry reaches for the door handle. It is locked. In a twinkling, the door vanishes. Great scene!

From the very first time that I read it, that scene was irrevocably etched into my memory banks. Ever since reading it, I've been hunting for magic theaters and the magic doors that open them. Perhaps that impulse is why I became a psychiatrist.

Later in the book, Harry finds the door unlocked. When he steps inside, he finds a mirror, in some respects much like the mirrors that we have been discussing, the ones that catch glimpses of thieves. It is the mirror that determines whether one is allowed entrance into the inner rooms of the Magic Theater.

If granted entry into the back rooms of Hesse's Magic Theater, one learns to think for oneself, to ask questions with the naivete of a child, to look for interlocking systems, to see patterns where others see things, and to place compassion and laughter at the center of it all.

I am reminded of the wonderful quotation by Rabbi Harold Kushner, "God is like a mirror. The mirror never changes, but everybody who looks at it sees something different." I am an unabashed lover of magic mirrors, whether found in the pages of the Kabbalah, the rooms of magic theaters or the wings of the human matrix, which brings me to my point.

Over the years, and through thousands of hours of listening and learning from my patients, I have come to realize something rather remarkable. There really is a magic theater just as Hesse described it. It is right in front of our eyes. All of the time. It is the human matrix. The human matrix is about as close to a real magic theater, even down to the magic mirrors, as one is likely to encounter on this planet.

Like Hesse's theater the human matrix is a place of wonderful possibilities—thousands of them. And as one would expect in a place of magic, the human matrix is also a structure that one must step into with an appropriate bit of caution, for it can get pretty tricky in there with all that magic buzzing about. This caution brings us to our first paradoxical principle called The Paradox of Serendipitous Control:

Use the principles of the human matrix to carefully choreograph and plan your life so that you can live life without plans.

Puzzling at first glance, as any good paradox should be. Hesse will help clarify its meaning and its relevance to our quest for happiness. If you will recall, once Harry enters the Magic Theater he is immediately confronted by a large mirror. Like a beefy bouncer at a Hollywood hotspot, this mirror decides who gets to pass into the inner sanctum of the theater and who gets a quick kick back out the front door. So what is one to do? It is a very serious matter, is it not? Hesse's answer is simple.

Laugh.

Laugh long and laugh loudly. And if you laugh at what you see in the mirror, if you laugh at yourself, the magic mirror will subsequently whisk you into the delightful and delectable rooms of the Magic Theater. If you don't laugh . . . well, let's just say things don't go so well.

Steppenwolf is filled with laughter. Harry Haller learns to laugh. His lover loves to laugh. The jazz musicians around him are always laughing. Even what Hesse calls the "Immortals," like Mozart, laugh all the way up to *the* immortal, God. And Hesse's message is clear. Don't take oneself too seriously.

I am immediately reminded of the Taoist sage who claimed that he began each day by looking in the mirror and letting rip with a long and resounding peal of laughter. I tried this technique for awhile, but found that every time I looked at my middle-aged belly, I felt more like crying. So much for that technique for enlightenment. But I think you get the message.

But what does all this mean? How does Hesse's laughter explain the Paradox of Serendipitous Control?

It does so by addressing one of my biggest concerns when I talk about the use of the human matrix. I am always worried that someone will take the whole thing too seriously, without laughter.

My concern is that those "overly controlling types" (I happen to be one of them) will think that the human matrix is a control-freak's heaven, a way of knowing exactly what to do when. But this attitude towards the human matrix couldn't be further from the truth.

Using the human matrix is not about controlling life. It is about learning how to best flow with life, how best to be well prepared so that one can relinquish control of life, so that one can feel comfortable enough to let life take its own course. In the last analysis, life will tell us where we should be flowing if we only know how to listen. The human matrix is our ears.

The human matrix model provides a reliable method for creating plans for effectively navigating life. These plans are born from an up-front knowledge of what is happening on all five wings of our matrix, so that the plans don't fight upstream but flow gracefully downstream with the currents of our very natures. Once this proactive and creative thinking is done, we can sit back and confidently let loose of the "thought thing." It has served its purpose. We can move through the rest of the day or week or month confident that we've made the best decisions at hand. If they prove faulty, so be it. Because of our understanding of the ins and outs of the human matrix, we are in the best possible position to flexibly change them.

Alan Watts was fond of calling this method of navigating life the "watercourse way." The Taoists had a name for it, wu-wei, which Watts translates variously as "easy does it," "go with the stream" or "don't force it." I like to call it "the soft way." Life does not always have to be hard. By understanding and using the ideas of the human matrix, we optimize the likelihood that as we "let go" we will flow softly, moving with grace, quietly swirling about life's everyday obstacles with the swift and sure movements of a sparkling stream.

As we have said before, understanding the human matrix opens the door to trust. Trust opens the door to confidence. Confidence opens the door to the soft way—to serendipity—where most of life should be played.

The human matrix model is a marvelous tool for making plans about life that allow one to move softly through it. But, there is a catch; it only works if one uses it judiciously. One plans with the matrix when one needs to plan with the matrix—as a proactive tool, during times of trouble or when stymied by a problem. This insight is the core wisdom awaiting us in the Paradox of Serendipitous Control. Hesse's laughter reminds us of the need for this critical balance.

By the way, effective use of the human matrix should be fun. If it is not fun, you are probably misusing it. We aren't built to be running around being mindful of the matrix every single second of the day. Some people unwittingly misunderstand the spirit of the Eastern wisdom of "mindfulness" and misconstrue that all moments should be mindful moments. How utterly frightening!

As any Taoist sage would advise, during most of the moments of the day I don't want to be mindful of what I am doing, I just want to be doing. Life is not meant to be a sequential exercise in mindfulness or an endless contemplation of the wings of the human matrix. You can't live in the present moment if you are desperately trying to be mindful of it.

When you talk, talk. When you listen, listen. When you cry, cry. When you laugh, laugh. When someone dies, weep. When someone kisses you, get excited. Whatever you do, be mindful that you are never too mindful. Pai-chang, a Zen master sums it up rather nicely: "Eat when you are hungry, sleep when you are tired." Sounds a lot like Benny.

Herman Hesse was right. Laughter—not taking oneself, or the human matrix for that matter, too seriously—is the secret password into the back rooms of the Magic Theater. It is also the secret key to using the human matrix model effectively. If we plan well and judiciously use the powerful principles of the human matrix, we will be free to stop planning and to begin living in the delightful fullness of the present moment.

Monkeying Around in Magic Theaters

It is now time to quietly slip away from pre-war Germany and Hesse's make-believe Magic Theater. It is time to find a real-life magic theater. Lo and behold, such a magic theater can be found in Keene, New Hampshire. Inside it, our last two matrix principles await us—the last two paradoxes of the magic theater.

We will find our next paradox in an everyday place of business—Big Boom Productions. Big Boom Productions is a videoediting company that provides great services and witty repartee, not necessarily in that order.

As a public speaker who trains mental health professionals and primary care clinicians in advanced interviewing techniques—such as how to help patients share painful suicidal thoughts or how to effectively transform angry interactions—I often demonstrate my techniques with videotaped clinical interviews. Naturally, I am always trying to enhance the video quality of the tapes—hence my frequent trips to Big Boom Productions.

The particular trip of interest to uncovering our next paradox involved the need to digitalize some of my archived interviews to make the color and sound sharper. The original tape had already been digitized. It was time for me to do my end of the work.

Ted, the video tech who was assigned to help me—probably not an assignment the boys at Big Boom Productions were fighting over, for I am electronically highly challenged—stepped over and directed me to a chair sitting in front of a bunch of knobs. Such knobs on computers and electronic stuff tend to scatter my neurons like ants fleeing a spray of Raid. It is not a pleasant sight.

For the sake of setting the scene, I should add that Ted, who was from the British Isles, was possessed of a tart English accent. I just love British accents and all such Celtic sounds. I'd adopt Sean Connery's voice in a second, but I don't seem to have the right moves to accompany it.

In any case, it was my duty to look at these knobs and adjust them till the videotape had the color and the look that I was aiming for. Each knob had a distinct characteristic of the tape that it enhanced and controlled. There was a knob for adjusting color. There was a knob for contrast. There was a knob for light intensity. There was a knob for sharpness. There was a knob for hue. There were too many darn knobs. I didn't like the look of this setup. I sensed an ambush.

Immediately after Ted entered the control booth, I gave him one of my confused looks. Such a highly refined look requires a subtle facial control — not unlike that of a mime. I was good at this look, and on this day I creatively combined a frowning of my forehead with a gaping of my mouth until I looked like a bass gasping for air in a fisherman's boat. Such a bass is clearly out of its element. So was I. My look impressed Ted. He knew at once that I was an electronic moron.

"Don't worry, Shawn, this is really easy," he said.

I nodded dully. I have a very convincing dull nod.

"I'm not kidding. It's fun. You'll be done in a couple of minutes."

The genuine kindness of his tone of voice was starting to convince me to relax just a bit.

"You don't have to fret. None of the changes are permanent. If you make a mistake or don't like what you see, we can change it in a jiffy."

Ahhhh . . . music to my ears. Ted had said the exact words an electronic moron needs to hear. My fantasies of mucking up my most important teaching tape, a mistake that would undoubtedly lead to the entire demise of my professional career, the loss of my house, and perhaps of my spouse, had just been vaporized. I was happy. I was excited.

I was like the proverbial duck before water. I jumped in.

Twenty minutes later, I jumped back out. I was an unhappy duck. Every time I would adjust one knob just the way I liked it, the videotape had a new problem. For instance, if I turned up the contrast knob, the tape would suddenly look too bright. If I proceeded to adjust the brightness knob downward, the colors got all dark and gooky. If I adjusted the color knob, well, I think you get the point.

Then I realized, how silly of me, I had not asked Ted how to scientifically approach the adjustment process. Surely there was a strategy and a technique that helped one along. There was a science to this thing. I needed some help. Time to get the lowdown on the high-tech approach.

"Hey Ted."

"Yeah?" a disembodied voice called from a distant room. I feel certain Ted had strategically maneuvered himself into a room that would increase the likelihood that he could avoid contact with me until the mayhem was done.

"How do you work these things? I'm having a little trouble here."

I could have imagined the look on Ted's face at this point, but I chose not to.

"Come in here a second. What's the technique, my man, what's the science behind this process?" I had a newfound excitement. Help was at hand. Science would surely save the day.

At that point, a smiling head of Ted—for he actually was kind of fond of the silly goose that he knew I was—peeked around the corner.

With that perky British accent he commented, "Well, I just sort of monkey around with them all until I get the picture I want."

His face disappeared. I heard his steps disappearing down the hall.

Okay—so much for the high-tech approach, I thought to myself.

And there is our next paradox. You see, the videotape equalizing system at Big Boom Productions is a genuine matrix. Each knob controls a specific process along a given continuum—a little light to lots of light, a little color to lots of color—but no process in a matrix can be changed without impacting the other wings of the matrix. Ouch! That is tricky. And it is important. It is so important that it has a name, the Paradox of the Multiplicitous Knob:

> Eagerly change the wings of the matrix yet make changes with caution for every knob you change is two.

When you are in the magic theater of your mind, remember that as you monkey around with one wing, you need to consider the potential impact on the other wings. Because of the Rules of Interdependence, Damaging Matrix Effects, and Healing Matrix Effects, every time you turn one knob— make a change on one wing of the matrix—you can pretty well count on the idea that you are going to need to turn another knob as well and make a change on another wing of the matrix.

As with my videotapes, a tiny change can result in a huge change in the overall functioning of the entire happiness machine. This generalized matrix effect can be good or bad, but at the very least we must learn to make changes with caution, wisely recognizing that each change has many possible ramifications, some potentially unforeseeable.

For example, if I convince a patient who lacks assertiveness to be more assertive by using psychotherapy on the psychological wing of the matrix (Knob #1), I better make sure that on the interpersonal wing of the matrix (Knob #2) we don't have a violent husband with alcoholism sitting at home. This abusive spouse may respond to the new assertiveness in his partner with the sharp edges of a broken wine bottle. Touch one knob . . . get the point? Clearly, while helping the patient with her assertiveness (turning Knob #1), one also needs to be intervening on the interpersonal wing by uncovering the alcoholism and addressing the domestic violence (turning Knob #2).

Generally speaking, most ramifications of the Paradox of the Multiplicitous Knob are much smaller and quite benign in nature. But it is important to maintain a healthy respect for the complexities of the human matrix, which simply means asking oneself what the possible ramifications of making a significant change in one wing may be on the other wings. Likewise, after making a change, always be on the lookout for both unexpected healing matrix effects and unsuspected damaging matrix effects.

Keeping these simple principles in mind, nine times out of ten your matrix interventions are going to help you uncover happiness in a much more effective fashion. The Paradox of the Multiplicitous Knob is not something to worry about. It is something to respect. It can help us.

Speaking of help, our experiences at Big Boom Productions directly conjure up our third and last paradox, the Paradox of Humbling Confidence:

Learn to move with incisive confidence in the human matrix, for
its insights provide you with a decisive edge; yet ask for help often.

Life is humbling if it is nothing else. Even though an understanding of the workings of the human matrix will undoubtedly result in a healthy gain in self-confidence, a matrix magician must never be afraid to do two things: (1) admit that he or she is wrong and (2) ask others for help.

As we have seen, the human matrix is a complicated, constantly shifting pattern that is filled with deceptive shadows and hidden trapdoors. As Alan Watts warned in his delightful book, *Taoism: Way Beyond Seeking*, "The world is everything happening altogether everywhere, and you just can't take all of that into consideration because there isn't time." I'd have to go ditto on that one.

I find it surprisingly useful, even with relatively easy matrix problems, to ask for help from Susan, my two boys, my friends, my colleagues and my books. It is always refreshing to get opinions from others.

A new pair of objective peepers may be better able to spot an untoward, or even a beneficial, matrix effect. From within our own matrices it is far too easy to see with the distorting eyes of self-interest. It's also just plain fun to see what others have to say and frequently intellectually stimulating to boot.

At other times, we are facing major life stressors that threaten to trigger seriously damaging matrix meltdowns. It is here that the Paradox of Humbling Confidence is most instructive. Without hesitation I can say that if you find yourself having persistent and painful feelings of depression and/or anxiety for more than a month, take the time to talk with your primary care physician or perhaps a mental health professional, even if you think you know exactly what is causing the pain. You might not. Red herrings are waiting everywhere. Or you might think that you know exactly what must be done. You might not. Hidden healing matrix effects are even more common than red herrings.

Over the years, with both my patients and with my own doings, I have found that the more difficult and the more complex the problem—the more intense the pain you are feeling—once you start monkeying around in the human matrix it can be surprisingly easy to become hopelessly lost in it. The magic theater can rapidly and, even dangerously, become a decidedly unpleasant magic maze. Here is where professionals like physicians, psychiatrists, psychologists, counselors, therapists and ministers may be vital to sorting things out and avoiding red herrings.

Remember Maria with her panic attacks following her child's birth? She had no idea that her pain was related to a biological maelstrom that had swept over a tiny lake in her brain. People were telling her to work through her obvious problems with ambivalence towards a child that she loved. People would have continued to harp indefinitely on this idea, misguided as it may be. It only took an hour with a professional for the correct wing of the matrix to be uncovered and appropriate intervention started.

Without that help Maria could have needlessly suffered for months or years. Without that help, who knows? Maria may have even eventually been lost to suicide—an incalculable loss to herself, her children, her spouse and all those that love her. Incalculable . . . . and absolutely needless.

You see, Ted from Big Boom Productions left something out. He might truly in his mind be "just monkeying" around with the knobs in his magic theater, but his monkeying around is being guided by years of understanding the results of such monkeying. He can anticipate matrix effects. He can spot red herrings. He can avoid damaging matrix effects. He can generate healing matrix effects. He can make the matrix work for him not against him. He can adjust the matrix so that it flows softly.

The beneficial consequence is that Ted's monkeying might produce splendid results in just a couple of minutes. My monkeying took, shall we just say, a little while longer. That is why on occasion, when it comes to an area like mental health, where I do have some expertise, it really is wise to knock on my office door or the door of your primary care physician. Health professionals are to damaged happiness machines what Ted is to mucked-up videotapes.

We have reached a waystation in our quest for happiness, the end of part III. If you will recall, we said that if we were successful, we should by this point have developed a rule book for our happiness quest. If lucky, this rule book would not only explain the rules of the game; it would provide strategic principles suggested by those very same rules—an owner's manual of sorts. And so we have.

It is worth taking a look at our rule book in its completed format, for such a survey will consolidate our understanding of the human matrix and better prepare us for our last and final step: a real world road test of our happiness machine.

The Rule Book for Happiness Machines: The Secrets of the Human Matrix

GUIDING RULES

#1 The Interdependence Rule

All wings of the human matrix intersect and are interdependent upon one another (think quantum mechanics).

#2 The Damaging Matrix Rule

Because there is interdependence in the wings of the human matrix, a problem on one wing can directly cause damage on a different wing (the social abuse done to Kaspar Hauser and its impact on his growth).

#3 The Red Herring Rule

Because of interdependence and damaging matrix effects, a problem on one wing of the matrix may cause such severe problems on a different wing that one is misled as to where the real problem lies (the tremendous damage done by the virions in Sally's brain on her thoughts, her mood and her behaviors to the point that people felt these wings of her matrix held her major problem).

#4 The Healing Matrix Rule

Because there is interdependence in the wings of the human matrix, a beneficial effect on one wing can directly cause a beneficial effect on a different wing (the power of cognitive therapy to heal the neurons misfiring in the brain of a little kid named Nick, who just had to spit).

STRATEGIC PRINCIPLES

#1 The Won't Get Fooled Again Principle

No matter how obvious it appears that one wing is the cause of the current state of unhappiness or disruption, search all other wings before deciding where the main problem lies (think of Maria and the mistaken assumption that she had ambivalent feelings about her child).

#2 The Cast a Wide Net Principle

No matter what the apparent cause of the immediate unhappiness, look at all wings of the matrix for contributing problems related to smaller yet still damaging matrix effects (the combined impact of Sally's problems from various wings of her matrix on her mood—in addition to the life-threatening emergency created by her encephalitis—including, long-standing interpersonal problems with kids at school, chronic feelings of insecurity and self-denigration, unintended tensions with her parents and the immediate social ostracism related to her slumber party fiasco).

#3 The Distant Healing Principle

When problems arise in the matrix look for healing matrix effects that can help a single distant wing—where the primary problem is originating—or on other distant wings—where secondary problems exist (Mrs. Perkins and the wisdom of tracking down God's telephone number).

#4 The Maximized Matrix Principle

No matter what the apparent cause of the immediate unhappiness, look at all wings of the matrix for possible healing effects. Maximize all possible healing matrix effects and the functioning of all the wings in a general sense. The more healing matrix effects that one can muster and the higher the general functioning on all the wings, the higher the likelihood of relief (once again think of Mrs. Perkins, with whom we eventually maximized all wings of her matrix using a combination of medications, individual counseling, group psychotherapy, a comforting hospitalization and the help of a caring local priest).

#5 The Universal Applicability Principle

Since every thing can be viewed from a quantum perspective as a matrix, all the principles that help to uncover happiness in the human matrix may be applicable to transforming dysfunction in other matrices: business problems, financial problems, community problems, even, at times, serious social problems (including crime, racism, poverty, and political discord). Matrix problem solving has the potential to be a "possibility generator" in a surprisingly broad range of situations (recall the power of matrix principles, when applied with great sophistication, to kick-start an entire social cycle of healing in the battle against AIDS in Haiti).

The Three Paradoxes of the Magic Theater

#1 The Paradox of Serendipitous Control

Use the principles of the human matrix to carefully choreograph and plan your life so that you can live life without plans (think magic mirrors, the importance of laughter, and flowing ever so softly around life's obstacles).

#2 The Paradox of the Multiplicitous Knob

Eagerly change the wings of the matrix yet make changes with caution, for every knob you change is two (remember Ted's sage advice to just twirl all the knobs).

#3 The Paradox of Humbling Confidence

Learn to move with incisive confidence in the human matrix, for its insights provide you with a decisive edge; yet ask for help often (knock on my door sooner than later if the situation warrants it).

The Fourth Paradox of the Magic Theater and Why Helen Keller Would Have Liked Our Rule Book

Now that we have reviewed our little book of rules and strategies for perusing magic theaters, I should mention something about Herman Hesse. I think he may have been holding back on us. His opening quotation barely hints at the wonders that await Harry Haller when he steps into the Magic Theater in search of himself.

Once inside, Harry will quickly discover that he is not just one Harry. He is two Harrys. There is Harry the human—an intellectual, thoughtful and timid being—and there is Harry the wolf—a lustful, sensual and bold being. Hesse believed that all people, not just Harry Haller, must recognize both sides of their natures and learn to integrate them so that these divergent natures do good things, not bad things.

Isolated from one another, they are prone to harm others by their big-otry and judgmental nature. Creatively synthesized they are capable of helping others by their openness and accepting nature. There are times in life calling for a timid approach and times in life calling for a bold approach. One must be able to do both.

But there is an even more powerful lesson to be learned in the back rooms of the Magic Theater. There is a fourth paradox waiting there. It has a great deal to do with our human matrix and the rule book we have worked so hard to uncover. I shall let Hesse introduce the paradox for himself:

> To explain so complex a man as Harry by the artless division into wolf and man is a hopelessly childish attempt. Harry consists of a hun-dred or a thousand selves, not of two. His life oscillates, as everyone's does, not merely between two poles, such as the body and the spirit, the saint and the sinner, but between thousands and thousands.

Paradoxically, each single human being is, in reality, a multitude of human beings. The Fourth Paradox of the Magic Theater is a powerful one:

The goal is not to know yourself. It is to know *yourselves.*

But the Fourth Paradox is even more far reaching, for Hesse was wrong on his math. As we now know from our knowledge of quantum mechanics and the resulting model of the human matrix derived from it, each person is a never-ending set of selves. Each self is defined by the unique intersec-tion of all five wings of the human matrix at each unique moment in time. Indeed, each self is a trillion trillion selves limited only by the number of seconds in a lifetime, for each second gives birth to a new being.

I believe it is our rule book that offers us one of our best shots at catch-ing a glimpse of this marvelously fleeting parade of selves; their competing needs, their powerful dreams and their divergent destinies. It provides us a chance to achieve a more resilient and practical education, much as Helen

Keller opined when she wrote, "The best educated human being is the one who understands most about the life in which he is placed."

With our rule book in hand, I believe that we have a reasonably good chance of understanding more about the life in which we have been so enigmatically placed. It is a tough life, but it is also a wonderfully good life—rich with compassion, mystery, and the endless twists and turns of serendipity.

I believe that Helen Keller would be very pleased with our education. She was a great believer in the power of trust. When you are blind, you learn a great deal about trust. You have no choice. You quickly learn the importance of the type of proactive planning that lies at the very heart of using the human matrix model effectively. And you learn how to "let go" after you have done your planning.

It was why Helen Keller, who was robbed of so much of what one would assume brings happiness to the world—sights and sounds—did not wait for the world to bring her happiness. She brought happiness to the world. She possessed the tough and enduring sense of happiness for which we have been so diligently searching. Despite a strangely dark and eerily quiet world, she learned to trust and, ultimately, to move with confidence.

As the quantum physicist Alfred North Whitehead said, "Nature is a theatre for the interrelations of activities." In part III we have learned how these activities interrelate. Whether it is the Magic Theater of Hesse, the video theater of Big Boom Productions or the awesome theater of nature described by Whitehead, they are all filled with wonderment and promise. We have our book of rules. We have our laughter. We have our magic mirrors. We have found the very things we need to free our souls. It is time at last to begin our quest, to take our happiness machine for a spin on the open road, where a thousand possibilities await us.

Part IV

The Quest Achieved:
Using the Human Matrix
to Uncover Happiness

*"Kindness is more important than wisdom,
and the recognition of this is the beginning of wisdom."*

THEODORE ISAAC RUBIN

*"The happiest excitement in life is to be
convinced that one is fighting for all one is worth on
behalf of some clearly seen and deeply felt good."*

RUTH BENEDICT
AMERICAN ANTHROPOLOGIST

15

Meet You at the
North Fork Dam

*"Know yourselves, and thou wilt know
the universe and the gods."*

PYTHAGORAS
MODIFIED TO A QUANTUM WORLD

The Third Coming of Michelle Kwan: A Prelude for Part IV

Performance. As we take our happiness machines out on the open road, our quest comes down to one word—performance. Does our understanding of the human matrix and its rules result in a successful quest—will it help us to perform better? Specifically, will it help us to more easily uncover an enduring sense of happiness?

But there is more to the story of performance than meets the eye. I am again reminded of Michelle Kwan's words, "I am excited about the program and confident of the performance." The initial words of this sentence are worth a second look. I'm not so sure that Michelle Kwan would perform so well unless she was genuinely excited about her program in the first place.

It is my guess that when Michelle Kwan steps upon the ice, she believes quite profoundly that she has choreographed a winning program. She knows in her gut that the design of her program effectively matches the needs of the competition with the skills that she brings to it. This empowering belief gives Michelle Kwan a dramatic competitive edge. It unleashes her confidence and her resulting power to skate in the present moment. But it also unleashes something new—excitement.

It is this excitement, generated by her unwavering belief in her program itself, that will translate all the years of hard work and practice into victory. Ultimate success is dependent not only on the choreography of the program, but on the excitement the skater brings to the performance of that choreography. It is this excitement that is a prerequisite for peak performance, whether the quest is for gold or happiness. In a similar sense, much of our success, in the quest for happiness, will depend upon the excitement we bring to our use of the model of the human matrix. How can we routinely and reliably generate such excitement?

Once again, much can be learned by examining how seasoned athletes generate their excitement. How do champions come to believe so intensely in the quality of their programs that they hit the ice bursting with an excitement that fires the blades of their skates, the hearts of the crowd and the scorecards of the judges? And, equally intriguing, how do they consistently maintain such excitement over the passage of their arduous careers?

As we begin to track down the answers to these questions, we come face to face with another example of an exquisitely beneficial positive feedback loop. Confidence breeds excitement. The excitement generated from this confidence leads to peak performances. These peak performances generate yet more confidence from which even more excitement follows and so on. We have seen a similar loop before—happiness begets happiness. It is the wisdom inherent in Kwan's comment, "I'm excited about the program and confident of its performance." One can enter this loop at any point by generating either confidence or excitement. Once in the loop, good things happen.

In the final chapters of our book—as we try to understand how to use the model of the human matrix effectively—we shall look in depth at the practices that bring excitement and confidence to our use of it. The end result is enhanced performance—increased happiness. Once again, we shall find that Michelle Kwan and her colleagues provide a useful metaphor for guiding our explorations. There are many methods that skaters use to step into the wondrous loop that interlaces confidence and excitement. All of these ways maximize performance both immediately— with the performance at hand—and longitudinally—with the performances of the future. I am struck by four particularly potent factors.

First, although I don't know Kwan personally, I feel certain that part of her ability to enter this critical loop comes from her sophisticated understanding of how to strategize, using her intimate knowledge of her own skating matrix, to create cohesive, functional programs that dazzle. No wings are left out. No wings are unattended. No wings are left broken. All wings are nurtured. The resulting choreography glows with the creative ingenuity born from her masterful ability to integrate the knowledge of the five wings of her skating matrix into winning programs.

Second, I suspect that Michelle Kwan has learned something that all master skaters must learn if they are to consistently produce winning programs. One doesn't want to be a brilliant flash in the pan that immediately becomes yesterday's news. To avoid this fate, the skater must learn how to improve. Improvement is a difficult feat if one is already skating near the level of perfection.

To do so, Michelle Kwan must carefully nurture the ability to tease out and improve the specific skills inherent to each wing of her skating machine. By doing so, when she is designing programs, she will be able to call on what skill is needed to create what effect she wants in any program that she designs. The result is a growing confidence and excitement that she can handle whatever challenges may come her way.

Third, Kwan has learned that not all the matrix effects within her skating machine are of equal importance. After years of discipline and competing she has happened upon a few particularly effective favorites. Her years of experience have taught her well. She has secrets, not damaging ones like Nick with his OCD, but winning ones like those Julian of Norwich used to whisper through her window. I feel confident that Kwan, like all seasoned skaters, has a knack for weaving these favorites into the fabric of her programs, yet another reason she skates with such excitement.

The fourth and final factor for enhancing confidence and excitement is an elusive one. It eludes all except those few athletes destined for sustained greatness: ferocious motivation. I suspect that Kwan, like all such champions, knows that to design winning programs and to skate them brilliantly over the long haul, you have to be a master at self-motivation. She knows what fuel propels a skating machine. She knows something that most of her competitors do not know. She knows "why." Because she knows why the skating machine skates, she is in a better place to make it do so well.

So it is with happiness machines when they are designing happiness programs. The same factors that help a skater to believe, to be excited, about his or her program will help us to be excited about ours.

But Kwan and other skaters use their understanding of their skating matrices to design skating programs. What is the equivalent task for happiness machines? What is the happiness machine's equivalent of a skating program? What exactly do we design when we use our knowledge of the human matrix? The answer is a simple one. We design plans of action. We design practical interventions. We design potential solutions to specific problems. If used effectively, the model of the human matrix can be used to generate possibilities on all of these fronts.

The model of the human matrix provides us with a surprisingly rapid and thorough method for sorting through many of the complexities of life in a systematic fashion. It is a model that is dependable and easily used at any time of the day or night. Through this lens, we hope to transform small problems before they become big ones. Indeed, once we have searched for matrix effects, red herrings and paradoxes on all five wings of the human matrix—from biological to spiritual—the potential success of our plans is greatly enhanced.

By shrewdly applying the principles of the human matrix we can, more often than not, generate creative plans for getting out of whatever mess we happen to be in at the moment. Such messes can range from the simple (feeling sort of "not with it today"), to the moderately complex (problems at work or with a marriage), to the really difficult and markedly complex (a divorce, a custody hearing, a severe mental illness).

This does not mean that we can eliminate all messes. Some messes are not going to go away. Some messes need to be left behind; some we walk around; and others we learn how to more gracefully accept. I am reminded of one of my favorite prayers, "God grant me the serenity to accept the things I cannot change, the courage to change the things I can, and the wisdom to know the difference." The application of the human matrix model can help bring the promise of the Serenity Prayer into the reality of everyday practice.

From a more personal perspective, when I have used the principles of the human matrix model in my own life, I have found that I have often performed better. I have increased my likelihood of feeling a little bit better and of coping a little bit more efficiently with whatever the particular mess is that I have encountered on that particular day.

To use the human matrix model wisely, like a skater, we must learn strategies for weaving our knowledge of the five wings of the human matrix into effective and cohesive plans of action. There are a variety of strategies that we can use. These strategies for applying the model of the human matrix range from strategies for immediately addressing short-term problems to strategies specifically designed for long-term problem solving and goal setting.

For instance, you can use the model of the human matrix proactively for the setting of long-term life goals, a strategy I like to affectionately call "matrix building." In matrix building we review each wing of our matrix and ask, "What do I want this wing to look like a year from now, or five years from now?"

After picking some goals, we decide which of life's tools (skills) will be necessary to get the job done, to most easily reach those goals. We take a look in our toolbox of personal skills. If the necessary tools are missing, we're off to the "hardware store." The hardware store may consist of a self-improvement book, advice from a mentor, a weekend retreat or, if you want the very best education that money can buy, you might choose to work with a therapist who can teach you advanced techniques for transforming life's inevitable obstacles.

There is no space in this book to do justice to all the many strategies for using and integrating our knowledge of the human matrix. Instead, I think it is most valuable to pick one such strategy and demonstrate it in detail, so that the reader has a model with which to develop other strategies. Ultimately, each person uses the knowledge of the matrix in uniquely flexible fashions that best suit their own proclivities, strengths and interests. In this chapter we will look at one of my very favorite strategies for using the human matrix model—the matrix spin.

But before we take a look at matrix spins, let us review our overall goals for part IV of our book, for they parallel nicely the four lessons we have learned from Michelle Kwan. By the conclusion of part IV we will achieve the following:

1.) We will have carefully explored a concrete example of a strategy—the matrix spin—for using our knowledge of the five wings of the human matrix to design concrete plans that transform specific obstacles to happiness. (We need to see a reliable strategy in action that uses the principles of the human matrix to tackle everyday problems.)

2.) We will have seen an example of how you can hone a specific skill on a specific wing of the human matrix. (We need to know how individual skills can be singled out, improved and used to enhance our ability to both create effective plans for uncovering happiness and effectively implementing them over time).

3.) We will have learned that not all the matrix effects in the happiness machine are of equal importance. Specifically, I shall share one of my favorite healing matrix effects. (We need to uncover a secret or two regarding the design of practical plans for use in the quest for happiness.)

4.) We will have a better idea of "why." Why does the human matrix move and what propels it to do so? (We need to know what fuel our happiness machine needs to work at peak performance.)

Armed with a working knowledge of these four factors, we will be ready to take our happiness machines out for a spin. But before we take our spin, I should add a cautionary note, for it would be very easy for a reader to wonder if the model of the human matrix is being presented as a system for beating life. The answer is a resounding, "Good God, no!"

You can't beat life, for life is not something to be beaten, it is something to be in cahoots with. As we learned in the Magic Theater, you don't want to be competing against life. You want to be laughing with life. Life is not the opposing team. It is the wondrously diverse group of teammates joking and roughhousing on the bus as we head for the stadium, some of whom we like, some of whom we dislike, all of whom are necessary for us to win the game. As with teammates, I have found it wisest to accept life as it is, the good with the bad. The art is making the good even better and the bad just a bit good, a fact that any successful baseball manager could tell us and Julian of Norwich already did.

Moreover, clever systems designed to beat the system almost never work—a lesson I learned from a most unlikely source, my dad. He spent much of his free time developing systems for beating the game of golf.

As was the case with about forty million other golfing addicts, every thirty or so days he developed a new system. My mother and I would always know of its arrival. From the dark recesses of the garage, where my dad had rigged a practice net, we would hear his jubilant voice bound down the hallway, "I've got it now!"

He did not. God bless his soul.

So the model of the human matrix is not a system for beating life. It is a marvelous lens for learning how to gracefully navigate and flow with life. It is a lens for seeing that we are life. Our brains are busily, with the diligent determination of honeybees, creating the universe. The universe, with the reliability of a honeybee colony, does its part. It busily creates brains. In a never-ending interplay of matrix effects, brain and universe, soul and world, "other" and "self" coalesce to form a kaleidoscope of reflections, creations and problems to be solved. The model of the human matrix provides a way, a wondrously soft way, of learning how to better transform these problems.

Bad Hair Days and the Fine Art of
Taking a Matrix Spin

Paradoxically, my first task is not so much to demonstrate that the application of the human matrix model can handle a big problem as it is to demonstrate that it can handle a little one. I believe that the example of transforming Nick's OCD—on a very human level—and transforming the AIDS matrix in Haiti—on a societal level—are already convincing illustrations of the power of applying the principles of the human matrix to big problems.

Indeed, returning to our skating machine metaphor, we have already shown that our model can help us to win world championships. But what about tiny, local skating competitions? I believe that, for our book to be completely successful, we must demonstrate that the human matrix can help us with the little dilemmas of life like, you know, bad hair days.

A matrix spin is a perfect strategy for uncovering happiness on bad hair days. To understand how a matrix spin works—how to use the rules, the principles and the paradoxes of our rule book.to "put it all together" with tiny everyday problems—we must go back in time. The year is 1961. I was seven years old.

When I was growing up, I had the good fortune that my father was not only a golf nut, he was a sports car nut. I particularly remember a silver

Porsche from the late 1950s. I don't even know what model it was. I just remember, with a child's magical vision, that it was silver, fast and looked like a Volkswagen Beetle on steroids.

My father enjoyed taking the Porsche for spins around the North Fork Dam. More important for me, he liked taking me along. Some of my fondest memories of both my childhood and my father were our spins. They usually took us to the North Fork Dam Road up past the Pickin' Chicken Diner and down past the abandoned coal mine, where on one very special day we stopped and went exploring.

Little did I know that forty years later I would be taking spins of a different nature—matrix spins—that would also prove to be of great importance to my happiness. In a matrix spin we don't go snaking around the tree-canopied roads that curve around North Fork Dam. Instead, a matrix spin simply means that we take a quick spin through all five wings of our matrix to see what's happening in each wing both recently and at the present moment.

These matrix spins are a responsive form of matrix work. I use them in response to feeling not so happy. If I'm having a rough moment in a day, I take five minutes out to take a quick matrix spin to see what might be causing the problem.

The first step of a matrix spin is to spot which wings may be having problems and what the problems may be. During this step, I always keep an eye out for damaging matrix effects while trying to make sure that I'm not taken in by a red herring or two.

The second step is to decide what I am going to do about the problems that I uncovered with the tools that I have immediately in hand: directly work on the problematic wings themselves, look for indirect healing matrix effects or perhaps just attempt to maximize every wing as best I can in as quick a fashion as possible. The final goal is to create a set of practical plans for all the appropriate wings of my matrix that can help me to reverse the direction of a day that is quickly going sour. A matrix spin is a strategy for rapidly creating such plans.

If lucky, within an hour after implementing the changes, I'll be feeling a bit better. Sometimes I am feeling remarkably better. Sometimes I don't feel any better; you can't win them all. On the other hand, matrix spins can often turn a bad hair day around, as sure as one of my father's spins around the North Fork Dam would perk up his spirits and mine as well.

For the sake of modeling a matrix spin, let me list the types of questions that might be of use on each wing for spotting specific problems. Please note, I don't need to ask myself all of these questions, because I'm experienced at using the strategy, nor will you after you get used to taking a spin now and then.

I usually just simply ask myself, "What's going on in my biological wing?" When I'm done answering that question I go on to the next wing, "What's going on with me interpersonally right now?" and so on, through each of the five wings.

Because you are just getting the knack for taking a matrix spin, a list of questions may be of value as you learn how to address issues on each wing of the matrix. Even now I sometimes ask myself some of these same questions. Remember, the first step of a matrix spin is to find out which wings of the matrix are troubled and what the trouble is. These are the kinds of questions that can help you find out quickly. See what you think:

1. Biological
    a.) Am I feeling wound-up physically?
    b.) Am I showing any nervous habits (like twitching feet, picking or biting at nails, twirling of hair) or signs of biological stress (a rapid pulse or rapid breathing rate)? Either of these findings may reflect the fact that I am wound-up physically but may not be fully aware of it.
    c.) Am I feeling tired, weary or sleepy?
2. Psychological
    a.) Am I fretting, worrying or otherwise stealing time from the present moment? Is there a thief in the mirror?

b.) Am I feeling demoralized, sad, tearful or depressed?

c.) Am I having negative thoughts?

d.) Am I feeling stressed? Worried that I won't be able to do something that I feel is important? Worried that I am going to let someone down, feel shame or be humiliated?

e.) Am I denigrating myself?

f.) Am I replaying unpleasant or hurtful memories?

g.) Am I fretting about someone I love?

3. Interpersonal

a.) How are things going today with the people who I have been just interacting with (partner, kids, friends, bosses, colleagues)?

b.) Are they enjoying my company?

c.) Am I enjoying their company?

d.) Am I feeling angry at anyone?

e.) Am I feeling jealous or bitter?

f.) Am I feeling sexually frustrated?

g.) Have I been talking negatively about someone?

4. Environmental (situations related to social groups or environmental situations not related to people)

a.) Is my nuclear or extended family causing problems?

b.) Am I angry at a group of people (family, bosses and administrators, employees, a group of friends, a set of neighbors)?

c.) Is my immediate culture bringing me psychological and/or physical violence (racism, sexism, ageism, homophobia)?

d.) Am I worried about finances, jobs, lawsuits or business deals?

e.) Am I literally being bothered by my immediate environment (the room I'm sitting in, the house I'm living in, the office space I'm working in)? For instance, am I feeling cooped up, or bothered that the house is a mess?

f.) Is there an immediate and serious nonsocial stressor (pollution, dangerous weather, physical illness)?

5. Spiritual

    a.) Are my spiritual needs being addressed?

    b.) Have I had any spiritual thoughts today?

    c.) Have I done any of the activities that calm or address my spiritual side such as listening to music, reading philosophy, praying, meditating, caring for or playing with a pet, walking or enjoying nature?

As you review each wing of the matrix (I can't emphasize enough that it is not as formal as the "cheat sheet" above suggests), you apply the rules, principles and paradoxes from our last chapter that may help transform the matrix with the tools at hand.

Notice that I can't tell you the details of how to pick out a set of specific strategies and tools to address the exact problems on each wing—for a very good reason. The types of problems encountered, which strategies from our rule book will be immediately applicable, and the set of potential tools you personally have available combine to create an endless array of situations and solutions.

We each have at hand different skills (our tools) for transforming each wing of the matrix: from working out to using psychological tools that we might have gained from a book; from remembering a bit of wisdom our mothers once said to saying a prayer we just read; from talking with a friend to seeking refreshment in the solitude of a woodland walk. Each person has a set of preferred tools (and talent in using those tools) in the same fashion that each figure skater has a set of skating skills and talent at using them.

A matrix spin is an advanced strategy for using the model of the human matrix to transform immediate threats to your happiness. It tells you where the problems are, the extent of the problems, and therefore what types of tools may be useful in solving them. It even suggests how to use the tools as a coherent unit through the strategic principles of our rule book. You then simply have to pick the tools that you ultimately want to employ.

Hopefully, this book will get you excited to go rummaging about for more and more tools for your toolbox, from diet plans to psychological frameworks for better understanding who you are and what you need. You may even discover that you have a relative paucity of tools for use on a specific wing or two. If this proves to be the case, you can proceed to beef up your toolbox through reading, therapy or spiritual endeavors. In the next chapter we will see how easy it is to acquire skills for use in a specific wing of the matrix.

Thus far we have accomplished two tasks. We have described the theory behind the use of the matrix spin strategy, and we have looked at specific questions that may help us to use it effectively. Our third and final goal is both simple and fun. Let's see our strategy in action.

Bedbugs, Deadlines and Porsches

I will demonstrate a matrix spin with my favorite guinea pig—me. Several weeks before penning this very page, I began the day, shall we say, badly. Let me set the scene. I had an extremely tight deadline for finishing part II of this book. It would require writing at a ferocious pace. Odds were against maintaining such a pace.

Although the job of writing has some definite similarities to my clinical work, in some ways I have found it to be quite unlike any job I have ever had before. Whether I feel like it or not I go to my clinic on clinic days. Once there, even if I am not feeling too great I can still do good work, because I can focus upon the needs of the patients. Naturally, even clinicians have "off days" when they would rather be at home listening to The Who, Third Eye Blind or Eminem—take your pick—but once there, the job comes easy.

Writing is not like this. If you don't feel like writing, it is unbelievably hard to write well. Oh, you can make yourself do it all right. But it is a slow and painful process. The results may be even more painful to read.

If you write when you really don't want to be writing, you are probably buying some pretty heavy-duty edit time. In the ensuing hours you will have more than a few chances to practice your "three-pointers" into nearby trash cans. You may find creative, catchy new expletives entering your stream of consciousness. You may even break some useless household items that needed to go anyway. But you won't write well.

On this particular day I was all excited about writing when I woke up.

Promptly at 8:30 A.M. my editor, Bret, called unexpectedly. Editors like to do that sort of thing. If your editor calls at 8:30 A.M., do not pick up the phone. They are calling because they did not sleep well. They had a bedbug the size of an orange in bed with them. They want to share this creature with you.

At 8:30 A.M. editors say things to you like, "I don't like the title you have chosen for your book." That phrase is exactly how Bret started my day.

He didn't like the title of my book.

That particular message is not music to any author's ears. But he had an even better tune to pass on. Nobody liked the title. "I showed it to about seven people here and nobody likes it. Oh, and by the way, good morning!" The good morning part is usually said with an annoyingly chipper sound.

Well now, isn't *that* just dandy. It's a great way to start off the morning—much better than a bowl full of Wheaties. For the sake of making the record clear, I should add that the title Bret eventually guided me toward, *Happiness Is.*, I absolutely adore. And I can't thank him enough for his wise guidance. (Bret made me add this last sentence. It's true, although personally I think it hurts the flow of this passage.)

Nevertheless, on this particular morning I was not a happy camper. I began pacing about the living room, mumbling to myself as one does when one is chewing out "no-good-nicks" in absentia. I didn't know who the seven people were that he had shown the title, but I damn well knew that they were no-good-nicks. After about ten minutes of convincing myself that the book was now doomed, for only the title that I had imagined could possibly work, I managed to settle myself down.

I had to settle down. You can't write good spiritual stuff when you feel like committing a felony, when your thoughts have moved to chainsaws, meat cleavers and hockey masks. The Dalai Lama frowns on this kind of thing. I had to get spiritual fast.

I knew that in a few minutes, if I wanted to have even a prayer of staying on schedule, I had to get my butt off to one of my favorite writing haunts. I still had a good thirty-minute drive down to Keene to reach it. The clock was ticking.

Once in Keene it would take me another good ten minutes to plop the aforementioned butt into a chair at either the Mason Library at Keene State or at Brewbakers, a local coffee shop. The latter thought brought a fleeting smile to my face as I imagined walking into Brewbakers to order my regular from Jason — "a café latte, double, no foam please" — the tasty treat that is always steaming before me when I do my best writing. But I had no time for such pleasantries. "My God, man! Precious time has been lost!" my superego quickly yelled at about thirty thousand decibels. I got the message.

I hopped in my car. As usual Susan came out to see me off for the day with a delicious kiss. After the kiss, she paused and then said, "You know, I'm not sure I want to go to Cape Cod this summer. I'm a little bit tired of it." Please note that for many months I had been looking forward eagerly, almost desperately, to our annual Cape Cod trip. It had become a family tradition for seven straight years. Never mess with a writer's core traditions as you are seeing the writer off for the day.

"Okay. I guess we'll have to see." That's all I said.

Of course, it was not okay.

By a quarter of a mile down the road, I was hot. Brewbakers could have used me to steam up those lattes. "Now why did she have to do that right now? I can't believe it. This really pisses me off. I just want to have a fun vacation. I've been working twelve-hour days all month, and I just want to enjoy my family at the Cape. That's all I want to do. Is that asking too much?" My two editors had given me back-to-back punches. It must be a conspiracy.

I turned the car sharply around.

When I stomped into the kitchen, doing my very best of imitation of

Ralph Cramden about to send Alice off to the moon, Susan looked surprised.

In a pleasant voice she asked, "What are you doing back? Did you forget something?"

With that demanding tone of voice that only Ralph Cramden, the epitome of maleness at its most annoying, was capable of conjuring up, I tersely said, "We've got to clear the air."

"About what?"

"About this Cape Cod business."

Yes, I was being an idiot.

Her response was a reasonable one, said with a reasonable tone of voice. "Oh that. I'm sorry if it upset you. It's not a big deal. I mean it. I still love the Cape. I just thought a change might be nice."

I just hate it when Susan keeps being reasonable when I'm being an idiot.

"Well, I don't." I snapped. I felt like adding, "And I like the damn title for the book," but it was the wrong editor.

Susan took the bait and testily responded, "I can see that now. I'm sorry. And it's not a big deal. We're off to the damn Cape. Forget it. It's *not* a big deal."

Then her facial expression softened. It had softened because, as is her habit, she had cut through the crap and intuited the real problem. I had a bedbug up my rear. A big one. Thanks, Bret.

She added, with a gentle tone of voice, "I can see now that my timing was a bit off." She paused, "I love the title of your book. You know that. Maybe they will change their minds. If they don't, I'm sure that Bret and you will come up with a great title. You're both smart guys. Remember, it's the writing on the inside, not the outside, that will eventually determine the success."

At times like this, she scares me. She must be a mind reader or something. In any case I grunted a thank-you and gave her a hug—one of my notorious "I love you but I'm still mad at you" hugs—and sulked out the door. I plunked down in the living room.

The ball game was over. I couldn't write now, that's for sure. I couldn't believe that the no-good-nicks at the publishing house did not like the title. It had Pulitzer written all over it. For gosh sakes, wake up, people. We're professional publishers here, aren't we? (My sarcastic side was now in full force.) And I was still mad at Susan. Why did she have to bring that Cape Cod stuff up now when I'm all off balance? I can't believe this is happening. I just can't believe this is happening to me (there's one of my favorites, the old "poor pitiful me." Gosh I love the oldies but goodies).

I looked in the mirror. He was there. The thief. He wasn't just smiling, he was gloating. My tether was so far away from the present moment that they'd need a motorized winch to haul my ass back in. He wasn't going to steal just a minute or two of the day from me. He could swipe an hour or two. Hell, he could probably steal the whole day. I was more than capable of making myself miserable for the next twenty-four hours. I was on a roll.

Of course the irony here was that, now, I did have a mess brewing. I was correct. I wouldn't be able to write effectively in this state of mind. I would be losing valuable time. The delay might actually jeopardize the deadline.

The even greater irony was the severity of my unhappiness. Do you remember Bob, the watchmaker, returning to his home after the flood? Both Bob and I had encountered disruptions on the environmental wing of our respective matrices. Bob experienced a devastating flood. I encountered a bedbug. Bob was a picture of courage. I was a raving lunatic. Hmmmmmm.

Yes, I was making a bigger and bigger mess for myself. But it's so easy to do, isn't it—in real life I mean? It is so easy to make more trouble for oneself than is actually there. If we are honest, we all probably do this more than we might like to admit. It is an easy thing to do because life is hectic. Life is stressful. People can be irritating. And it is easy to get so caught up in the rat race—like Timothy from our first chapter—that everything, and I mean everything starts to look like a personal affront.

In fact, it is so easy to do that our culture has a long-standing metaphor to describe it. "Don't make a mountain out of a molehill." Yes, indeedy, I didn't just build mountains. I built Alps. And I could do it with just about any stress life handed me if I really put my mind to it.

What could I do? What could I do to turn this mess around? And what can you do, when this type of escalation happens to you? The answer is simple. Reach for the keys to the Porsche.

It's time for a matrix spin.

The View Around North Fork Dam

As I put the keys into my metaphorical Porsche, I felt a bit of a rush. These spins were usually fun. A matrix spin can clear one's mind as sure as the wind shooting past the open ragtop of a silver Porsche can clear the soul.

What was cooking on my biological wing? Me. My brain was frying.

When I'm wound up, far from the present moment, I am a hair twirler. When I'm really wound-up I twirl with both my hands. "Look, Ma! Both hands!" Looks incredibly silly. Thank God I only do it when I'm alone. If I had the prehensile dexterity of a chimpanzee with my feet, on this day, I would have undoubtedly been doing a two-hander/two-footer. I also noticed that my pulse was racing.

Apparently, my biological wing was a bit out of kilter. It had been at the receiving end of some damaging matrix effects from the other wings, where the more serious problems were lurking.

I noted this point and decided that perhaps I needed to do something that might help me calm my physical sense of being wired. I had just the trick in my toolbox. I enjoy using a deep-breathing exercise that only takes about five minutes; it really works for me. I have often shared it with my patients.

I decided not to wait. I might as well calm down a bit right now, so I took ten deep breaths—very slowly, very deeply, so that I could literally feel the breath slowly slipping through my lips with each exhale. When I was done, I was still wound up, but I was less wound up. The Porsche turned a corner to a new part of the matrix.

On my psychological wing, things weren't looking too good, I can tell you that. This wing was in real turmoil, yet another example of a damaging matrix effect. This time the leak had set a torch to the kindling. The result—a raging bonfire on my psychological wing, and my pep rally days were decades behind me. The primary problem in my matrix was undoubtedly related to my social wing, "editorial issues," but the resulting flames on the psychological wing were threatening to engulf me, my laptop, and any hope of a productive day.

Psychologically, I was trumping up all sorts of bigger mountains, none of which were true, none of which needed to be climbed. But, all of which were now creating tension and anxiety. All of which had zapped me out of the present moment and catapulted me into the furious future.

Here was the train of thoughts toodling through my brain: "That's it, I can't write now. . . . The whole day is screwed. . . . Oh my gosh, I can't make this time up tomorrow. . . . Oh no, I'm going to miss the deadline. . . . They'll be really upset. They're going to lose interest in the book. . . . They are not going to push the marketing of the book. . . . That will doom sales! . . . Oh my gosh. All this work for absolutely nothing. . . . I'm never going to make it as a writer!"

Boy, this is getting sick. The only thing that I did not think this title change would cause was my ultimate physical demise. Although, at the rate my mind was running with this one, death, perhaps at my own hands, was surely only a few years off—after Susan divorced me for screwing up the book deal and my kids were too ashamed to go out in public with such a loser for a dad. The human mind is a wondrous thing, especially when it is industriously constructing mountains out of molehills.

You see, if any of my latter statements about "bad sales" and "lost dreams" were true, then there would be a legitimate reason to be upset. But all of these thoughts were nonsense. Unfortunately, my mind didn't know that they were nonsense, because I wasn't even really aware that they were shooting through my consciousness until I took the matrix spin. I had been just worrying about the consequences that they implied.

Hence, my extreme anxiety. Hence a two-handed/two-footed chimpanzee on LSD twirling exhibition. You don't see that in your living room every day.

Here was an example of a damaging matrix effect created by my cognitions leaking into my fingers and the pulse-rate centers of my heart. Also note that when your mind takes off and creates such stressful thoughts, then your anxiety is not so hard to explain. Bob was facing the aftermath of a flood. I wasn't facing a bedbug. In my mind, I was facing the loss of my writing career.

Such runaway false cognitions, usually caused by processes such as over-generalizing, black/whiting, and catastrophizing, have been well studied by a branch of therapy called cognitive therapy. Cognitive therapy teaches you to quickly spot such damaging and distorted thoughts.

Once you find them, you repair them. You find out what the real situation is. The real, undistorted situation is often a good deal less threatening. Consequently, your anxiety plummets.

In my case, I took the time to re-evaluate what had really just happened to me—I might have to change my book title, but Bret and I will probably come up with another good one. It is impossible for there to be only one good book title. Impossible. There are thousands. Then there is no reason to be so upset.

As I truly realized this fact in my gut—that nothing catastrophic was happening—a deep and totally spontaneous sigh left my lips. The matrix spin was leading to plans of action that were already helping to transform my stress. The mountain had just become a hill. The Porsche sped around the next corner.

On the interpersonal level, it was a chip shot—what needed to be done, that is. I had just created stress between Susan and myself. I was experiencing a stressful event—some unexpected negative feedback on the book—and it was a time when I could sorely use the interpersonal support.

Susan is an amazing support system at just such times. I could have used her support to create an immediate healing matrix effect on the environmental and psychological wings of my matrix. So what had I done instead? I took a potential supportive wing of the matrix and made it into a new problem. Hmmmmmm.

The ball in the interpersonal wing of my matrix was totally in my control. I could create a new stress or I could create a healing matrix effect.

I got my butt up, walked into the kitchen and gave Susan a hug—my best, "I really can be an idiot, but I adore you" hug. After my apology, I quietly returned to the living room. There was no stomping this time, and the hill was looking more and more like a mound.

As I turned the most southerly corner of North Fork Dam, I came upon the environmental wing of the matrix. What was happening here? This was the center of the maelstrom. This was the wing—in this case my career environment—that was the source of the initial insult to the system. Here was our trigger point from which all the damaging matrix effects had flowed.

Truth be told, this area was still a bit unpleasant. There were no red herrings in this particular matrix spin. The stress was real here, and this wing had always appeared as the primary troublemaker responsible for this particular bad hair day—my publisher did not like my title. But, by this time in my spin, it all seemed much easier to navigate.

Here I made a good decision. Trust the process.

Originally, I was going to spend the rest of the morning trying to generate new titles. Then I felt a need to call Bret up in the afternoon and get this thing all fixed—RIGHT NOW. Not smart.

When I'm feeling vulnerable, one of my immediate natural proclivities is to take control. I'm good at it, too. Been practicing for years. Sometimes this is okay. Usually, it is not. This situation was a definite "it is not."

You can't just come up with a great title on the spot. Moreover, I was too wound up and invested in the topic to have the serendipity and playfulness needed to generate a creative solution. I decided to sit on it for a day or two. Play with it, and then give Bret a call. Plus, he often had great ideas. We work well together, and we work well off of each other's ideas.

For the record, a couple of days later, an unexpected letter arrived. It was a good letter. In it Bret carefully and meticulously laid out his concerns about my original title suggestion. He then, in a sensitive, lively and organized fashion discussed exactly the goals that our title should accomplish. A sentence later, the letter whispered, *Happiness Is*. There was a pause in my mind. I thought. The words juggled about my neurons. I smiled. A half-year later, they had jumped onto the dust jacket of this book.

Of course, at the time we are talking about, I had no idea that this would be the turn of events. But it didn't matter. I had a plan for the environmental wing of my matrix. It seemed like a good plan. It took the heat off. As I hopped off to the kitchen to make some tea, I glanced in the hallway mirror. No thief.

The Porsche was really flying now. I could feel the road through my hands. I could hear the engine purring as only a sports car engine can purr. The gearshift went through its paces with the gentle lightness of a clicking light switch. I was in control again. It felt good.

As I put the pedal to the metal, down the long straightway into the spiritual wing, the mountain had, for all intents and purposes, become a molehill again.

On my spiritual wing, nothing too bad had been happening in this particular mess. But the spiritual wing did hold some promise for maximizing my matrix. I often find music to be a powerful calming influence.

Gregorian chant, in particular, casts a stained glass beauty over my eyes. With these goggles on, the Emerald City is ablaze with a rainbow of colors. I find it all quite magical and soothing. I decided to listen to the good brothers while I supped upon my tea.

I pulled the Porsche into the driveway.

About twenty minutes later I grabbed the keys to my real car—not a Porsche (I wish). Forty minutes later, I was sitting in Brewbakers. There was a cup of café latte—double, no foam—steaming on my table. I was ready to rock and roll. The keys started clicking away with a gentle fury.

Closing Caveats, Brandenberg Concertos and the Quandary of the Quantum Pythagoras

I would like to add a few final reflections about matrix spins. When designing plans of action, for use both directly on damaged wings or indirectly via healing matrix effects, try to make sure that your plans are reasonable and doable. An ideal plan that is not doable is not ideal, it is foolish. It is also frustrating. And, as you implement the plans of your happiness programs, implement them gently. See how they work. Adjust them as you go along. Almost all interventions will be an ongoing series of adjustments for, as we know from our quantum view of the universe, everything flows, everything changes, and so must our plans and expectations.

As we near the close of our discussion of matrix spins, the connection between their use and the generation of confidence and excitement becomes more palpable. Earlier, we discussed this relationship in a general sense. The point was made that the intelligent application of matrix principles often leads to an increased sense of trust, confidence, excitement, and ensuing happiness, because the human matrix model is a possibility generator par excellence. Now, with our illustration of the matrix spin strategy under our belts, we have a wonderful example of this process directly in our sights.

You see, one of the problems when one is in a miniscule crisis (bad hair day) or in a major crisis (a divorce) is that everything can get merged into one big, black, overwhelming thunderhead. The immensity of this storm cell feels extremely unsettling. Of course, this unsettling sensation only adds to our problems. It gunks up the matrix. It is hard to generate trust or move with confidence when one is fleeing lightning bolts or flailing away at hailstones.

As we drive through the wings during a matrix spin, I believe that we benefit not only from the destination we reach (our new plans for action) but from the process of driving itself. People in Porsches, with the top down during a matrix spin, seem to benefit from the organization given to their lives as they deftly swing through the curves around North Fork Dam. As we become more and more familiar with taking matrix spins, we become more adept at spotting specific problems, avoiding red herrings, generating healing matrix effects and choosing effective tools. All of these skills cut down any storm cell that comes our way into a more manageable rain cloud. By the end of the spin, the very fact that we have some concrete plans for action in hand is greatly reassuring.

We start up our Porsches feeling chaos. We turn them off feeling trust. This newfound trust comes from our tenacious belief that we have a reliable strategy—the matrix spin—that we feel confident can generate reasonable plans of action no matter what the demands of our problems nor the limitations of our tools. Armed with this belief, as is the case with Michelle Kwan as she steps onto the ice to begin her programs, we are excited about our abilities to develop sound plans of action and confident that we can successfully implement them. Consequently, we are able to live a good deal more of life in the present moment.

It is now time to return to our friend Pythagoras, whose Porsche we tricked-out with a few quantum hubcaps and headers. Pythagoras began our chapter with his updated epigraph, "Know yourselves, and thou wilt know the universe and the gods."

It is clear that we are indeed an endless parade of selves unfolding from the universe as naturally as buds blooming from cherry trees. According to Pythagoras it is also clear that if we get to know these selves, we will know a lot of neat things and meet some important people. It is here that, if we try to follow the maxim of Pythagoras, we hit a quandary.

We can't do it.

It is ludicrous to think that any human being can study each passing self as it zips by in the parade of life. To attempt to do so is a little like listening to a Brandenberg concerto while trying to enjoy it note by note, stopping to savor each note before going on. Soon enough, there will be nothing to savor. The notes are not what make Bach's masterpieces enjoyable. It is the way the notes move together that fascinates our ears. One cannot capture the magic of a Brandenberg concerto by trying to capture the individual notes. The magic comes from listening to their flowings, their patterns, their whimsy.

So it is with selves. The bad news is that no matter what the quantum Pythagoras tells you to do, you can't capture and know each of your individual selves as they dance by you. But you can watch the dance. The good news is that if you watch enough of the dance, say a good ten minutes of it, you will have a surprisingly good composite picture of all the dancers. Matrix spins allow us to do just that.

One of the most famous principles of quantum mechanics was coined by Werner Heisenberg, and is aptly called Heisenberg's Principle of Uncertainty. He noted that one can never perfectly measure anything in a quantum universe, because the very act of measuring the thing changes it. In the time you take the measurement, the pattern has shifted, a new self was born, lived and died. Moreover, the elusive self that you were trying to measure was changed by the very poking you were doing to it while trying to measure it. Things squirm when poked.

Matrix spins are our answer to the monkey wrench thrown into the dictum of Pythagoras by Heisenberg's Principle. We don't need to accurately know each of our individual selves if our composite understanding—created by our matrix spin—gives us an accurate picture of what they are all doing as they dance past us. In an indirect fashion, we really *can* know ourselves as Pythagoras implored. The matrix spin strategy is a powerful tool towards that end. When we use it, we shall meet on the gracefully curving road that hugs the banks of the North Fork Dam. I can't promise you that we will have seen any gods, but I do think we will be a good deal happier.

The Trouble with Cats and Dogs

16

"After all, there is nothing in the world as interesting as people, and one can never study them enough."

VINCENT VAN GOGH

Wisdom from Nickelodeon and the Plight of Mr. Ramsey

As we noted in the prelude to part IV, one of the key ingredients for creating effective matrix generated plans (using strategies such as matrix spins) is the ability to successfully improve your skills in each wing of your matrix. For a skater approaching a key competition, there is hardly anything more exciting than learning to land a brilliant jump that others are incapable of doing. The thrill of victory is close at hand. As we saw, this ability to learn new skills, one by one, is a vital factor in generating and maintaining both excitement and confidence over the long haul in the tough world of competitive figure skating.

We too live in a tough world: the tough world of making a living, making ends meet and making deadlines on time. And, like our skating friends, excitement, confidence and victory often come from our ability to learn to land specific types of skills in each of the wings of our matrix. We want to expand the tools waiting for our reach in our toolboxes. We want to have sufficient tools at hand to implement whatever interventions will help best for whatever moment of unhappiness we happen to be transforming. The more tools we have, the more creative our designing of interventions, solutions and plans of action can be.

Every wing of the human matrix has a nearly inexhaustible set of tools that can be of use. Consequently, it is well beyond the scope of this book to provide numerous skills for each wing of the matrix. I also believe that such an overly ambitious goal would be . . . overly ambitious. On the other hand, it is well within our scope to garner a sound introduction to the fine art of matrix skill building. Indeed, I feel we would be remiss if we did not do so. And the good news is that developing individual skills, although not always, is often surprisingly easy to do, much easier than learning to land a triple spiral jump on ice. The goal of this chapter is to show just how easy it is.

Over the years with my patients, I have found that one of the best ways to accomplish this goal is to pick a single skill from a single wing of the matrix to use as a prototype. My patients like this approach for it is clear, concise, fun and not overwhelming. It is also easily doable in a single session or, in this instance, a single chapter.

By the end of this chapter we will have accomplished the following: (1) You will have gained a useful skill for use on one of the wings of the matrix. (2) You will have seen modeled a process for gaining future skills of your choice. (3) You will be convinced that skill building (despite the daunting number of options) is not only desirable, but feasible. (4) And you will be more excited and motivated to do so. Looks like a game plan to me. But what wing of the matrix and which skill?

I have decided to focus on the interpersonal wing of the matrix, for so much of our happiness seems to be somehow or other always connected— sometimes seemingly determined—by who shares our beds, sits at our dining room tables, works at our office suites, teaches at our schools or plops out of our bellies. Our happiness is inextricably bound to the whirling fancies of the interpersonal wing of the human matrix—the escapades as it were of our parents, siblings, children, friends, lovers and coworkers.

When it comes to the interpersonal wing of the matrix, the available tools fall into two broad categories: 1) Tools that help us to more effectively communicate our needs to others and better listen to their needs. 2) Tools that improve our ability to understand ourselves and others so that we can make more informed choices on whom we want to employ, work for, socialize with, date and mate.

In the first category, improving our abilities to communicate, the types of skills are varied, numerous and, fortunately, so behaviorally specific that they can be easily learned if the book author, parent or therapist presenting them is talented at teaching. Invaluable tools await the avid seeker in this category. You can learn techniques for communicating more directly, for presenting your needs with the appropriate amount of assertiveness, for providing constructive criticism gently, for enhancing the power and impact of your praise, for transforming arguments into reasonable discussions, for empathizing and listening better, and for learning how to effectively bargain and compromise. And there are many more. These tools are equally invaluable for transforming tensions in the living room, the boardroom or the bedroom.

In the second category—better understanding of yourself and others— the types of skills available are equally numerous and fun to learn. There are practical tricks of the trade that can help you to better understand who you are, what you need and what you have to offer. Conversely, there are skills for deepening your understanding of who the person on that first date, sitting across from you in the candlelight, really is, what he or she needs from you and what he or she has to offer you.

All of this reminds us of a fact too often forgotten: We are our own matchmakers. Matchmaking is complex business. It pays to learn the business well. In short, the more skills we learn about how people are compatible or not can greatly enhance our likelihood of picking a compatible spouse or partner—one of the absolutely most complicated and critical decisions that a human being ever makes.

Unfortunately, this decision making often first confronts us when we are in our adolescence or early adulthood, a time of roaring hormones, sexual firestorms and still-unformed perspectives on life. To complicate the matter more, most adolescents and young adults are taught next to nothing about the skills described above that can be so valuable in navigating these treacherous interpersonal waters. Having not been taught these tools early on in life, most adults, in the wake of divorces and deaths, face this critical decision-making process for a second time armed with no further advances in their skill set.

For instance, I have become convinced after twenty years of clinical experience that everyone, and I mean *everyone*, should be taught about the delicious yet lethal jaws of infatuation. Infatuation has destroyed more lives by leading people to make poor choices in their mates, more than Homer Simpson's eating impulses have led to empty doughnut boxes—a staggering thought. It is a lack of the exact tools described above that render the unsuspecting human vulnerable to the whimsical furies of infatuation.

As a psychiatrist I make my living teaching both of the above sets of skills so useful for navigating the endlessly fascinating interpersonal wing of the matrix. Consequently, I find myself faced with a dazzling array of possible offerings to use as our prototype skill. I hope that you enjoy my choice and find it to be of immediate use in your own life and in helping others, such as your children or friends.

The skill you are about to learn is a special one. It comes from our second category of interpersonal tools—better understanding of self and others. It is a snippet of self-knowledge that many people do not know, a fact that is most unfortunate, for this bit of self-knowledge is an absolute must for any frequenter of the magic theater who is about to look for a mate. It has to deal with your ability to understand your needs for receiving affection and your proclivities for giving it, for people vary greatly on this continuum. If a prospective couple does not resonate on this continuum, some very bad juju will often result.

Our goal is to show that this skill for gaining self-knowledge can be easily learned and easily applied. It can be invaluable in helping one to make the correct decisions when choosing a long-term partner and can help one not to be fooled by the ecstasy of infatuation. An added perk is the fact that if one has already made a poor decision, this particular insight may help one to recognize what the problem is, a key first step towards potentially transforming it.

Without further ado, allow me to bring you face to face with a magic mirror. Like all good magic mirrors, it will make you laugh. But its main value is to make sure you don't need to cry—you don't make future bad choices in partners. We will find our mirror in a most unlikely place, for we are not standing in some back alleyway outside a bar in Hesse's mist enshrouded city. We are sitting in the TV room of your house. This lesson begins on a Saturday morning. We are watching cartoons.

It doesn't take much of a discerning eye to see that cartoons have changed a great deal since the age of Bugs Bunny and QuickDraw McGraw, not all for the better, I might add. But there is always something to learn from what is unique, and what could be more unique than the wildly popular cartoon show *CatDog* on the Nickelodeon Channel.

The premise is simple. For some reason that is never fully explained, a creature jumps from the TV screen into our living rooms that is part cat and part dog, joined like a mutant Oscar Meyer wiener at the mid-section. This idea is simply not something that would have crossed the minds of the writers of the *Rocky and Bullwinkle Show* forty years ago, but it certainly leads to some zany plot developments, concerning how this pair of merged enemies goes about the business of their everyday lives, from chasing cars to choosing friends.

Needless to say they have strikingly different tastes. Dog, as the dog half is creatively called, simply cannot understand why Cat does not enjoy chasing garbage trucks or retrieving sticks from wonderfully wet lakes, while Cat cannot understand how Dog could possibly be bored by the opportunity to wrestle with a catnip mouse for hours on end. They are, in essence, a modern-day *Odd Couple* with Tony Randall and Jack Klugman cast not as apartment mates but as Siamese twins. It is strange, is it not? Of course, the humor becomes vastly more bizarre as each head of the creature expresses more nontraditional tastes—Dog adores monster truck shows and Cat is a connoisseur of polka music. Bottom line: They hate each other profoundly but have to live together because some pathetically twisted artist drew them united at the waist.

As funny as this situation is on a TV cartoon, I unfortunately have had a goodly number of CatDogs walk into my office for counseling, tied together not by an artist's doodlings but by a pair of snugly fitting wedding bands. They are not laughing. They are not pleased to see me. And I've yet to meet one that is a devotee of the *CatDog* show on Nickelodeon. The cartoon probably hits too close to home. As it should, for I am convinced that some people are cats and some people are dogs. Generally speaking, they don't belong together.

Let me explain. We all hear about people being "cat people" meaning they love to have cats as pets but don't really enjoy dogs; vice versa, dog people don't like cats but adore dogs. This is not the situation we are concerned with in this chapter. It is not so much whether or not a person likes cats or dogs that interests us as it is whether a person is a cat or a dog.

In particular, we are interested in one specific continuum that seems to separate most cats from dogs in the animal kingdom—the continuum of how cats and dogs like to receive and give affection. As noted earlier it is one of the most vital areas of self-knowledge that one can acquire before picking a mate. Let's see why.

Mr. Ramsey had been in therapy for quite some time, working on a variety of issues, from problems with depression to a propensity to drink too much. His six-foot-three frame cut an imposing figure as he would fill the doorway of my office, pausing just long enough in the doorway to suggest that, like Samson, he could easily push apart the door frame if the need ever arose. Control was a bit of an issue here. He had a good-old-boy sensibility, a quick sense of humor and a genuine love of people. I liked him right off the bat. Despite a prospering business, a waiting list of friends and a stock market portfolio that I wished I had had, he was unhappy.

By this point in the therapy, with a late-summer light sneaking through the blinds of my office windows, we had turned our attention to his marriage.

"Mr. Ramsey, you had said earlier there were some real difficulties with your marriage. Tell me a little bit about that."

"Well, Doc, it's hard to explain. Terry and I have many shared interests. She loves working in the yard, so do I. She loves socializing, so do I. She loves *The Sopranos*, so do I. She even loves football."

"Sounds like a marriage made in heaven," I quipped with a good-natured humor that Mr. Ramsey always seemed to appreciate.

"Yeah, yeah. Exactly." He suddenly shook his head in a tight side-to-side nod, continuing, "But it isn't."

"What are some of the problems?"

"It's odd. I just don't feel appreciated. She never just comes up to me and tells me she loves me, but I know she does. At least I think she does. Sometimes I find myself telling her that I love her, just to hear her say it back. It pisses me off."

"What's it like for you at parties and when the two of you go out?"

"Well, Doc, she likes going out, and she looks great and has fun and all, but she doesn't want to be with me the whole time, you know what I mean?"

"I'm not entirely certain, Mr. Ramsey. What do you mean?"

"Well, I like to stand around talking and joking, but I like her to be beside me, with her arm through mine or holding hands, you know, stuff like that."

"Is she generally affectionate?"

"Well, she loves sex, which is great, but she's not really what I would call affectionate."

By this time I was pretty sure I was on the trail of a CatDog. But I needed a few more leads. "Give me an example of what you mean when you say she's not that affectionate?"

"Well, let's say I come into a room and she's reading a book. I'll come up to her and wrap my arms around her from behind and say that I love her, and you know what she'll do?"

I nodded for him to continue.

"She'll shake me off and say something like, 'Not now, Honey, I'm reading.'"

"Sort of like a cat that doesn't want to be petted?"

Mr. Ramsey furrowed his brow for a second. Then he looked at me with a smile of insight. "Exactly."

Diagnosis made: CatDog Syndrome. As a well-trained professional who watches a lot of cartoons, I had seen it coming a mile away.

The CatDog Syndrome: Diagnosis, Prognosis and Treatment

So far I've been presenting this material with a rather light tone, but it is actually surprisingly serious. In fact, the CatDog syndrome has ended more than a few marriages, for people vary dramatically on how much outward affection they need and how much outward affection they show.

Some people are like dogs. Dogs just love giving and receiving affection. They thrive on it. It is second nature. Around other dogs they constantly lick each other and do curious things like sniff each others' behinds. They play with each other and sleep in big dog mounds of entwined bodies. Around people they are just as endearing, if indeed you consider sniffing butts an endearing behavior. They live to be petted. They will walk up to you and slurp you on the face without much discrimination as to who the slurpee is. If you stop petting them they will put their paw up daintily to let you know that the "kissy-fest" is not over yet. They love you, and they let you know they love you.

Dog people are very similar except for the sniffing stuff. They like to hold hands. They like to cuddle. And if they love you, you are in for a real treat if you like to feel special. Many times a day they will tell you how much they love you. And they have the uncanny knack of saying just the right thing at the right time, such as a whispered, "You are the most special thing that ever happened to me." And they mean it. In a nutshell, they need a lot of affection and they give a lot of affection. It's just the way they are. They are dogs.

Other people are cats. Cats like to be petted, as long as they choose who will do the petting and when. They like nothing better than to stroll over and as you reach down to say, "Nice kitty," they scamper away, tails twitching in the air. If they feel like receiving affection, they can curl up in your lap and produce one of the most entrancing sounds in the animal world—the purr of contentment. But, in a moment's notice, they will jump off your lap, for, quite frankly, there are more important things to do than please you. They are independent and self-confident. There is something mysterious about their aloofness. It is not mere coincidence that they were viewed as a sacred goddess, Bastet, by the Egyptians.

Cat people are equally intriguing. They are not big on the touching thing, unless they know you well. Like their feline counterpart, they carefully wait and choose when and how to give affection. If married to one, a cat person might spontaneously say, "I love you" or "You're the best thing that ever happened to me" once or twice a year, but don't count on it. On the other hand, if you say, "I love you," they'll generally respond in kind, but please don't over do it. From their perspective you should know they love you, because they do. It frankly puzzles them as to why you would need to keep hearing it. Surely you are not so insecure that you don't trust their love. They can seem cool and aloof like a cat, but their sense of love is just as deep as that of a dog. In a nutshell they simply do not need to receive nor show much affection. It is not their nature. They are cats.

Neither cat nor dog is a superior human. It is okay to be a dog. It is okay to be a cat. There is no sexual predisposition either—I have seen men who are cats and men who are dogs. The same with women.

And it has little to do with sexuality itself. As one would expect, dog people are essentially born horny. But cat people can be just as wickedly delightful in bed—the difference being they are particularly picky about who lands in their bed. And, even with mates, you probably won't find your-self in bed as often with a cat, for sexual encounters will be doled out as per their needs and on their time schedules.

As stated earlier, it is okay to be a cat or a dog, but it is very important to figure out which you are and what species is your dinner date. Keep in mind that most people are combinations of a sort. Some people are nearly 50/50. Nevertheless, most people are either more cat or more dog.

Over the years I have discovered that although things like shared inter-ests, shared dreams and shared beliefs are all quite important in creating enduring relationships and successful marriages, I am not convinced they are the main glue. The main glue in a marriage is less likely to be those things we like about our partners and more likely to be the fact that there are very few things we don't like about our partners. In short, in highly suc-cessful marriages and relationships, one of the most common features I find is the fact that the partners feel comfortable with the other person's quirks, eccentricities, propensities and even their flaws. They are seldom bothered by the other person's behaviors. Hence they are seldom hurt or disap-pointed. Anger is not common. There is no need to change the other part-ner. More important, neither partner feels pressure to change. It is safe to be oneself. These marriages stick.

Now it should be obvious why cat people and dog people have a rough go of it, for how humans need and show affection is at the very cornerstone of interpersonal happiness. A dog person like Mr. Ramsey is going to feel constantly underappreciated and disappointed by a cat person such as his wife. Equally damaging, a cat person is going to feel constantly pressured to show affection in ways that are not natural — to be somebody that he or she is simply not meant to be. It is, unfortunately, a lose-lose proposition for both. The tragedy is that neither is right and neither is wrong, but both will be deeply hurt.

The above observations translate into some practical suggestions for addressing unhappiness in the interpersonal wing of the human matrix. If one is feeling unhappy in a relationship, it may be of value to look for evidence that one has unwittingly stumbled into a CatDog relationship. The first step, consistent with our Pythagorean adage to know ourselves, is to determine if one is primarily a cat or primarily a dog. The following questions may help:

1. Do I tend to spontaneously tell my significant other that I love him or her more than two times a day?
2. Do I spontaneously kiss or hug my significant other several times a day?
3. Do I like to hold hands?
4. Do I feel comfortable hugging my significant other in public places?
5. When my significant other enters the room, do I smile?
6. Is cuddling with my significant other right before we go to sleep or right after we wake up one of my absolute favorite things to do in the whole world?
7. Do I sometimes just look at my significant other when he or she is asleep, feeling grateful they exist?

The more of the above questions that you answered with a "yes," the more likely that you are predominantly pooch material as opposed to feline and vice versa. One then must make a determination of the species of ones mate or date.

If you are a dog, ask yourself the following questions:

1. Do I often feel underappreciated by my significant other?
2. Do I wish my significant other would say, "I love you" more often.
3. Do I sometimes say "I love you" to my significant other just to hear him or her respond with an "I love you?"
4. Do I sometimes feel my significant other does not like it when I hug/touch him or her?
5. Does my significant other seem to want "alone time" much more than I do?

"Yes" answers to the above questions suggest that you may be dating or living with a cat person.

If you are a cat (in other words, answered "no" to most of the questions in the first set above), ask yourself the following questions:

1. Does my significant other seem to be needlessly insecure about how much I love him or her?
2. Is my significant other overly sentimental?
3. Is my significant other too dependent on me?
4. Does my significant other tend to be jealous?
5. Do I sometimes feel pressured by my significant other to be affectionate?
6. Do I feel smothered sometimes by my significant other's constant attention?
7. Does my significant other touch me too often?

"Yes" answers to the above questions suggest that you may be dating or living with a dog person.

Can CatDog relationships work out? Absolutely. Truth be told, if you watch enough weeks of the *CatDog* show, you'll discover that there is a bond between our two mutant protagonists that is rather touching—a bond I don't think is missed by the young minds that giggle at their zany antics. Also keep in mind that the intensity of the differences in CatDog relationships can vary dramatically depending upon how pure a cat and how pure a dog are involved. There are many other factors that might make it worth trying to make a CatDog relationship work. But the truth is, it will take a lot of work.

The cat will need to increase his or her outward displays of affection. The cat will also have to learn to both expect and accept that his or her mate will be more affectionate than the cat person deems necessary or even desirable. Vice versa, the dog is just going to have to learn "to tone it all down" a notch or two. In addition, the dog will have to accept that his or her cat mate loves him or her even though affection is not shown on a daily basis. It all can work, but it is hard.

If a CatDog mismatch is really causing you a significant problem, I strongly suggest counseling. A marriage or couples counselor can help you decide whether or not it is worth pursuing the relationship and, if so, can help both of you develop the communication skills that will be necessary to make a CatDog relationship work effectively so that both parties can grow.

If while dating you discover that you are in a CatDog relationship, consider dating others as well, so that you experience what it is like to be in a CatCat or a DogDog relationship before committing to a more permanent CatDog relationship. I have found that nine times out of ten, people are shocked at how much easier such same species relationships feel. They are often much less friction bound, and all parties feel both safer and more themselves.

In the last analysis, it is hard to find two happier people than two dog people who have found each other after each enduring some frustrating years of cat love. At long last they have found somebody who makes them feel like the most special person in the world. They charge out into the day, hand in hand, playful as pups and eager to face life's challenges. Their excitement can only be matched by two cat people, who after long years of feeling pressured and misunderstood by dogs, find in each other a calm, sure love. It is a love based on mutual admiration and a sense of respect, where each is free to grow even in different ways—two cats in the night, sitting on different fences, in love with the same moon.

17 Looking for Tom

"The eyes are the mirror of the soul."

YIDDISH PROVERB

Bushy Eyebrows, Buried Typewriters,
and the Young Man Behind the Barn

In chapter 15 we saw the impressive power of a quantum strategy—matrix spins—to usefully design plans of action and intervention. In chapter 16 we saw the utility of learning new tools—such as the ability to gain self-understanding by perceiving where one sits on the CatDog continuum—to help us better implement such plans, in this case, picking partners. With the passage of time you will find that both of these factors (using matrix strategies to design plans of action and developing new tools on each wing of your matrix) will contribute considerably to your confidence, excitement and effectiveness when using the human matrix model.

Your belief that you can design programs that are up to snuff and can reliably help you to uncover happiness will undoubtedly grow. And with its growth, you will find yourself more frequently entering the positive feedback loop in which confidence and excitement build and revitalize each other.

The next factor that provides entrance into this wonderful loop is a tad unexpected. It is called insider information. Not the illegal type, mind you. We are interested in the legal type. We are interested in so-called trade secrets. Armed with such secrets, we can be further assured that we will design happiness programs of unusual power.

The trade secrets we seek are those healing matrix effects that have consistently proven themselves to be potent, reliable and readily available. Some of these effects we consciously design. Others we stumble upon. It is the latter effects that sometimes are the most memorable and often prove to be the most useful. Of course, every experienced wanderer in the magic theater will have his or her own favorites.

In this chapter my goal is to share with you one of my favorite healing matrix effects so that you can use it for your own matrix planning. It is one of the most striking matrix effects that I have personally encountered. Its imprint was memorable on me at the time I first encountered it, and its ramifications for me have grown even more so as time has gone on. There is no better way to explore this effect than to watch it in action.

Consequently, in this chapter we will explore the powerful impact that a change initiated in the interpersonal wing can have on the spiritual wing of the human matrix. The frequent use of this matrix combination, interpersonal wing to spiritual wing, is one of my most potent trade secrets. In this case, we will see how this particular healing matrix effect can help us to pursue one of the most difficult of all quests in the spiritual wing of the matrix, defining the nature of the soul.

It also serves as a poignant reminder that the enduring happiness we seek—a profound sense of trust and a refreshing feeling of confidence—can take root in the strangest of forms in the most unexpected of situations: at times of physical or emotional pain, during moments of intense empathy that may bring tears to our eyes and during times when we come upon aspects of ourself that may not be pleasant to uncover but are vital to our growth. The seeds of our happiness are sometimes sown in the tracks etched by our tears.

So it is with those moments when we experience a palpable sense of the presence of our souls—sacred times—times sometimes called numinous because the thunderous power of their marvelousness can be almost frightening in nature. For once we touch our soul, like touching the exposed flesh of our first love, we are forever changed.

At such moments, happiness is often ignited and fortified, for the fire of the soul can revitalize both trust and confidence. Souls are powerful things. Their touch can create purpose. Their breath can engender meaning. With their touch we suddenly trust that we are on the right track and are confident that it leads to our destiny.

As one would expect, the powerful healing matrix effect we are about to explore in detail is one of those matrix effects that I did not seek purposefully. I stumbled upon it. Indeed, it may be more accurate to say that it stumbled upon me.

It all began when I was making a home visit to a patient I had never met before—an attempt to make an impact on the interpersonal wing of the matrix. I was with one of my favorite clinicians, Barney, driving on the winding back roads of New Hampshire many miles north of Keene, as aging birches, stone walls and sugar houses darted past us. It took almost an hour before we were close to our destination. Barney's much-beleaguered red Subaru had once again proved its dogged reliability on the potholed roads of Cheshire County, where the frost heaves were finally settling like the bubbles of a hot pastry as it cools.

We were uncertain what type of situation lay before us. We knew there was a young man, Tom, who apparently had developed schizophrenia. We knew he lived in a very poor house with his father, who had kept him going over the years, but now his father felt he needed help caring for Tom. Admitting that one needs help does not come naturally to a New England native. We knew that things had to be bad.

Barney and I were a part of a continuous treatment team (CTT). The

CTT was designed to be an outreach team for people suffering from severe psychiatric diseases such as schizophrenia and bipolar disorder. Each CTT clinician worked with only ten people at a time and was expected to provide all of the casemanagement, social work, family therapy, liaison with the police and other community resources, substance abuse counseling, supportive counseling and psychotherapy if indicated. Only the worst of the worst situations came our way, and we loved it.

We were somewhat of an odd band of clinicians, for all of the CTT clinicians were master-level therapists, many of whom, at some future point, wanted to move into more traditional roles as outpatient therapists. But for whatever reason, these clinicians had come together to dedicate years of their lives at low pay and long hours to help the people and families that had been beaten down by these illnesses. The clinicians came for the experience, the education and for the mission, for they all knew that not many clinicians were available to do this type of work.

As we pulled into the driveway, we stood face-to-face with true rural poverty. To our left, the house of Mr. Jennings and his son, Tom, courageously held its ground against the preying winds. It was gray, tiny and literally falling apart.

We were met at the door by a tall, gray-haired man, who managed a warm but haggard smile. "Glad you could make it." He had a strong handshake. But the first thing that caught my notice was the wonderfully green eyes that sat calmly beneath his large white eyebrows, eyebrows so bushy they looked like moths ready to take flight. They were the most strikingly green eyes—alive with a searching intelligence—I have ever seen. Many a *Vogue* aspirant would have killed for them.

His hands were weathered, and the dirt had lodged in nails that would never yield their hard-earned blackness. We passed by a porch hung with gaping screens. The floor was covered with rusting farm equipment, rakes, boxes, crates and a strange-looking engine that Mr. Jennings said had been an old and valuable steam engine. I noticed a bike propped upside down on its handlebars without its rear wheel.

Mr. Jennings caught my eye. "That's Tom's. Been working on it for a year now. Can't do nothin with it. Hard to believe he used to build computers."

Mr. Jenning's clothes were gray, baggy and soiled. They hung from his frame almost like a scarecrow's seconds. I don't know when it was, but somewhere during this first meeting, an association went through my mind. I do not mean it in any sense of stereotyping or condescension. It just appeared. Mr. Jennings looked, for all the world, like Jed Clampett from the old TV show *The Beverly Hillbillies.* And he shared the rugged yet good-natured outlook of Jed as well. If ever there was a hard-working man who was the salt of the earth, this was he.

Somewhere along the line I also noticed his limp. We would eventually learn that he'd gained it from a war-related injury. We also learned that Mr. Jennings, who looked much older than his sixty-two years, still supported himself as a subsistence farmer begging the tired soil for whatever meager yields it offered. To our amazement he did almost all the work single-handedly with help from a few hired hands a couple of months each year. And he wanted nothing to do with welfare. Indeed, he viewed our help with a suspicious distance.

As we entered the kitchen, we found it to be thick with clutter. Dirty pots and pans were piled everywhere. The cheap Formica table was littered with junk and was filthy with years of stains. All the plastic-coated kitchen chairs were torn with the stuffing peeking out. A typewriter sat buried on the table.

He showed us into a tiny study filled with languishing furniture and, to our surprise, books everywhere. The yellowed shelves were teeming with yellowed books stacked every which way. Good books, such as *The Return of Sherlock Holmes* and *Huckleberry Finn*. Books of all kinds and topics. Mr. Jennings caught my eye again. "I read a lot. The winter's long. Not as much work to do then." I nodded.

It would be months of slowly building trust before Mr. Jennings would share a special secret about his life. He was writing a book. He tapped it out on the hard keys of the manual typewriter hiding on the kitchen table. It was about his days growing up on his father's farm in Vermont, a farm teeming with cattle, chickens and much hard work for a small boy of seven. Much later I would read some of the rough draft. It was well written. It would not surprise me to see it published someday.

After an appropriate amount of chitchat, Mr. Jennings began to tell us about his son. It was quite clear that he loved Tom. Tom's mother had died a long time ago, leaving Mr. Jennings with the task of taking care of his only son, who had begun to deteriorate about six years earlier. Apparently, Tom had voluntarily been hospitalized about five years ago and had responded quite well to prolixin. Although his schizophrenia had been laced with some auditory hallucinations and paranoid process back then, except for some under-the-breath mumbling, these typical psychotic symptoms were not prominent now.

We asked to see Tom. Mr. Jennings shrugged, "Good luck. He didn't want to see you, so he took off. Might try behind the barn at the edge of the woods down by the back field. That's where he goes to be by himself sometimes. I'll take you down."

The skies were gray. The wind had picked up a bit. There was a feel of rain in the air. Hidden from the road behind the house, a huge barn lay dilapidated, collapsing inward, as the woods inexorably reclaimed their birthright. Over the years its shingles had fallen imperceptibly, like a quiet rain upon the ghosts of the many sheep it had once sheltered. After we crossed the field, Mr. Jennings hung back. I suspect he didn't want to be in the way. Barney and I saw no sign of Tom. The huge barn seemed to lumber in its foundations. It was dark, filled with shadows, broken timbers and mechanical creatures slowly rusting away. Barney and I became animated in our conversation, as was our habit, temporarily becoming less aware of our surroundings. We were talking with some gusto when we turned the corner.

It would take some doing to find two people who shut up more abruptly. Tucked away in a shadowy recess of a loft, Tom was watching us.

He was squatting, just staring at us. His hair was matted with dirt. Shoes bandaged with white tape. His red-plaid shirt and dirty jeans, with a hole in their knee, were all part of a perfectly framed still life. Tom didn't move a muscle. No smile. No gesture. It was as if two wild animals had stumbled upon each other. Neither party knew what to do.

It is hard to describe the moment. It had a disquietude to it that goes beyond words. Eventually, we spoke and Tom nodded. He approached us slowly. We attempted to chit–chat. Tom could carry on a reasonable conversation but was clearly not particularly interested in a long encounter. But what bothered me the most were his eyes.

There before us were his father's eyes. But they were empty. It was as if one could crawl into them and out of them without being noticed. It was as if he was not in there. It was as if he lived not inside his skin but on top of it. We had met the outside of Tom, but Barney and I would spend the next several years looking for the real Tom hidden deep inside those vacant eyes.

It was truly disturbing to see the ravages of the disease. Tom's condition was most consistent with an older diagnosis, no longer even described in the current psychiatric diagnostic system, known as "simple schizophrenia," something I had never really seen before. In this condition, psychotic symptoms, such as hallucinations and delusions, play little role. Instead, the symptoms of the schizophrenia take on an insidious and debilitating aspect. Slowly the patient becomes less animated, thinking becomes more and more simplistic with an increasingly concrete quality, hygiene deteriorates and the inner world of the person becomes progressively empty. In some respects the very structure of the person's personality begins to disappear.

Our immediate dilemma with Tom was painful, for there was essentially nothing we could do for him. He wanted nothing to do with us and certainly nothing to do with our psychosocial interventions or our medications. He denied suicidal or violent thoughts. Although it was questionable how well Tom could take care of himself away from his father, while he was with his father he presented no danger to himself. Even if he did, his father would probably be, as any parent would, hesitant to commit his son against his will. Consequently, it become our goal over the ensuing months to try to help Tom feel safe with us with the thin hope that someday he would trust us enough to be willing to try some medications.

From the moment we first met Tom, Barney and I felt the need to help him and his father. It was phenomenal to realize what we were seeing. A molecular storm had stolen across the oceans of Tom's brain, disrupting the firing of billions upon billions of cells. As the molecules of dopamine and serotonin were buffeted about in the winds of this organic storm, the violent waves were literally reshaping the shoreline. The sands of his personality were being stripped away and possibly lost forever. Just as we stand in awe at the destructive power of a hurricane, Barney and I were humbled by the destruction of personality caused by the biochemical lesions of this disease. And for the moment, we felt the fear of helplessness, for without the medications we could only stand on a hilltop and watch the destruction below.

And herein lies the connection with our search for a trade secret, an unusually powerful matrix effect. You see, I thought that I was there to transform Tom, but it was me who was being transformed. Not only did I meet Tom behind that barn, I stumbled upon my soul. What had begun as an intervention on the interpersonal wing of the matrix—trying to provide medical aid to someone in need—had become an intervention on the spiritual wing of my own matrix—receiving help that I didn't even know I needed.

Like the reality of the wind tossing my hair, I realized the existence of my soul by the impact it was having upon me. I was being compelled by some force to feel. I was being compelled by some force to experience compassion. I wasn't choosing to care for Tom, I just did. I didn't need to search for my soul, it had found me.

Wind-Trees, Scarecrows and Fingers Made of Tears

Our old friend Alan Watts used to describe the similarly puzzling search for the "self" as an eye looking for its own eyeball or teeth attempting to bite themselves. It ain't gonna happen. But eyes and teeth exist even if they cannot find themselves. Perhaps the soul is such a creature.

When we try to describe the soul with words, it seems to vanish into principles that are as hollow as the look in Tom's eyes. The words make sense, but they lack meaning. They seem to confuse the process. A quizzical philosopher of nineteenth-century Europe, with the delightful name of Ludwig Wittgenstein, stated the truth of this enigma succinctly. "Concerning that which cannot be talked about, we should not say anything."

I am reminded of a tart summer day in my backyard, after having just moved to New Hampshire. The sky was crisp with blue. A wind tossed pleasantly, playing with trees like a sea surf pushing and pulling on the tumbling sands. My three-year-old son, Brenden, and I were playing in the sun. I decided to test his constantly growing curiosity, so I asked, "Brenden, what do you think causes the wind?" As the words passed my lips I had the suddenly disruptive realization that I was not entirely sure of the answer myself, but nevertheless it seemed like a pithy father-like question to ask. Brenden looked around, as if the answer lay in his surroundings, squinting his eyes with contemplation, a peculiarly human thing to do. Suddenly, his eyes lit up as he said, "That does." And he pointed.

"What does?" I asked.

"That." He looked triumphant in his discovery as he verbally accented his pointing, "A wind-tree."

So it is with words that try to describe the soul. He was convinced he was correct, yet he was wrong. Trees don't cause the wind. He had mistaken an effect for a cause and then combined the two. But somehow he seemed almost intuitively right. Perhaps he was right. Perhaps the problem was that Brenden was trying to describe a "process," wind, with words better designed for describing "things." This problem may be at the heart of why philosophers and theologians have been arguing about this "thing" we call a soul, that, in truth, may be more of a process, a way of being more clearly viewed with a quantum lens. In this sense, for a human to try to define his or her soul, using words, might be akin to the eye looking for its own eyeball.

There is another Eastern parable that speaks clearly to this dilemma. One hears this story told in many ways, and it goes something like this. A novice Zen monk approached a Zen master sitting quietly beneath a night sky. The novice was interested in philosophically understanding what is the nature of beauty. Not one to be awed by an elder, he quickly approached the master and asked, "What makes the moon beautiful?" The young novice waited, fully expecting the wizened monk to provide wise words. The master opened his eyes. He raised his arm. He pointed to the white moon in the black sky. He shut his eyes.

Words were unnecessary.

In fact, words would have confused the issue. This parable is often used as a warning to avoid an over-reliance on meanings and definitions. It highlights the fact that sometimes one can become so lost in defining the myriad of exciting processes and things that make up life that one can mistake the definitions as life itself. In a like manner, this idea is what I meant earlier when I suggested that perhaps the soul must be felt, not described.

Where does this leave us? Well, it takes us away from that haunting barn where we first met Tom. It plops us into a somewhat enchanting parlor in a creaking New England house with white clapboards and black shutters, sitting beneath the white moonlight of a winter's night. The house was built before the Civil War by a cobbler in a small town in New Hampshire. The original owner now lies buried in a tiny cemetery about a quarter of a mile down a shady dirt road.

On this particular evening, the current owner of the house, myself, was sitting alone in the dim light, listening to a CD. The song was by

Sinead O'Connor, "Black Boys on Mopeds," and it tells of a very sad tragedy in which a boy is killed in a political demonstration in Northern Ireland. The artist deftly portrayed the parents' anguish as they first heard the news of the senseless slaying of their child. Of course, the death of a child is a pain that goes well beyond words, and O'Connor's skilled artistry drew me imperceptibly into this moment. And then a strange thing happened. Sinead O'Connor, the boy, his parents and even the distant island of Ireland disappeared.

The image changed. I found myself thinking about a young man I had treated many years ago as a resident in psychiatry back in Pittsburgh, who had a severe case of paranoid schizophrenia. His name was Frankie. His world was filled with biblical injunctions and true demons of the night. He would become intermittently convinced that he was the whore of Babylon and that the Great Beast was nearby. He felt that God was punishing him for his weaknesses by harming innocent people. Indeed, God had killed a pair of Pittsburgh residents in a car wreck as retribution for his own sin of smoking. Such torments had led Frankie to thoughts of "justified" suicide, and in the past his paranoia had led to assaults. On this particular night, his face came up to haunt me like a ghost from a forbidden hallway, and I did not know why.

It was a gaunt face. At one time Frankie had been blessed with a rakish handsomeness, complemented by a beguiling sense of humor and a thick match of sumber-blond hair. He was built like a sculpture by Giacometti, wiry and wisp-like. But like Tom's visage, the pain of the inner torments had, over the years, cut deep scars. Unlike Tom, his still-sharp intelligence shot from his eyes, challenging my every word, for he and I held very different beliefs. Every time he had come off of his medicines he had become psychotic again, and dangerous to himself or others. But he absolutely loathed the medicines. I have never seen anybody hate medications so deeply. By court order I was part of the system that was keeping him on what he perceived as wretched drugs.

On occasion he would become furious with me, stomping out of the clinic yelling, "You're messing with me. Your drugs are hurting my body. Nobody has a damn right to do that. You're messing with my body." In the past he had threatened to bomb the police station and in one instance, before I knew him, he had broken several windows in a local shopping mall. When he was angry, Frankie scared me.

But that feeling was not typical. Usually I felt very good around Frankie. We had worked together for some time, talked long and hard about everything from God to house painting to football (he was an avid fan of the Pittsburgh Steelers). And, for the most part, Frankie genuinely liked me. Outbursts such as the ones described above were rare. I believe he truly thought I was giving him the meds because I thought they were helping him. He just thought I was out of my mind. We shared this opinion of each other.

Frankie had a sparkling wit and intelligence. He read everything he could about his medications and would catch me off guard with queries such as, "Isn't it true, Dr. Shea, that haldol can, in some cases, cause a sub-cortical dementia?" I would go scurrying off to my books to track down my retorts. We had become opponents who grew fond of each other from our respect for the other's unrelenting tenacity and skills.

The bottom line was that there was something endearing about Frankie. He was so persistent about wanting to get off the meds (despite over seven failures without them) that his arguments would tug at my decision, but I would remind myself of the ethical need to maintain my stance. He had been repeatedly tried off the meds, and it had resulted in danger-ous situations.

But none of these thoughts were on my mind that night in my parlor. Instead, his image just popped into my mind, like the first fireworks explod-ing on a hot Fourth of July night. Like the first boom that follows the fiery splinters, there was a rumbling of my psyche. I thought of all of Frankie's lost dreams, the jobs lost, the carefree dating days gone, the schooling long since abandoned and the intense loneliness of his nights.

Suddenly I saw a field in my mind. There was a scarecrow in it. The scarecrow was forlornly hung, almost Christ-like, crucified on its stake. As I approached it, I sensed it wanted down but knew it could never happen. As I looked at it, I realized it was Frankie. Images of his parents appeared. They looked unbelievably pained by what they saw, their small child, no longer recognizable, alone in the field at the mercy of the disease, no end to his pain in sight. And I began to weep. I wept for Frankie. I wept for his parents. Perhaps I even wept for myself.

I still do not fully understand the moment nor the emotions. But I do know it was an important night for me, for as sure as the hand of the Zen monk had pointed to the beauty of the moon, my tears were pointing to the presence of my soul.

18 The Journey Outward

"The purpose of life is to serve and to show compassion and the will to help others. Only then have we ourselves become true human beings."

ALBERT SCHWEITZER, M.D.

Optical Illusions, Prison Bars and Billowing Sheets

With my struggles to reach out to Tom, who was wrestling with the unseen demons that whirled about the shadowy lofts of his barn, and to Frankie, who was fighting back the crows of madness that swirled about the restless regions of his brain, we saw the power of one of my favorite trade secrets. What started out as an attempt to help another person in the interpersonal wing of the matrix ended up as a journey into the spiritual wing of my own matrix. What I found there was my soul.

One can't find a much more potent brew of matrix magic. Finding one's soul is reasonably serious business. You can readily see why I chose this particular healing matrix effect as one of my favorites. But I sometimes worry that the rather dramatic result displayed by the use of this specific effect— finding a soul—can overshadow its more enduring practical wisdom. The power of this trade secret is not a one shot deal: See the soul and say good-bye. It is an invaluable tool for daily use. Used in this fashion, it often leads to many other dazzling effects. What does it really mean, in the practical sense of designing plans for overcoming everyday obstacles, that one should *frequently* use a matrix effect that moves from the interpersonal wing to the spiritual wing?

The answer to this question returns us to some of the key secrets for successfully working the complexities of the human matrix. Imagine for a minute that you have uncovered the fact that your immediate state of unhappiness is primarily originating on the spiritual wing of your matrix. Perhaps you are feeling an acute loss of meaning or an alarming estrangement from God, as Mrs. Perkins was feeling, before she picked up the phone and gave Him a call.

Generally speaking, one way to address pain localized to one afflicted wing, a very logical and often productive way, is to address the troubles within that wing with direct interventions on that wing. In fact, I almost always recommend this approach as a good first step. Thus, if the trouble is brewing on the spiritual wing of the matrix, use spiritual tools to help transform it: pray, meditate, read philosophy, enjoy a church service, take a walk in the woods or a park, meet with a pastor or a rabbi or do what Mrs. Perkins did—call up God and have a long conversation. These are all excellent methods, which I heartily endorse. They are what I call "inward paths" to wisdom, to spiritual enrichment. This path is also the obvious way: deal with a spiritual problem by spiritual means.

But there is another way. A less obvious way.

It is a way that many people, untrained in the nuances of matrix working, would not quickly think of using. One could choose to additionally focus, perhaps primarily focus, on using an intervention on a completely different wing of the matrix, perhaps a wing that is not even troubled at present. In short, you could put your money on the indirect forces of a healing matrix effect.

The goal of such an intervention is to create an impact on a distant wing that, through the influences of a healing matrix effect, will initiate healing on the afflicted wing. This is the message that one should take away from the trade secret I offered in our last chapter. When I am troubled spiritually, I often focus on the interpersonal wing of my matrix. The changes I create there have a surprising ability to heal my spiritual wing.

It has taken me many years of matrix work—of helping my patients cope with spiritual problems and helping myself to do the same— to come upon this little gem of a matrix effect. But I swear by it.

If, when designing your plans for intervention, you learn how to routinely use this approach—intervene on the spiritual wing by focusing on the interpersonal wing—I think you will gain more and more confidence in the power of your designs. As we have seen, it is just such a belief that will ignite excitement, in you, in your plans and in your performance. It is this excitement that will bring a daring sparkle to your skating. And like Michelle Kwan, you will skate to gold. You will more frequently and more easily uncover the happiness waiting within the moment.

The use of this rather mysterious matrix effect may also bring you some surprises. In fact, examining my experiences with Tom and Frankie will bring us something quite unexpected—the final piece of the puzzle. It brings us face-to-face with the answer to the very last question in our book: Why? Why does the human matrix move, and what propels it to do so? We are about to discover the fuel that drives the human matrix, the secret that enhances every aspect of our journey as questing beasts.

In our last chapter, the healing matrix effect that began on the interpersonal wing took us directly to my soul, but what interests me even more is not what I found behind that barn but what took me there—compassion. We have touched upon compassion throughout our book. Sir Frederick felt it toward John Merrick. John Merrick felt it toward those who had abused him. Saint Francis felt it toward all the creatures and plants he touched from sweeping swallows to bending grasses. Even our quantum physicists felt the power of compassion, for once the boundaries between men come down—once we realize that we are all part of one quantum pattern—then it is only natural to feel compassion for others for they are we.

Albert Einstein captures this essential truth elegantly:

> *A human being . . . experiences himself, his thoughts and feelings as something separated from the rest—a kind of optical illusion of his consciousness. This delusion is a kind of prison for us, restricting us to our personal desires and affection for a few persons nearest to us. Our task must be to free ourselves from this prison by widening our circle of understanding and compassion to embrace all living creatures and the whole of nature in its beauty.*

Saint Francis of Assisi could not have put it any better. Curiously, one of the inescapable conclusions of both the quantum mechanics of Einstein and the mystical realities of Saint Francis is that compassion is not only a good thing to do, it is the logical thing to do.

Alan Watts frequently addressed this mystery as follows. Imagine that the universe is represented as a giant billowing sheet. At various points this sheet pulls itself up into tall peaks. The peaks represent those moments in time when all of the forces of the universe so intersect that human consciousness comes into being. Each moment of human consciousness thus unfolds from the matrix of the universe in the same fashion that a flower unfolds from a bud.

Further assume that these moments of consciousness are limited by their senses so that they are not able to see the connection between themselves. In short, because our eyes and brains cannot see pions and muons, we cannot see that we are all patterns in one large matrix. If such was the case, when two of these moments of consciousness would look upon each other, they would assume that they are separate entities looking at one another. In point of fact, they are bits of the universe looking at itself.

All sentient beings, are, in essence, the eyes and ears of the universe. We are all, from ants and grasshoppers to dolphins and humans, magnificent sets of peepers. We are God's eyeballs. We are peepers that spend a great deal of our time peeping at all the other peepers, gasping at their absurdity, their beauty and their paradoxes. Nor do we realize the greatest of the paradoxes, that when we look into the eyes of another creature, whether it be the adoring eyes of a dog, the shimmering eyes of a dragonfly or the enchanting eyes of someone we love, we are looking at ourselves.

It is dangerously easy to not see oneself at such moments. It is even easier to forget that the bits of human consciousness out of sight down the street, a couple of miles away or across the ocean, several thousand of miles away in Haiti, are connected to me, a part of the same matrix as myself.

But they are.

Whether mystic or quantum physicist, the answer is the same. It is wise to care for others, to feel and show compassion, for to do so is to care for ourselves. All creatures on this planet share the same pains, share the same dilemmas, share the same fears. I am reminded of one of my very favorite quotes, voiced by John Watson. I love it because it is so simple:

Be kind; everyone you meet is fighting a hard fight.

I love it, because it is so true. I believe it, because it makes sense. But I feel it, because I know that we are all a part of the same matrix. I feel the pain in others, because I recognize it as my own.

And now I must share a bias of mine. Throughout this book I have tried not to emphasize the importance of one wing of the matrix over any other wing. But now I must. I believe that where our last chapter started—on a back road in New Hampshire on a mission to help a father and his son—may be pointing towards the most important wing of the matrix. It is on the interpersonal wing that compassion waits for us. And I believe that compassion is the very soul of the human matrix and the happiness machine for which it is a blueprint.

Compassion is the soul of the human matrix because it consistently and ferociously ignites all the other wings of the matrix with its fire. The striking matrix effect we just saw with Tom—my reaching out to another brought me to see what was inside myself—happens all the time. Compassion, and the sense of mission that often accompanies it, is the fuel for which we have been questing in this journey of ours. It is the fuel that makes the entire happiness machine run, and it surges through each and every wing of the matrix.

Compassion is deeply imbedded in the biologies of our brains. We are hardwired to be social animals. When we care, we come to life, as do the circuits of our brains. It is the cornerstone of the psychological wing of the matrix. Huge amounts of our thoughts and beliefs deal with our relationships with others, and the effort to make the world a better place for them. It is the drive of the interpersonal wing of the matrix. We are made to hold and to be held; to care and to be cared for. It is the wellspring of the environmental wing of the matrix. We are built to create families, communities and environments that we nurture. And of course, compassion is at the very heart of the spiritual wing of the matrix. Some would argue that it is the mirror of the soul.

Compassion, the ability to feel the pain of others and the desire to do something about it, is the fuel of the human matrix. Despite all our flaws, and Homo sapiens have many, we are a wondrously compassionate lot. Whether we are showing compassion in a tiny fashion—Sir Frederick's kindness to John Merrick—or in a grand fashion—Paul Farmer's dedication to the people of Haiti—it is always a glorious aspect of the human condition. We skate our best, we shine our brightest, we achieve our greatest when we know that we skate to help others not just ourselves. Compassion is the surprising answer to one of the most practical of all questions, "Why skate at all?" And Albert Schweitzer in our opening epigraph had the answer: We skate because we are human, and it is our compassion that makes us so.

I am reminded of my very favorite passage in the annals of medicine. Throughout my medical training, I always turned to it when I felt swamped by heavy case loads, long hours and sleepless nights.

It was written by a physician almost 70 years ago. In my opinion, it is message that is as meaningful to us in 2004 as it was when it was first written by Francis Peabody in the *American Journal of Medicine*, 88th volume, in 1927, just about the time that Albert Einstein and his friends were stepping inside the atom:

> *One of the essential qualities of the clinician*
> *is interest in humanity, for the secret of the care of the*
> *patient is in caring for the patient.*

We have ourselves some fuel now, and I believe it is high-octane stuff. It gives life to the human matrix and it gives excitement to our performances. Undoubtedly, some of the most wondrous feats that I have seen performed by humanity are those feats fueled by compassion.

One could argue that one of the primary messages, some would argue *the* primary message, of almost every God of every major religion has been the message of compassion. When the Christ commented, "Love your neighbor as yourself," was he not possibly speaking of the reality of the matrix, that we are all interconnected with one another and the world around us: man with beast, beast with plant, cloud with wind, and God with all? Saint Paul followed it up with a most impressive endorsement when he was addressing the Corinthians:

> *If I knew all the mysteries of the future and*
> *knew everything about everything, but didn't love others,*
> *what good would I be? . . . There are three things that will endure—*
> *faith, hope, and love—and the greatest of these is love.*

The Dalai Lama, with the unerring aim of a Zen monk, releases an arrow that passes directly through the bull's-eye of this truth when he writes:

This is my simple religion. There is no need for temples;
no need for complicated philosophy. Our own brain, our own
heart is our temple: the philosophy is kindness.

We live in an age where there is a lot of talk about spirituality and self-growth. Our bookshelves teem with information about how to grow spiritually, and many of these books are about the inward paths we discussed earlier—yoga, meditation, prayer and the power of solitude. As I said before, all of these are useful and wonderful additions to our contemporary search for meaning and spiritual growth.

But over the years, I have come to a realization. I found it in the vacant eyes of Tom and in the tortured loneliness of Frankie. I saw it in the late hours that Mack spent night after night tending to his hospitalized patients back in Pittsburgh. And I still see it in the unwavering intensity of Paul Farmer and his friends as they battle AIDS in Haiti. Happiness is to be found in the present moment, and compassion is the single most powerful way to slip into that moment.

In the last analysis, spiritual growth is less a searching inwards than it is a reaching outwards. The inward path to spiritual growth is empty unless one also travels the outward path. And, if one has to choose which path to spend more time upon when seeking spiritual growth, without hesitation I would choose the journey outwards.

Sir Frederick knew it. That is why he spent his Sundays helping the poor on the back wards of London Hospital. Julian of Norwich knew it. That is why she sacrificed her freedom to pray for others. Benny knew it. That is why he doggedly helped his wife when her multiple illnesses would flare. Francis Peabody knew it. That is why he wrote those timeless words in the *American Journal of Medicine* back in 1927. And now, so do we.

Reprise: Altars for Unknown Gods and the Importance of Kaleidoscopes

It was with great pleasure that I stumbled upon the writings penned by a most curious Swiss philosopher, Henri Frederic Amiel, who was walking the cobbled streets of Bern in the 1800s.

Amiel was as little known and isolative as Alan Watts was well known and charismatic. He lived not so much in the company of others as he did in the company of his books and, of course, in the company of the constantly reproducing pages of his journal—fourteen thousand of them to be exact.

If you have never read sections of the journal of Amiel, you are in for a rare treat. Like Watts, he was not only a wise man but also a gifted wordsmith. Some of my favorite quotes have come from his pen. It is why I have decided to end our book with two of them, both of which seem to capture important elements for questing beasts as we pursue happiness along the wings of the human matrix.

The first quote, by all intents and purposes, should be hanging on the wall of the entranceway to Hesse's Magic Theater. It is a quote that reminds us of the importance of wonderment and mystery, two of my favorite elements of the human matrix. The wonders of quantum mechanics and the endlessly shifting patterns of the human matrix assure us that there will always be mystery. No one can know every nuance or combination that the human matrix will bring us. We only know that it will ultimately bring us surprise, for each unique combination of the five wings has plenty of shadowy nooks and hidden places for the heart. Amiel reminds us:

> *Let mystery have its place in you; do not be always turning up your whole ploughshare of self-examination, but leave a little fallow corner in your heart ready for any seed the wind may bring, and reserve a nook of shadow for the passing bird; keep a place in your heart for the unexpected guest, an altar for the unknown God.*

An understanding of the complexities of the human matrix will always remind us of the importance of looking for these altars, pausing at them and reflecting upon the wonderment they promise. And I hope that the introduction to the human matrix that we have jointly explored in this book will serve as a gateway for you to these altars. If so, I will have done my job well.

Henri Frederic Amiel has one more offering for us as our book rapidly draws to a close. After many hours of perusing his seemingly endless journal I came upon the following little gem. It makes me smile every time I read it, for I have always loved kaleidoscopes. Many years before quantum mechanics, Amiel seemed to see the emerging outline of the human matrix and even foresaw the wisdom of Heisenberg's Principle of Uncertainty:

> *Between us and things, how many screens there are! Our mood, our health, all the tissues of the eye, the window-panes of our cell, fog, smoke, rain or dust, and even light itself, and all this infinitely variable! Heraclitus said that one never bathes twice in the same river. I will say that one never sees the same landscape twice, for a window is one kaleidoscope and the observer is another.*

I have never thought of myself as a kaleidoscope, but I guess I am. Each questing beast—each happiness machine—is a constantly changing kaleidoscope with each wing of our matrix bringing us an almost infinite number of bits of shifting glass. Each moment is defined by the intersection of these bits of glass. Each moment is unique and fleeting.

At times now when I stop to peek in the mirror in my hallway, I sometimes think of this quotation by Amiel. When I look, I occasionally see a thief. Most times I simply see my own self. But at other times—much more special times—as I look in the mirror I find my features softening, and as they soften I begin to see my other selves.

I see the eyes of Sir Frederick as he first felt the pain of his new friend John Merrick. I see the tears of little Nick as he struggles not to spit. I see Mrs. Perkins opening a long-closed drawer, reaching for her rosary beads. I see a watchmaker bending down picking up a bit of broken propeller and cracked wing. I see his wife, Judy. I see that smile that I have never forgotten, that singular moment in time when I saw a smile soften a world that had grown hard. And I see the look in Susan's eyes on our very first date so long ago beneath the gargoyles and magnolias of Duke. I see all these moments, all these fleeting glimpses of the universe.

And then I see, if I'm very lucky, one of my favorite images. I see a man with a misshapen head wildly clapping, tears running down his eyes, for he has seen what others often miss. And if I listen—ever so carefully—a most wonderful thing happens. I hear the clapping of John Merrick as he sits in his box overlooking his precious pantomime. I hear the whispers of Julian of Norwich passing through her window. I hear the banging of Benny's limo door. And I smile.

I sometimes laugh, too, for I realize I have found the magic mirror for which I have spent my life searching. The magic theater is in my hallway. It is in the constantly shifting patterns of my matrix where it was always waiting for me.

I realize that all of these images and sounds are bits and pieces of me, and I of them. We are all part of a marvelous quantum world where we look at each other, change each other as we look and never cease to be awestruck by what we see.

At such times I slip inside the present moment, where happiness lies quietly hidden. It lies inside my trust, my laughter, my excitement, my belief, my acceptance of the good and the bad, and my wonderment. To find it, I need only look through the kaleidoscope of Amiel, for he was correct. We are all kaleidoscopes. The wings of the human matrix are the bits of colored glass, the facets of dream and hope. Compassion is the hand that turns the lens, bringing it all to wondrous life.

I trust that all will be as it is meant to be, and I move, thanks to my newfound understanding of the human matrix, with a gentle and refreshing confidence. I understand, deep in my soul, that Happiness Is. I need only uncover it.

Suggested Readings and References

Christian Mysticism and Philosophy

Manuela Dunn, *Christian Mysticism* (Hyperion) 1998

Ursula King, *Christian Mystics, the Spiritual Heart of the Christian Tradition* (Simon & Schuster Editions) 1998

Julian of Norwich, *Revelation of Love* (Image Books/Doubleday) 1997

Fiona Maddocks, *Hildegard of Bingen* (Image Books/Doubleday) 2003

Mother Teresa, *Meditations from a Simple Path* (Ballantine Books) 1996

Classic Books of Spirituality

Alan McGlashan, *Savage and Beautiful Country: The Secret Life of the Mind* (Hillstone) 1967

Sam Keen, *To a Dancing God: Notes of a Spiritual Traveler* (HarperSan Francisco) 1990

M. Scott Peck, *The Road Less Traveled: A New Psychology of Love, Traditional Values and Spiritual Growth* (A Touchstone Book/Simon & Schuster) 1978

T. Byram Karasu, *The Art of Serenity: The Path to a Joyful Life in the Best and Worst of Times* (Simon & Schuster) 2003

Jon Kabat-Zinn, *Wherever You Go There You Are: Mindfulness Meditation in Everyday Life* (Hyperion) 1994

Eastern Religion

Stewart W. Holmes and Chimyo Horioka, *Zen Art for Meditation* (Tuttle Publishing) 2002

Chang Chung-yuan, *Creativity and Taoism: A Study of Chinese Philosophy, Art, and Poetry* (Harper Torchbooks) 1963

C. Scott Littleton, *Shinto: Origins, Rituals, Festivals, Spirits, Sacred Spaces* (Oxford University Press) 2002

Alan Watts

Alan Watts, *The Meaning of Happiness* (Harper & Brothers Publishers) 1940

Alan Watts, *The Book On the Taboo Against Knowing Who You Are* (Vintage Books) 1989

Alan Watts, *Taoism: Way Beyond Seeking* (Tuttle Publishing) 1997

Alan Watts, *The Culture of Counter-Culture* (Tuttle Publishing) 1998

Alan Watts, *Cloud-Hidden, Whereabouts Unknown* (Pantheon Books) 1973

Henri Frederic Amiel

Henri Frederic Amiel, *The Private Journal of Henri Frederic Amiel* (The Macmillan Company) 1935

Quantum Mechanics and Modern Physics

Fritjof Capra, *The Tao of Physics, 25th Anniversary Edition* (Shambhala) 2000

Thomas J. McFarlane, editor, *Einstein and Buddha* (Seastone) 2002

James Gleick, *Chaos: Making a New Science* (Viking) 1988

Neurobiology and Philosophy

Jeffrey M. Schwartz and Sharon Begley, *The Mind and the Brain: Neuroplasticity and the Power of Mental Force* (Regan Books) 2002

Michael Reagan, editor, *Inside the Mind of God* (Templeton Foundation Press) 2002

Obsessive-Compulsive Disorder (OCD)

Jeffrey M. Schwartz and Beverly Beyette, *Brain Lock: Free Yourself from Obsessive-Compulsive Behavior* (Regan Books) 1996

Placebo Effect

R. Fuente-Fernandez et al., Expectation and Dopamine Release: Mechanism of the Placebo Effect in Parkinson's Disease, *Science*, volume 293, 2001

Andrew F. Leuchter et al., Changes in Brain Function of Depressed Subjects During Treatment with Placebo, *American Journal of Psychiatry*, volume 159, January 2002

Helen S. Mayberg et al., The Functional Neuroanatomy of the Placebo Effect, *American Journal of Psychiatry*, volume 159, May 2002

Paul Farmer and Haiti

Tracy Kidder, *Mountains Beyond Mountains: The Quest of Dr. Paul Farmer, A Man Who Would Cure the World*, (Random House) 2003

Paul Farmer, *The Uses of Haiti, 2nd Edition* (Common Courage Press) 2003

The Johnstown Flood 1889

David G. McCullough, *The Johnstown Flood* (Simon and Schuster) 1968

Victorian England and John Merrick

Wolf Von Eckardt, Sander L. Gillman and J. Edward Chamberlin, *Oscar Wilde's London—A Scrapbook of Vices and Virtues: 1880-1900* (Anchor Press, Doubleday & Company Inc.) 1987

Roger Hart, *English Life in the Nineteenth Century* (G. P. Putnam's Sons) 1971

Karl Beckson, *London in the 1890s: A Cultural History* (W. W. Norton & Company) 1992

Ashley Montagu, *The Elephant Man: A Study in Human Dignity* (Outerbridge & Dienstfrey, distributed by E. P. Dutton & Co.) 1971

Permissions